TRANSFORMING LAW AND INSTITUTION

How did indigenous peoples secure the right to self-determination in international law? Morgan's analysis shows how the "discursive activism" of the global indigenous movement within the UN succeeded in transforming accepted understandings and definitions of human rights norms. Theoretically sophisticated and rich in empirical detail, this analysis will appeal to scholars in social movement studies, international relations and the sociology of law.

Rachel Sieder, Centro de Investigaciones y Estudios Superiores en Antropología Social (CIESAS), Mexico

Rhiannon Morgan's exciting, scholarly and elegantly written book on the indigenous peoples rights movement is a pleasure to read. Using a wide span of interdisciplinary knowledge and her own research at the UN, Dr. Morgan vividly explores the struggles between indigenous peoples, national governments and international bodies. Her analysis of the emerging spaces for the recognition of new rights that challenge the authority of the state is a genuinely original contribution.

Colin Samson, University of Essex, UK

Rhiannon Morgan's Transforming Law and Institution *is timely and scholarly. It is not just that indigenous rights are in themselves significant. As Morgan correctly points out, their passage into law heralds a change in the nature of state sovereignty and its territorial borders, pointing to the growth of legal pluralism and to claims for self-determination on a global scale. A compelling and authoritative work.*

Bryan S. Turner, The City University of New York, USA

Non-State Actors in International Law, Politics and Governance Series

Series Editors

Professor Dr Math Noortmann, *Oxford Brookes University, UK*
Dr Bob Reinalda, *Radboud University Nijmegen, The Netherlands*
Professor Dr Bas Arts, *Radboud Wageningen University and Research Centre (WUR), The Netherlands*

The proliferation of non-state actors in the international system over the last three decades has increased the need for a broader theoretical analysis and empirical validation. The series explores the capabilities and impact of non-state actors, such as privately-based transnational corporations, non-governmental organizations (NGOs), international criminal organizations, and liberation movements, as well as intergovernmental organizations (in which NGOs often participate). The series seeks to address this need and to deepen the knowledge and understanding of non-state actors by scholars, practitioners and students in the fields of international law, politics and governance. By emphasizing legal, political and governance aspects of non-state actors' activities at the international (global or regional) level, the series intends to transcend traditional disciplinary and organizational boundaries.

Also in the series

Non-State Actor Dynamics in International Law
From Law-Takers to Law-Makers
Edited by Math Noortmann and Cedric Ryngaert
ISBN 978 1 4094 0316 6

Making Corporate Social Responsibility a Global Concern
Norm Construction in a Globalizing World
Lisbeth Segerlund
ISBN 978 0 7546 7707 9

Partners in Peace
Discourses and Practices of Civil-Society Peacebuilding
Mathijs van Leeuwen
ISBN 978 0 7546 7743 7

Civil Society and Nuclear Non-Proliferation
How do States Respond?
Claudia Kissling
ISBN 978 0 7546 7300 2

Transforming Law and Institution

Indigenous Peoples, the United Nations and Human Rights

RHIANNON MORGAN
Oxford Brookes University, UK

Routledge
Taylor & Francis Group
LONDON AND NEW YORK

First published 2011 by Ashgate Publishing

Published 2016 by Routledge
2 Park Square, Milton Park, Abingdon, Oxon OX14 4RN
605 Third Avenue, New York, NY 10017

Routledge is an imprint of the Taylor & Francis Group, an informa business

British Library Cataloguing in Publication Data
Morgan, Rhiannon.
Transforming law and institution : indigenous peoples, the United Nations and human rights. -- (Non-state actors in international law, politics and governance series)
1. United Nations. 2. Indigenous peoples--self determination.
3. Indigenous peoples--Legal status, laws, etc.
I. Title II. Series
341.4'852-dc22

Library of Congress Cataloging-in-Publication Data
Morgan, Rhiannon.
Transforming law and institution : indigenous peoples, the United Nations and human rights / by Rhiannon Morgan.
p. cm. -- (Non-state actors in international law, politics and governance series)
Includes bibliographical references and index.
ISBN 978-0-7546-7445-0 (hardcover)
1. Indigenous peoples--self determination 2. Indigenous peoples--Legal status, laws, etc. 3. Indigenous peoples (International law) 4. United Nations. 5. Human rights. I. Title.

JZ4974.M67 2011
323.11--dc23

2011032858

ISBN 13: 978-0-7546-7445-0 (hbk)

Contents

List of Figures

List of Abbreviations

ATSIC	Aboriginal and Torres Strait Islander Commission
CERD	United Nations Committee on the Elimination of Racial Discrimination
CRC	United Nations Committee on the Rights of the Child
CBD	Convention on Biological Diversity
CEACR	ILO Committee of Experts on the Application of Conventions and Recommendations
CHR	United Nations Commission on Human Rights
CSCE	Conference on Security and Cooperation in Europe
CSD	Commission on Sustainable Development
ECOSOC	United Nations Economic and Social Council
EMRIP	United Nations Expert Mechanism on the Rights of Indigenous Peoples
GA	United Nations General Assembly
HRC	United Nations Human Rights Committee
IASG	Inter-Agency Support Group on Indigenous Peoples' Issues
ICC	Inuit Circumpolar Conference
ICCPR	International Covenant on Civil and Political Rights
ICESRC	International Covenant on Economic, Social, and Cultural Rights
ICJ	International Court of Justice
IFAD	United Nations International Fund for Agricultural Development
IIPFCC	International Indigenous Peoples Forum on Climate Change
IITC	International Indian Treaty Council
ILO	International Labour Organization
ILRC	Indian Law Resource Centre
IPO	Indigenous peoples' organization
IWGIA	International Work Group for Indigenous Affairs
MDG	Millennium Development Goals
MRG	Minority Rights Group
NGO	Non-governmental organization
OHCHR	Office of the United Nations High Commissioner for Human Rights
PFII	United Nations Permanent Forum on Indigenous Issues
REDD	UN Collaborative Initiative on Reducing Emissions from Deforestation and Forest Degradation on Developing Countries
SMO	Social movement organization
UDHR	Universal Declaration of Human Rights

UNDG	United Nations Development Group
UNDP	United Nations Development Program
UNDRIP	United Nations Declaration on the Rights of Indigenous Peoples
UNESCO	United Nations Educational, Scientific, and Cultural Organization
UPR	Universal Periodic Review
WCC	World Council of Churches
WCIP	World Council of Indigenous Peoples
WGDD	United Nations Working Group on the Draft Declaration
WGIP	United Nations Working Group on Indigenous Populations
WHO	World Health Organization
WSSD	World Summit on Sustainable Development

Introduction

Indigenous Peoples, the United Nations and Human Rights

In recent decades, and in response to the mobilization of indigenous peoples in and around the United Nations, the rights of indigenous peoples have assumed a highly visible place within the United Nations overall treatment of human rights. In this time, a plethora of instruments, bodies, and mechanisms relevant to indigenous peoples' rights have come into being, highlighting the importance that the United Nations and the international community more broadly have come to place upon the protection of indigenous peoples, who are widely recognized to be amongst the most vulnerable and at risk human communities in the world today. This heightened international concern takes its most concrete form in the United Nations Declaration on the Rights of Indigenous Peoples (UNDRIP), which was adopted by the UN General Assembly in September 2007 after some 25 years of intensive negotiations between independent human rights experts, indigenous peoples' representatives, and state delegates. The Declaration broadly reflects the aspirations of indigenous advocates, leaders, and community representatives participating in its production, in particular in recognizing a right of indigenous peoples to self-determination, and is already considered by some experts to have achieved – in part at least – the status of customary international law. In addition, the United Nations has declared two International Decades of the World's Indigenous People, appointed a UN Special Rapporteur on the Human Rights and Fundamental Freedoms of Indigenous People, and, in an unprecedented move, established a UN Permanent Forum on Indigenous Issues (PFII), which has been the vehicle for the further mainstreaming of indigenous rights within the United Nations system.

These are remarkable developments, even when taken in the context of the ever increasing normative ambitions of international society, giving rise in recent times to the dramatic expansion of the international human rights regime and the development of ever new objects and subjects of human rights. Contemporary indigenous rights reflect a radically reformed international law, which – though at temporal junctures exhibiting an attitude of humanity toward non-European peoples as illustrated, for example, in the early writings of Las Casas and Vitoria – can be regarded as having played a central role in the dispossession of indigenous peoples, legitimizing historical patterns of colonization and conquest that usurped indigenous peoples' sovereignty and deprived them of their lands and territories. As recently as the immediate post-World War II period, indigenous peoples were subject to legal discourses characterizing them as obstacles to progress, 'populations' to be governed and controlled prior to their eventual assimilation and integration into national society. New norms of indigenous peoples' rights also represent the bridging of a paradigmatic gulf between traditional liberal conceptions of human rights and the privileging of individualism and the collective claims of historically grounded human associations, amounting to a radical transformation as to the nature of human rights. They suggest, moreover, a fundamental realignment of sovereignty within state borders, in particular the right of self-determination, which calls for new, more creative approaches to sovereignty and political ordering within states – shared, dispersed, and less exclusive. Stemming from the activities of the global indigenous movement, these unprecedented developments call for an explanation.

Indigenous peoples, associated as they often are with locality, powerlessness, and marginalization, may seem improbable candidates for a global movement orientated towards the United Nations and international law. Yet emerging predominantly from the Anglophone world in the mid- to late-1970s and expanding in scope in subsequent decades, the global indigenous movement is now one of the most visible civil society groupings across the United Nations and its specialized agencies. More than any other social movement sector, the global indigenous movement has succeeded in representing indigenous concerns across a range of policy areas from human rights to the environment, sustainable development, HIV/AIDS, and climate change, and in carving out spaces and mechanisms in the UN institution through which indigenous peoples may seek redress, including a permanent space consistent with the recognition of indigenous peoples' special status in international society. The PFII is a unique body in the UN system, comprised of eight indigenous representatives and eight state representatives working on an equal basis, and allowing for the exercise of indigenous peoples' international legal personality.

The success of the global indigenous movement speaks to the justice of the indigenous cause. There is little disagreement that the contemporary plight of indigenous peoples is not of their own making, but stems from historical forces that have decimated their numbers, dispossessed them of their lands and resources, and suppressed their political and cultural institutions, actions that have been carried out without legitimate basis, and which translate today into the disadvantage, marginalization, and poverty experienced by indigenous peoples globally. The achievements of the global indigenous movement also underscore the virtues of its strategic approach, which has involved movement activists in a discursive undertaking aimed at challenging entrenched understandings, particularly around the right of self-determination, and developing new, more nuanced meanings capable of embracing the claims of indigenous peoples. Linking strategic form to location, discursive activism has proved apposite in the institutional context of the UN, where disruptive or unruly forms of protest more usually associated with social movements make little sense but where creative framing may draw upon a wealth of discursive opportunities, not least in the form of legal norms and rules.

The chapters that follow explore the emergence and strategies of the global movement of indigenous peoples and its impact at the United Nations and upon international law: under what conditions did indigenous peoples, amongst the world's poorest and most marginalized peoples, gather themselves into a global movement? What methods has the global indigenous movement pursued in its efforts to influence the UN and international law to address the lamentable situation of indigenous peoples? How does the movement act, and what is its appeal? What can we say about the impact of the movement, including its ultimate impact, namely beyond the international stage of the United Nations, in the concrete settings where indigenous peoples live?

Chapter 1 sets the backdrop for the study with a discussion of the main UN developments in the area of indigenous peoples' rights. Chapter 2 discusses the core analytical concepts and frameworks employed throughout the book, which derive from three main bodies of literature: social scientific writing on human rights, social movement theory, and the literature on transnationalism, norms, and identities in international relations. In Chapter 3, I discuss the emergence and constitution of the collective actor that is the global indigenous movement. Here, I trace the development of the movement in terms of both incentive and opportunity, present the main organizations that comprise the movement, and discuss the characteristics of the movement in terms of activist composition. Chapter 4 discusses the core claims and campaigns of the movement, focusing on goals of a substantive and institutional or procedural character. Chapter 5 is dedicated to the strategic level, which finds the movement engaged principally in discursive forms of activism appropriate to a context of international law-making. Chapter 6, the concluding chapter, considers the impact of the movement and in particular assesses the prospects for implementation.

Research Strategy

Data for this book were collected mainly through fieldwork, interviews, and extensive documentary research. Fieldwork took place chiefly between 2001 and 2004, and involved participant observation at various UN meetings and conferences dealing with indigenous issues. These included the UN Working Group on Indigenous Populations (WGIP), the Open-Ended Inter-Sessional Working Group of the Commission on Human Rights on the Draft Declaration (WGDD), the UN Permanent Forum on Indigenous Issues (PFII), the UN World Conference Against Racism (WCAR) and its Third Preparatory Committee, the UN Human Rights Committee (HRC), the UN Committee on the Elimination of All Forms of Discrimination and Racial Discrimination (CERD), and the former UN Sub-Commission on the Promotion and Protection of Human Rights.[1] I also attended an International Conference of Experts on the Implementation of the Right

1 Formerly the Sub-Commission on the Prevention of Discrimination and the Protection of Minorities (until 1999), its mandates and functions were assumed by the Human Rights Council Advisory Committee as of June 2006.

to Self-Determination organized by the United Nations Educational, Scientific, and Cultural Organization (UNESCO). These meetings and conferences took place at a range of venues around the world, including Geneva, New York, and Durban, calling for a kind of multi-sited ethnography characterized more by similarity than difference across the various research sites. Whether in South Africa, Geneva, or New York, the de-territorialized world of UN conferences and NGO activism presented similar processes and practices, focused principally though not exclusively on the making and monitoring of international human rights. At each, I observed similar deliberations and meetings, including formal plenary sessions comprising all accredited participants, smaller, more informal subcommittees consisting of governmental delegations, and lobbying meetings involving indigenous and state delegates. At each, I encountered similar protocols and procedures for participation and decision-making, and, in the production of consensual documents, for building agreement and working out differences on competing language (e.g. 'getting rid of brackets'). I also attended an array of panel discussions and side events, and sat in on daily indigenous caucus meetings, from which I gained indispensable insights into movement goals, strategy, and organization.

In addition to participant observation, I undertook interviews with state representatives, indigenous delegates, and representatives of non-indigenous advocacy and support organizations, and spoke with fellow scholars involved in the movement. A majority of interviews might be described as 'informal', involving 'conversations conducted in the field' (Bernard 2001, 190). As a rule, I found this appropriate to the conditions of the research sites, where core actors were generally engaged in intensive struggle and where interpretation of events was best sought as they unfolded. Informal interviews were conducted in a variety of places, including the vast, yawning plenary spaces of the Palais des Nations in Geneva, in the corridors and cafeterias of the UN headquarters in New York, over photocopying machines and document tables, on public transport to and from conference venues, and so on. Informal interviews were combined with semi-structured interviews, which allowed for more in-depth discussion of participants' goals, motivations, strategies, and positions, as well as the collection of historical data.

Access to UN meetings was facilitated through two NGOs, the Essex Human Rights Centre based at the University of Essex and the International Movement Against All Forms of Racial Discrimination (IMADR), a Tokyo-based NGO with consultative status at the United Nations. IMADR provided access in exchange for report writing and coordination of their team of interns. With few exceptions, the UN provides no capacity for individuals to attend UN meetings, thereby necessitating affiliation with an accredited NGO. The WGIP posed no access difficulties, being unique in the UN system for its open and flexible accreditation procedures. Parallel NGO conferences and counter summits, such as the Durban NGO Forum Against Racism held in September 2001, provided no real access difficulties.

Further data were gathered from relevant documentary sources. These included a range of official and restricted UN documents, literature produced by various UN specialized agencies, press reports, and brochures and publications produced by indigenous and non-indigenous NGOs. I also made extensive use of literature distributed by the indigenous caucus, including strategy papers and legal interpretations. Additional data in the form of written interventions and oral statements from previous UN meetings were accessed through the Geneva-based archives of the Indigenous Peoples' Centre for Documentation, Research, and Information (doCip). Finally, material was accessed from the websites of a range of indigenous organizations. Indigenous peoples' communities of resistance, both internationally and nationally, rely substantially on the virtual field of the Web.[2]

2 For a discussion of the implications of ICTs for indigenous peoples' movements, see Havemann (2000).

[illegible]

Chapter 1
United Nations Engagement with Indigenous Issues

Indigenous peoples' interests are progressed in part through general, undifferentiated human rights instruments in the human rights canon, which, as Article 1 of the UNDRIP affirms, apply equally to indigenous individuals and peoples as to all other individuals and peoples (United Nations 2007a, Art. 1). These are not the main concern of this book, though the question of the extent to which general human rights instruments can advance indigenous concerns is a relevant one, not least because indigenous advocates have been relatively successful in utilizing such instruments, as highlighted elsewhere (e.g. Thornberry 2002). This notwithstanding, the central focus throughout this book is on UN instruments and initiatives specifically dedicated to the promotion and protection of indigenous peoples' rights, which have come into being in the last thirty years or so principally as a result of the activities of the global indigenous movement within the UN system. This chapter provides an overview of these developments, beginning with the core human rights instruments concerning indigenous peoples before progressing to further supporting initiatives.

Core Indigenous Rights Instruments

Developments within the ILO: Conventions No. 107 and No. 169

The issue of indigenous rights first arose in the UN in the context of the International Labour Organization (ILO) – a UN specialized agency that predates the UN – and its concern with the exploitation of indigenous labour. An interest of the ILO dating back to the 1920s, during the 1930s the ILO produced a number of instruments protecting indigenous workers before adopting, in 1957, the ILO Convention No.107 Concerning the Protection and Integration of Indigenous and Other Tribal and Semi-Tribal Populations in Independent Countries (ILO Convention No. 107) and its accompanying Indigenous and Tribal Populations Recommendation No. 104.[1] The first comprehensive set of international standards on indigenous rights,

1 The ILO showed interest in indigenous labour as early as 1921, when it undertook a series of studies on the conditions of indigenous workers. In 1926, it established the Committee of Experts on Native Labour to set standards for the protection of indigenous workers. A number of instruments on indigenous labour followed, including the (1930)

ILO Convention No.107 attempts to address the marginalization of indigenous peoples through a range of special protective measures, but overwhelmingly reflects the dominant 'indigenist' (Gray 1997, 49) approach of the time in promoting the eventual integration of indigenous peoples into national societies and economies. Article 2 sets forth the main thrust of the Convention, as follows:

> 1. Governments shall have the primary responsibility for developing co-ordinated and systematic action for the protection of the populations concerned and their progressive integration into the life of their respective countries.
> 2. Such action shall include measures for:
>   a) enabling the said populations to benefit on an equal footing from the rights and opportunities which national laws or regulations grant to the other elements of the population;
>   b) promoting the social, economic and cultural development of these populations and raising their standard of living;
>   c) creating possibilities of national integration to the exclusion of measures tending towards the artificial assimilation of these populations.
> 3. The primary objective of all such action shall be the fostering of individual dignity, and the advancement of individual usefulness and initiative.

The protections recognized in ILO Convention No.107 are varied and include the right to both individual and collective ownership of traditional lands (Art. 11), preservation of language (Art. 23), and some degree of protection for indigenous customs and institutions, but special measures are viewed as temporary and 'not to be used as a means of creating or prolonging a state of segregation' (ILO 1957, Art. 3.2). The balance between protection and integration is therefore very much biased towards the latter, and in way that is wholly at odds with contemporary norms of indigenous peoples' rights.

ILO Convention No. 107 is no longer open for ratification, though it remains in force for eighteen countries.[2] The ILO has, however, long recognized the fundamental limitations of the Convention; for over a decade, the Committee of Experts on the Application of Conventions and Recommendations (CEACR)

Forced Labour Convention, the (1936) Recruiting of Indigenous Workers Convention, the (1939) Contracts of Employment (Indigenous Workers) Convention, and the (1939) Penal Sanctions (Indigenous Workers) Convention. From 1952–1972, the ILO also led a multi-agency enterprise directed at peasants in the Andes, the Andean Indian Programme, an essentially integrationist endeavour claimed by the ILO to have assisted some 250,000 indigenous people (ILO 2003, 3).

2 These are: Angola, Bangladesh, Belgium, Cuba, Dominican Republic, Egypt, El Salvador, Ghana, Guinea-Bissau, Haiti, India, Iraq, Malawi, Pakistan, Panama, Portugal, Syrian Arab Republic, Tunisia (ILO 2008a).

responsible for monitoring compliance has interpreted government obligations under the Convention in a way that dispenses with its integrationist and paternalistic elements in favour of more current developments,[3] and especially in accordance with the ILO Convention No.169 Concerning Indigenous and Tribal Peoples in Independent Countries (ILO Convention No.169) of 1989. Accordingly, the live status of the Convention in the aforementioned eighteen states does not create an anomaly in international law and implementation.

The revision of ILO Convention No. 107 and its replacement with ILO Convention No. 169 was brought about in the context of growing indigenous mobilization within the UN system and reflects a responsiveness to indigenous peoples' demands for recognition of their collective rights to exist as distinct communities and peoples. ILO Convention No.169 formally rejects the integrationist and assimilationist intentions of its predecessor, which were described at the 1986 Meeting of Experts convened to discuss revision of the Convention as 'destructive in the modern world ... in practice it [integration] had become a concept which meant the extinction of ways of life which are different from that of dominant society' (cited in Anaya 1996, 47). Its basic orientation is reflected in the preamble, which recognizes the aspirations of indigenous peoples 'to exercise control over their own institutions, ways of life and economic development and to maintain and develop their identities, languages and religions, within the framework of the States in which they live' (ILO 1989, preamble). Its provisions establish a wide range of rights, including individual rights of non-discrimination (Art. 3), personal security (Art. 4), and political and civic participation in national society (Art. 4), and collective rights to cultural, institutional, and linguistic integrity (Arts. 8, 9 and 28) and ownership and possession of lands and resources (Arts. 14, 15, 16, 17 and 18).[4]

Unlike ILO Convention No.107, ILO Convention No.169 uses the term 'peoples' rather than 'populations' to denote the beneficiaries of the Convention. This represented a significant breakthrough insofar as the former is associated

3 Illustrative examples of the CEACR's approach in this respect can be found in its series of observations concerning Brazil and Bangladesh, in which it has reiterated the need for reform of government policy to recognize the land rights and cultural integrity of the Yanomami of the northern Amazon and the tribal peoples of the Chittagong Hill Tracts, respectively. See CEACR, Individual Observation concerning Convention No. 107, Indigenous and Tribal Populations, Brazil, published 1990, 1991, 1993, 1994, 1995, 1996, 1997, 1998, and 1999; also CEACR, Individual Observation concerning Convention No. 107, Indigenous and Tribal Populations, Bangladesh, published 1990, 1991, 1993, 1994, 1996, 1998, and 1999.

4 As of 2009, ILO Convention No.169 has been ratified by the following twenty states: Argentina, Bolivia, Brazil, Chile, Colombia, Costa Rica, Denmark, Dominica, Ecuador, Fiji, Guatemala, Honduras, Mexico, Nepal, Netherlands, Norway, Paraguay, Peru, Spain, Bolivarian Republic of Venezuela (ILO 2009). In the cases of Argentina, Bolivia, Brazil, Colombia, Costa Rica, Ecuador, Mexico, Paraguay, and Peru, ILO Convention No. 169 replaces ILO Convention No. 107.

with the right to self-determination in international law. Its inclusion, however, was strongly resisted by some states, resulting in an eventual compromise in the form of a clarification, as follows (Art 1.3):

> The use of the term 'peoples' in this Convention shall not be construed as having any implications as regards the rights which may attach to the term under international law.

The qualifying language of Article 1.3 disappointed indigenous advocates, who also expressed dissatisfaction with the lack of effective participation of indigenous peoples in the 1988 General Conference. Only international NGOs were allowed to participate, and these were permitted to address the conference on a limited basis only (Berman 1988, 52). Nonetheless, as Anaya (1996, 48–49) notes, even the qualified use of the term 'peoples' represented significant progress in implying 'a greater and more positive recognition of group identity and corresponding attributes of community', while a number of the Convention's provisions go a significant way to protecting aspects of the right of indigenous peoples to self-determination. Nor is it the case that the qualifying language should be seen as having been intended to limit the meaning of the term; as is evident from the legislative history and several statements since, the ILO considered the issue of the right to self-determination of indigenous peoples to be a political rather than a labour issue, and therefore best left to procedures within the UN.

UN Declaration on the Rights of Indigenous Peoples

Progression through the UN System

Within the UN proper, the earliest significant engagement with indigenous issues dates to 1971, when the UN Economic and Social Council (ECOSOC) requested the UN Sub-Commission on the Prevention of Discrimination and Protection of Minorities (Sub-Commission) to undertake a study on discrimination experienced by indigenous peoples. The study was allotted to Special Rapporteur José R. Martínez Cobo of Ecuador and took thirteen years to complete.[5] It was issued in instalments between 1981 and 1983 and published in consolidated form under the title *Study on the Problem of Discrimination Against Indigenous Populations* (United Nations 1986a). Containing 22 chapters covering diverse areas of concern for indigenous peoples including land, political rights, language, health, and culture, the study makes a number of conclusions and proposals, and offers the noteworthy view that 'self-determination, in its

5 Augusto Wilemsen Diaz, a Guatemalan jurist on the staff of the United Nations Centre for Human Rights in Geneva, is regarded as the principal drafter of the study (Sanders 1998, 75; Stamatopoulou 1994, 68).

many forms, must be recognized as the basic precondition for the enjoyment by indigenous peoples of their fundamental rights and the determination of their own future' (United Nations 1983, para. 580). A major consideration in the process of preparing the report was that it take into account the views and aspirations of indigenous peoples, which, by the late 1970s, were increasingly being voiced in international fora.

In 1982, urged on by the findings of the Cobo report, as well as the growing advocacy of indigenous and non-indigenous NGOs, ECOSOC authorized the establishment of the UN Working Group on Indigenous Populations (WGIP) as a sub-organ of the Sub-Commission.[6] Comprised of five rotating members of the Sub-Commission, who are individuals working in the capacity of independent human rights experts rather than state representatives, the WGIP was charged with a twofold mandate: i) to review developments concerning the promotion and protection of the human rights and fundamental freedoms of indigenous peoples; and ii) to formulate standards that could guide relations between indigenous peoples and states. In 1985, the latter task was given greater focus with the Sub-Commission's approval of the WGIP's decision to draft a UN declaration on the rights of indigenous peoples.

The WGIP's original intention was to complete work on a draft declaration within a few years, allowing enough time for a declaration to progress to the General Assembly for adoption in 1993. In the event, the WGIP did not agree on a final text until 1993. Critical to the overall task was the esteemed Chairperson-Rapporteur of the WGIP from 1984 to 2000, Erica-Irene A. Daes, who steered the working group through the drafting process. Also regarded as the principal drafter, Daes produced a first set of preambular paragraphs and principles in 1988 (United Nations 1988). Discussion of this and subsequent drafts continued until the final revision in 1993. Following technical review by the Secretariat,[7] the final draft was adopted without changes by the Sub-Commission at its 46th session in 1994.[8]

During the process of composing the Draft United Nations Declaration, the WGIP accepted interventions from states, intergovernmental organizations, UN specialized agencies, and organizations of indigenous peoples, with the latter

6 The creation of the WGIP was proposed by the Sub-Commission in Resolution 2 (XXXIV) of 8 September 1981, endorsed by the Commission on Human Rights in Resolution 1982/19 of 10 March 1982, and empowered by ECOSOC in Resolution 1982/34 of 7 May 1982.

7 See *Technical Review of the Draft United Nations Declaration on the Rights of Indigenous Peoples*, U.N. Doc. E/CN.4/Sub.2/1994/2 (1994).

8 The final text adopted by the WGIP was published in an annex to the *Report of the Working Group on Indigenous Populations at its Eleventh Session*, U.N. Doc. E/CN.4/Sub.2/1993/29, Annex 1 (1993). Following its adoption by the Sub-Commission, the draft declaration appeared in an annex to the Sub-Commission Resolution 1994/45 of 26 August 1994 as 'The Draft United Nations Declaration on the Rights of Indigenous Peoples', U.N. Doc. E/CN.4/1995/2, E/CN.4/Sub.2/1994/56.

having equal rights to express their views on the content of the text. As such, the draft that emerged substantially reflected the aspirations of indigenous peoples, especially as, over time, states gradually withdrew from the drafting process, attending in smaller numbers as the draft developed (Barsh 1996, 783). Of particular note is the right of self-determination, which was eventually included in the final draft text in the following format (Art. 3):

> Indigenous peoples have the right of self-determination. By virtue of that right they freely determine their political status and freely pursue their economic, social, and cultural development.

This language reproduces the classic language of Common Article 1 of the International Human Rights Covenants of 1966 on the right to self-determination, and was met with a standing ovation from indigenous participants (Daes 2008, 18). Besides the right to self-determination, the Draft United Nations Declaration recognized amongst its 45 articles a range of collective rights, including protection from genocide and ethnocide (Arts. 6 and 7), the right to practice and perpetuate their culture (Arts. 12, 13 and 14), the right to comprehensive control over lands, territories, and resources (Arts. 25, 26, 27, 28 and 30), intellectual property rights (Art. 29), and the recognition of distinct indigenous political and legal systems (Arts. 31 and 33).

The text of the Draft United Nations Declaration produced by the WGIP has been described as radical by a number of commentators. Thornberry (2002, 375), for example, has stated that, 'in the spectrum from reform to revolution [the Draft Declaration] reaches towards the upper revolutionary end, among the passionate colours'. Xanthaki (2007, 102), similarly, describes it as 'an ambitious text that challenges state sovereignty at a deep level'. Nonetheless, at the twelfth session of the WGIP in 1994, some indigenous participants criticized the draft for not going far enough, with criticism focusing in particular on Article 31, which some argued might be read as imposing a limitation on the exercise of Article 3 (United Nations 1994a, para. 37). Article 31 states that:

> Indigenous peoples, as a specific form of exercising their right to self-determination, have the right to autonomy or self-government in matters relating to their internal and local affairs, including culture, religion, education, information, media, health, housing, employment, social welfare, economic activities, land and resources management, environment and entry by non-members, as well as ways and means for financing these autonomous functions.

Others, including the 1992 Nobel Peace Prize winner Rigoberta Menchu Tum, interpreted Article 31 as identifying autonomy as just one, presumably minimal, form of exercising a right to self-determination (United Nations 1994a, para. 39), while the text itself states in Article 42 that 'the rights recognized herein constitute the minimum standards for the survival, dignity, and well-being of the indigenous peoples of the world'. For their part, few state representatives fully endorsed the draft text. Following adoption by the Sub-Commission, the latter submitted the Draft UN Declaration to its parent body, the Commission on Human Rights (CHR).[9] Comprised of the representatives of 53 states, the CHR was unable to accept the text as received, and established, by Resolution 1995/32 of 3 March 1995, 'an open-ended working group of the Commission on Human Rights with the sole purpose of elaborating a draft declaration, considering the draft contained in the annex to Resolution 1994/45 of 26 August 1994' (United Nations 1995a). The main concerns of state representatives revolved around issues of self-determination, which many states regarded as posing serious threats to their territorial integrity, land and resource rights, and collective rights more generally.

An initial concern raised by the creation of the Working Group of the Draft Declaration (WGDD) was that the stricter rules of accreditation and participation applied by the CHR would limit the extent of participation of indigenous representatives and that the draft text would therefore become substantially diluted. After much lobbying on the part of indigenous delegates, however, the Commission established a procedure to allow indigenous organizations lacking consultative status with ECOSOC to attend sessions of the WGDD (United Nations 1995a, Annex). Though not meeting the degree of openness characterized by the WGIP, the procedure enabled over 100 indigenous organizations to participate, while, over time, indigenous delegates were also able to significantly influence the modalities of their participation and the working methods. These 'procedural claims of the resistance' (Tennant 1994) will be discussed in Chapter 4. Here, suffice to say that struggles to secure participation have been critical to the achievement of substantive goals, whilst also being emblematic of the wider struggle for self-determination.

Meeting annually from 1995 to 2006, the eleven years of deliberations in the WGDD managed to reduce some important fears of states, especially relating to self-determination, control over natural resources, and collective rights more generally. Yet at the first reading of the draft text at the opening session in 1995, only two articles met with no objections from states, while 26 articles were entirely objectionable to at least one government (United Nations 1996a; see also Barsh 1996, 804–805).[10] As anticipated, indigenous NGOs and states were particularly polarized over the right to self-determination, which immediately arose as a difficult issue with Brazil's objection to the use of the term 'peoples' in the title of the drafting group as it appeared on the draft agenda: 'working group on a draft United Nations Declaration on the Rights of Indigenous Peoples' (Barsh 1996, 796). A term that carries implications in

9 The Human Rights Commission was replaced in 2006 by the Human Rights Council.

10 Legal scholar Russell Barsh (1996) has produced a scorecard of states' discursive positioning on the draft articles as articulated at the first session of the WGDD in 1995. The official report for the session cites the range of positions, but fails to identify which positions belong to which states (United Nations 1996a).

international law, to avoid a stalemate all documents were revised to: 'working group established in accordance with Commission on Human Rights Resolution 1995/32' (United Nations 1996a, para. 14). During discussions on Article 3, only Australia, Bolivia, Cuba, Denmark, Fiji, Finland, and Norway supported its wording. Of the remaining states, five countries, including Iraq, Peru, the Philippines, the United States, and the Ukraine, took the view that the language of self-determination would need to be substantially qualified to protect the territorial integrity of states before being acceptable, while a remaining nine states comprising of Argentina, Brazil, Chile, Colombia, Ecuador, Japan, Mexico, Morocco, and Russia voiced fundamental objections that went to the underlying principle (United Nations 1996a, para. 45; Barsh 1996, 809). Of the group requiring amendments to the effect that the territorial integrity of states would not be affected, the Philippines proposed that the text explicitly state that self-determination be exercised 'within the framework of national unity', while the United States argued that the language of self-determination could only be supported if limited to internal self-government (United Nations 1996a, para 48; Barsh 798). Of the latter group, Argentina suggested deleting all references to 'peoples' and 'self-determination', whilst the Russian Federation favoured restricting the text to terms such as joint decision-making and self-management (Barsh 1996, 797–800). The report for the session states that 'certain Governments took the position that the right of self-determination as referred to in article 3 needed to be qualified, or elaborated in a way which preserves the territorial integrity of States and their constitutional frameworks, where these meet current human rights standards' (United Nations 1996a, para. 46).

Later sessions of the WGDD witnessed gradual changes in the positions of many states, though not always in a direction favourable to indigenous peoples. At the third session in 1997, for example, Australia, under the new conservative government of John Howard since March 1996,[11] allied with the United States, Canada, and New Zealand in opposing much of the text, forming the so-called CANZUS group of states. More generally, however, shifts in states' discursive positioning can be seen to gradually lean towards a growing recognition of indigenous peoples' collective rights, including acceptance of the right to self-determination for indigenous peoples. Thus, by the fifth session in 1999 a majority of states speaking on the language of Article 3 indicated that they could accept its inclusion subject to certain textual amendments intended to protect the territorial integrity of states, while the Chairperson-Rapporteur was also able to conclude that 'the participants in general agreed that the right of self-determination was

11 An early supporter of the declaration process under Prime Minister Paul Keating, Australia's position shifted dramatically under the administration of Prime Minister John Howard, whose government was also responsible for a range of regressive policies in relation to Aboriginal and Torres Strait Islander peoples.

the cornerstone of the draft declaration' (United Nations 2000a, para. 82).[12] By the time of the eighth session in 2002, moreover, a significant number of states were prepared to accept the language of Article 3 as drafted by the Sub-Commission without any amendments or qualifications, including Denmark, Norway, Switzerland, Sweden, Spain, Finland, Fiji, Pakistan, Guatemala, Mexico, Cuba, Costa Rica, Bolivia, Chile, Ecuador, and Peru. In the same year, the United States, Canada, New Zealand, and the Russian Federation continued to insist on limits on the meaning and exercise of self-determination as a prerequisite for their support, while Australia stood out as singularly opposed to any mention of a right of indigenous peoples to self-determination.

Notwithstanding a clear but gradual progression among states within the WGDD towards an acceptance of indigenous peoples' collective rights, including the right to self-determination, by the end of the first UN International Decade on Indigenous People in 2004 – the initial time frame specified for the adoption of a declaration – the working group had still only managed to adopt two articles.[13] The following year, the WGDD held its final session, at which participants considered various proposals with the aim of reaching consensus on the text, including Chairperson-Rapporteur Luis Enrique Chávez's 'proposals on articles'. The session was characterized by an emerging consensus on many but not all of the text's 45 articles, with key issues such as self-determination, lands, territories, and resources continuing to create discordance. As a result, at the end of the session, Chávez took the decision to submit his own revised proposed text to the newly constituted Human Rights Council (the Council), containing articles provisionally agreed upon in the WGDD and his own proposals on outstanding issues.[14] At its first session in June 2006, the Council, over the objections of some states with sizeable indigenous populations, adopted the Chairperson's proposed text by its

12 States at the fifth session in 1999 indicating acceptance of the right to self-determination, subject to certain limits, included Argentina, Brazil, Canada, Colombia, Ecuador, Finland, France, Guatemala, Mexico, New Zealand, Norway, Pakistan, the Russian Federation, and Switzerland, of which Pakistan and Switzerland specifically endorsed Article 3 without changes (United Nations 2000a). Australia was relatively isolated in unequivocally rejecting the inclusion of self-determination on the basis that 'for many people it implied the establishment of separate nations and laws' (United Nations 2000a, para. 62).

13 These were Article 5, which states that every indigenous person has the right to a nationality, and Article 43, which guarantees that rights and freedoms should be granted to both males and females. Articles 5 and 43 were adopted at the third session of the WGDD in 1997 (United Nations 1998a, paras. 41 and 42).

14 This is contained in the official report for the meeting as Annex 1 'Revised Chairman's Summary and Proposal'. See United Nations (2006a), *Report of the Working Group Established in Accordance with Commission on Human Rights Resolution 1995/32*, U.N. Doc. E/CN.4/2006/79 (22 March 2006).

Resolution 1/2 of 29 June 2006, by a vote of 30 in favour to two against and 12 abstentions (United Nations 2006b).[15]

Following adoption by the Council, the text was submitted to the 61st session of the General Assembly (GA). The process towards adoption within the GA included a number of delays and considerations, which are outlined in some detail in Daes (2008, 18–22). Notably, at the behest of the group of African states led by Namibia, which expressed a number of concerns with the text as adopted by the Council, particularly as regards the status quo of existing state boundaries,[16] consideration of the text was deferred until the end of the 61st session of the GA in September 2007, thereby allowing time for further consultations.[17] These were convened in part by the Permanent Representative of the Philippines to the UN, Hilario G Davide Jr., who undertook informal consultations with and received feedback from governments (Daes 2008, 19–21). Consultations also took place between so-called 'friends of the Declaration', which included member states of the European Union and most Latin American states, and those seeking amendments (*ibid.*, 22). The latter group comprised of the group of African states and another group generally referred to as 'CANZUS and others', composed of Australia, Canada, Colombia, Guyana, New Zealand, the Russian Federation, and Surinam (*ibid.*). Consultations were successful in addressing the issue of greatest concern to African states, which was dealt with through the addition of a new provision in the form of Article 46(1), to be discussed in the following section. Subsequently, the United Nations Declaration on the Rights of Indigenous Peoples (UNDRIP) was adopted on the 13 September 2007 by GA Resolution

15 The text is contained in an annex to the Resolution (United Nations 2006b). The Council consists of 47 state members, three of which were absent during the vote. The states voting in favour were Azerbaijan, Brazil, Cameroon, China, Cuba, Czech Republic, Ecuador, Finland, France, Germany, Guatemala, India, Indonesia, Japan, Malaysia, Mauritius, Mexico, the Netherlands, Pakistan, Peru, Poland, Republic of Korea, Romania, Saudi Arabia, South Africa, Sri Lanka, Switzerland, UK, Uruguay, and Zambia. The states abstaining were Algeria, Argentina, Bahrain, Bangladesh, Ghana, Jordan, Morocco, Nigeria, the Philippines, Senegal, Tunisia, and the Ukraine. Canada and the Russian Federation voted against. Australia, New Zealand, and the United States are not members of the Human Rights Council and so could not vote, though they voiced opposition.

16 At the 8th session of the Assembly of the African Union in January 2007, the Assembly of the Union adopted a decision in which it decided to 'maintain a united position on negotiations on amending the Declaration and any further negotiations and constructively work alongside other Member States of the United Nations in finding solutions to the concerns of African States' (African Union 2007, para. 8). The decision identifies a number of areas of particular concern for African states, including: (a) the definition of indigenous peoples; (b) self-determination; (c) ownership of lands and resources; (d) establishment of distinct economic and political institutions; and (e) national and territorial integrity (*ibid.*, para. 6).

17 The decision to defer action was enacted by General Assembly Resolution 61/178 of 20 December 2006.

A/61/295 by a landslide affirmative vote of 143 in favour with four against and 11 abstentions (United Nations 2007a). Australia, Canada, New Zealand, and the United States voted against the Declaration. Azerbaijan, Bangladesh, Bhutan, Burundi, Colombia, Georgia, Kenya, Nigeria, the Russian Federation, Samoa, and the Ukraine abstained. Australia, New Zealand, Canada and the United States have since endorsed the UNDRIP, in April 2009, April 2010, November 2010, and December 2010 respectively.[18]

Key Provisions

The UNDRIP is a comprehensive instrument containing 23 preambular paragraphs and 46 articles, making it the longest human rights instrument to emerge from the UN to date. It is also the only specifically collective human rights instrument recognized by the UN, this being the essence and distinctive character of the text and 'indispensable' for the 'existence, well-being and integral development' of indigenous peoples (preamble). Key collective rights recognized by the UNDRIP include the right of indigenous peoples to self-determination, the right to protection and preservation of their lands, territories and resources, and the right to maintain and protect their cultural heritage and expressions. Whilst being at core a collective rights instrument, the UNDRIP also recognizes the right of indigenous individuals to equality and non-discrimination (preamble, Art. 2). Moreover, though the text focuses predominantly on the 'traditional and the territorial', it does also provide protections for indigenous individuals who have been marginalized from their communities by social and development processes (Thornberry 2002, 378), for example in relation to conditions of employment and labour (Art. 17).

As noted in the previous section, indigenous peoples' core demand for the right to self-determination is contained in Article 3, which, as in the Draft UN Declaration, restates without any qualification existing international law concerning the right to self-determination. Article 3 is to be read in conjunction with a number of articles, in particular Articles 46(1), 4, and 5, which together define the meaning and content of self-determination intended by the Declaration. The main interpretative provision is arguably Article 46(1), which is recognized as reconciling indigenous peoples' demands for a full and equal expression of self-determination as contained in the language of Article 3 and states' concerns regarding their territorial integrity.

---

18 See Australia (2009) 'The Hon Jenny Macklin MP, Statement on the United Nations Declaration on the Rights of Indigenous Peoples, 03 April 2009'; New Zealand (2010) 'Hon Pita Sharpe, Minister for Maori Affairs, New Zealand Permanent Mission to the United Nations, Statement to the Ninth Session of the United Nations Permanent Forum on Indigenous Issues, 19 April 2010'; Canada (2010) 'Canada's Statement of Support on the United Nations Declaration on the Rights of Indigenous Peoples'; (United States 2010) 'Statement by Ambassador Susan E. Rice, U.S. Permanent Representative to the United Nations, on the Announcement of U.S. Support for the United Nations Declaration on the Rights of Indigenous Peoples'.

Article 46(1) was introduced primarily in response to the concerns of African states, and essentially establishes that indigenous peoples do not have the right unilaterally to secede from existing states:

> Nothing in this Declaration may be interpreted as implying for any State, people, group or person any right to engage in any activity or to perform any act contrary to the Charter of the United Nations or construed as authorizing or encouraging any action which would dismember or impair, totally or in part, the territorial integrity and political unity of sovereign and independent States.

Article 46(1) draws on the language of Article 1 of the 1970 Declaration on the Principles of International Law Concerning Friendly Relations and Cooperation among States (Declaration on Friendly Relations), also known as Resolution 2625 (XXV), but diverges from the latter in omitting any suggestion of states' obligations in securing their territorial integrity and political unity. As per Article 1 of the Declaration on Friendly Relations, the territorial integrity and political unity of states is generally not regarded as an absolute principle that can be invoked under all circumstances, but as dependent upon states' respecting the 'principle of equal rights and self-determination of peoples' (United Nations 1970, Art. 1), as follows:

> By virtue of the principle of equal rights and self-determination of peoples enshrined in the Charter of the United Nations, all peoples have the right to freely determine, without external interference, their political status and to pursue their economic, social and cultural development, and every State has the duty to respect this right in accordance with the provisions of the Charter.
>
> Nothing in the foregoing paragraphs shall be construed as authorizing or encouraging any action which would dismember or impair, totally or in part, the territorial integrity and political unity of sovereign and independent States conducting themselves in compliance with the principle of equal rights and self-determination of peoples as described above and thus possessed of a Government representing the whole people belonging to the territory without distinction as to race, creed, or colour.

As discussed in some detail in Chapter 4, this provision opens up the possibility of secession in cases where a government is engaged in systematic discrimination or exploitation against a defined sub-national group, and forms the basis of a doctrine of remedial secession in international law. The omission from Article 46(1) of any such reference to the remedial circumstances under which sub-national groups may pursue self-determination through secession means that Article 46(1) of the UNDRIP is considered more restrictive than the 1970 Declaration, and indeed, its intention is to 'rule out any interpretation of the right to self-determination of indigenous peoples that might allow for secession' (Eide 2009, 42).[19] However, Article 46(1) does not supersede general international law, particularly where it constitutes international customary law, as in the case of Resolution 2625 (XXV). The stipulations of Resolution 2625 (XXV) in obliging states to comply with the 'principles of equal rights and self-determination of peoples', and the conditionality of the principle of territorial integrity implied by this, are reaffirmed in the 1993 Vienna Declaration and Programme of Action (United Nations 1993, Principle I, Art. 2):

> In accordance with the Declaration on Principles of International Law concerning Friendly Relations and Cooperation among States in accordance with the Charter of the United Nations, this shall not be construed as authorizing or encouraging any action which would dismember or impair, totally or in part, the territorial integrity and political unity of sovereign and independent States conducting themselves in compliance with the principle of equal rights and self-determination of peoples and thus possessed of a Government representing the whole people belonging to the territory without distinction of any kind.

The importance of Art 46(1) to the adoption of the UNDRIP in September 2007 is reflected in states' voting explanations on the Declaration, many of which express an understanding of the right of indigenous peoples to self-determination as exercised with regard for the territorial integrity and political unity of states. Paraguay, for example, asserted that 'the Declaration's reference to self-determination referred to acts and rights that would not interfere with the sovereignty or political unity of States' (United Nations, Department of Public Information 2007.). The Philippines, similarly, declared that its support was premised on the understanding that 'the right to self-determination shall not be construed as encouraging any action that would dismember or impair the territorial integrity or political unity of a sovereign or independent State' (*ibid.*). Argentina, more specifically, described 'the inclusion in paragraph 1 of Article 46 of conditions for the application of the Declaration' as making the UNDRIP 'fully compatible with principles pertaining to the territorial integrity, national unity, and organizational structure of each State' (United Nations 2007f, 19).

19 It is worth noting that secession is not synonymous with the concept of 'external self-determination', and that, moreover, the fact that indigenous peoples are not entitled to secession – other than under the very limited conditions discussed here – does not mean that they are not entitled to exercise other aspects of external self-determination. This is reflected in particular in Article 36(1) of the UNDRIP which affirms that, 'indigenous peoples, in particular those divided by international borders, have the right to maintain and develop contacts, relations and cooperation, including activities for spiritual, cultural, political, economic, and social purposes, with their own members as well as other peoples across borders'.

Though states' concerns regarding their territorial integrity seem to point to aspirations on the part of indigenous peoples for secession, in point of fact secession – with few exceptions[20] – is not what indigenous peoples have been demanding, and in this respect the core content of indigenous peoples' right to self-determination is dealt with in Articles 4 and 5. Article 4 recognizes the right of indigenous peoples to autonomy and self-government, which is generally looked upon as constituting the political precondition for preserving and developing indigenous peoples' cultures, identities, and ways of life. The scope of self-government is set out in Article 4 as encompassing 'matters relating to their internal and local affairs'. The extent or range of autonomous governance is not made clear from Article 4, presumably a positive detail in that it allows for flexibility in the face of the variety of indigenous peoples' circumstances and aspirations, but it can be assumed, when taken in the context of the wider declaration and its provisions on culture, religion, education, media, health, housing, employment, social welfare, membership, and lands and resources, that it contemplates the most extensive and comprehensive possible self-government. There is no reference in Article 4 to a right to territorial self-government, but again, this should be thought of as implicitly contained in any right of indigenous peoples to self-government. As expressed by the authors of the recent International Law Association (ILA) report on the meaning, scope, and status of the UNDRIP, 'in light of the extent to which the social, economic, and political life of indigenous peoples is connected to land, it appears unreasonable that the effective guarantee of the right to autonomy or self-government may be achieved without some recognition of control by indigenous peoples of the lands they have traditionally owned, occupied, or otherwise used or acquired' (ILA 2010, 13).

Article 5 offers further clarification as to the meaning of indigenous peoples right to self-government and self-determination, particularly in regard to its 'dual aspects', whereby indigenous peoples are 'appropriately viewed as simultaneously distinct from, yet joined to, larger units of social and political interaction, units that may include indigenous federations, the states within which they live, and the global community itself' (Anaya 2010, 193). Thus, on the one hand Article 5 provides that indigenous peoples have the 'right to maintain and strengthen their distinct political, legal, economic, social, and cultural institutions', which are not defined but which can be taken to refer to the various customs, laws, traditions, and practices of indigenous peoples through which political, social, economic, and cultural life is regulated. On the other hand, Article 5 asserts the right of indigenous peoples to 'participate fully, if they so choose, in the political, economic, social and cultural life of the State'. 'Inward- and outward-looking associational patterns' (Anaya 1996, 112) are also manifest in Article 18, which affirms the right of indigenous peoples to 'participate in decision-making in matters which would

20 One exception includes the conditional claim of the James Bay Cree, who have threatened to secede from Quebec if the latter succeeds in its intention to secede from Canada.

affect their rights, through representatives chosen by themselves in accordance with their own procedures, as well as to maintain and develop their own decision-making institutions'.

Other provisions pertinent to autonomous governance include Article 19, which calls upon states to 'consult and cooperate in good faith with the indigenous peoples concerned through their representative institutions in order to obtain their free, prior, and informed consent before adopting and implementing legislative or administrative measures that may affect them'. Article 20(1) provides that 'indigenous peoples have the right to maintain and develop their political, economic, and social systems or institutions, to be secure in the enjoyment of their own means of subsistence and development, and to engage freely in all their traditional and other economic activities'. Article 34, further, recognizes that indigenous peoples have the right to 'promote, develop and maintain their institutional structures and their distinctive customs, spirituality, traditions, procedures, practices and, in cases where they exist, juridical systems or customs, in accordance with international human rights standards'.

Provisions relevant to the safeguarding of indigenous peoples' lands and territories are for the most part clustered in Articles 25–30. The profound and 'distinctive spiritual relationship' that indigenous peoples have with their environment is highlighted in Article 25, which is a principle that applies to 'lands, territories, waters and coastal seas and other resources' that may or may not be presently owned, occupied or used, and which highlights the interrelationship between indigenous peoples' land, resource, and territorial rights and indigenous peoples' cultural worlds. Article 26 is arguably the most significant provision dealing with lands, territories, and resources, and recognizes, in Article 26(1), the general right of indigenous peoples to the lands, territories and resources that they have traditionally owned, occupied, or used, and, in Article 26(2), indigenous peoples' right to own, use, develop, and control the lands, territories and resources they currently possess. An ordinary interpretation of Article 26 offers a robust right, making it highly contentious with a number of states, though to the extent that the reference in Article 26(1) to 'lands, territories and resources that they have traditionally owned, occupied, or used' might appear in some cases to include the whole of a state's territory, the Declaration evidently does not intend to mean all of the territory once used or occupied by indigenous peoples but since lost – a concern noted by certain states in their interpretative statements on the UNDRIP. Notably, in explaining its negative vote on the UNDRIP in September 2007, Australia voiced the concern that (United Nations 2007f, 11):

> With regard to lands and resources, the declaration's provisions could be read to require the recognition of indigenous rights to land without recognition of other existing legal rights pertaining to land, both indigenous and non-indigenous. It is important to stress that any right to traditional lands must be subject to national laws, otherwise the provisions would be both arbitrary and impossible to implement, with no recognition being given to the fact that ownership of

land may lawfully vest in others – for example through grants of freehold or leasehold interests in land.

Two provisions in particular clearly contemplate that some lands, territories, and resources cannot be returned, namely Article 27 establishing a process of adjudication of indigenous peoples' territories no longer in their possession and Article 28, which establishes that:

1. Indigenous peoples have the right to redress, by means that can include restitution or, when this is not possible, just, fair and equitable compensation, for the lands, territories and resources which they have traditionally owned or otherwise occupied or used, and which have been confiscated, taken, occupied, used or damaged without their free, prior and informed consent.
2. Unless otherwise freely agreed upon by the peoples concerned, compensation shall take the form of lands, territories and resources equal in quality, size, and legal status or of monetary compensation or other appropriate redress.

Other land rights provisions include Article 10 prohibiting the forcible removal of indigenous peoples from their lands and territories, or their relocation 'without the free, prior, and informed consent of the indigenous peoples concerned and after agreement on just and fair compensation and, where possible, with the option of return'. Article 29, further, affirms the right of indigenous peoples to the conservation and protection of their environment and the productive capacity of their lands and resources, and calls on states to 'take effective measures to ensure that no storage or disposal of hazardous materials shall take place' without their consent. The right of indigenous peoples to determine and develop priorities for the development and use of their lands, territories, and resources is recognized in Article 32, which also requires that states obtain the 'free, prior, and informed consent' of indigenous peoples prior to the approval of any project affecting their lands and territories, particularly where involving the exploitation of mineral, water, or other resources'.

References to the cultural integrity of indigenous peoples are scattered throughout the text, making the protection and celebration of indigenous cultures critical to an understanding of the UNDRIP. Key protections can be found in Articles 7 and 8, which protect indigenous peoples from genocide and ethnocide, respectively, though without using the latter term. Article 7(2) asserts that indigenous peoples have 'the collective right to live in freedom, peace and security as distinct peoples and shall not be subjected to genocide or any other act of violence, including forcibly removing children of the group to another group'. The reference to the removal of children recalls Article II(e) of the 1948 United Nations Convention on the Prevention and Punishment of the Crime of Genocide (UN Genocide Convention), and responds to the widespread and now well-documented experiences of indigenous children, particularly in the Anglophone world, subjected to forcible removal from their families and placement in schools and institutions where efforts were made to rid them of their cultural attachments and identity as a means to bring about the eventual disappearance of the group (see e.g. Human Rights and Equal Opportunities Commission 1997). Article 8(2), similarly, which emphasizes the obligations of states in 'providing effective mechanisms for prevention of, and redress for' actions liable to lead to the destruction of indigenous cultures, responds to the multiple forms of cultural violence that indigenous peoples have been subjected to, including forced assimilation and integration, forced population transfers, propaganda intended to promote or incite ethnic discrimination, and 'actions with the aim or effect of dispossessing them of their lands, territories or resources'. The latter clause – Article 8(2)(b) – recalls Article 10, mentioned above, affirming the right of indigenous peoples not to be forcibly removed from their lands and territories, a form of violence widely understood to threaten the very survival of indigenous cultures and ways of life. Article 8(2) does not refer to either 'ethnocide' or 'cultural genocide', though the actions described constitute ethnocide as per UNESCO's 1981 Declaration of San José, drawn up by a meeting of experts, which serves as a standard reference (UNESCO 1981):

> Ethnocide means that an ethnic group is denied the right to enjoy, develop and transmit its own culture and its own language, whether collectively or individually. This involves an extreme form of massive violation of human rights and, in particular, the right of ethnic groups to respect for their cultural identity, as established by numerous declarations, covenants and agreements of the United Nations and its Specialised Agencies … We declare that ethnocide, that is cultural genocide, is a violation of international law equivalent to genocide, which was condemned by the United Nations Convention on the Prevention and Punishment of the Crime of Genocide of 1948.

Articles 11–13 are key to the protection of indigenous peoples' cultural integrity, dignity and flourishing. Article 11 affirms the right of indigenous peoples to practice and revitalize their cultural traditions and customs, which includes the right to 'maintain, protect and develop the past, present and future manifestations of their cultures, such as archaeological and historical sites, artefacts, designs, ceremonies, technologies and visual and performing arts and literature'. The implementation clause requires that 'States shall provide redress through effective mechanisms, which may include restitution, developed in conjunction with indigenous peoples, with respect to their cultural, intellectual, religious and spiritual property taken with their free, prior and informed consent'. As with many other rights encompassed within the general cultural integrity norm, implementation of the right calls not only for restraint on the part of governments to refrain from continuing harmful actions but entitles indigenous peoples to some form of positive or affirmative action intended to 'remedy the past undermining of their cultural survival' (Anaya 1996, 102). Article 12 recognizes the right of indigenous peoples to 'manifest, practice, develop and teach their spiritual and religious traditions, customs and ceremonies', 'maintain, protect, and have access in privacy to their religious and cultural sites', 'use and control of their ceremonial objects', and repatriation of human remains. Article 13 focuses on living cultural heritage or intangible heritage, defined in the UNESCO Convention on the Safeguarding of the Intangible Cultural Heritage as (UNESCO 2003, Art. 2.2), 'the practices, representations, expressions, knowledge and skills – as well as the instruments, objects and artefacts and cultural spaces associated herewith – that communities, groups, and, in some cases, individuals recognize as part of their cultural heritage', and which is 'transmitted from generation to generation', 'constantly recreated by communities and groups in response to their environment, their interaction with nature and their history', and which 'provides them with a sense of identity and continuity, thus promoting respect for cultural diversity and human creativity'. Article 13 affirms the right of indigenous peoples to 'revitalize, use, develop and transmit to future generations their histories, languages, oral traditions, philosophies, writing systems and literatures' and to 'retain their own names for communities, places and persons', and calls on states to 'ensure this right is protected'. Article 13 reflects the general tenor of the Declaration in recognizing the dynamism of indigenous cultures, and in conferring upon indigenous peoples the right to determine the direction of their own cultural evolution.

A number of further provisions reflect a concern for cultural protection and transmission. Linguistic integrity is protected in Articles 14 and 16 in the context of media and education, respectively, while Article 15 recognizes the right of indigenous peoples to the 'dignity and diversity of their cultures, traditions, histories, and aspirations', which are to be 'appropriately reflected in education and public information'. As for indigenous intellectual property, Article 31 affirms the right of indigenous peoples to 'maintain, control, protect and develop their intellectual property' over their 'cultural heritage and traditional knowledge', but falls short of recognizing ownership.

Limits on the right to cultural autonomy are present in Article 34, which recognizes that indigenous peoples have the right to 'promote, develop and maintain their institutional structures and their distinctive customs, spirituality, traditions, procedures, and practices', as well as their juridical systems and customs, 'in accordance with international human rights standards'. This limitation is applicable to the UNDRIP as a whole, as established in Article 46(2), which states that 'in the exercise of the rights enunciated in the present Declaration, human rights and fundamental freedoms of all shall be protected'. Any limits must, however, meet the criteria set out in the Article that they are 'non-discriminatory and strictly necessary solely for the purpose of securing due recognition and respect for the rights and freedoms of others and for meeting the just and most compelling requirements of a democratic society'.

Other United Nations Initiatives

Other Relevant Normative Content

In addition to the core instruments outlined above, there are a number of programmatic statements, comments, resolutions, and recommendations on indigenous peoples' rights that can be considered as both representing indicators of and contributing to developing international law and practice.

Amongst the most influential of these are a number of concluding observations and general recommendations issued from within the UN treaty system, which carry weight to the extent that the UN human rights treaties generate legal duties incumbent upon ratifying states and constitute forms of 'hard law'. Though not taking indigenous issues as the main subject matter, the International Covenant on Civil and Political Rights (ICCPR), the International Covenant on Economic, Social, and Cultural Rights (IESCR), the Convention on the Elimination of All Forms of Racial Discrimination (CERD), the Convention on the Elimination of All Forms of Discrimination Against Women (CEDAW), and the Convention on the Rights of the Child (CRC) have all been considered by their corresponding committees as relevant to indigenous concerns, creating a mass of UN treaty body jurisprudence on indigenous rights. Too dense to recount in full here (see e.g. MacKay 2009, 2006, 2005), arguably the most significant observations have impinged on issues of self-determination, land and resource rights, and equality and non-discrimination. Of particular note, the Human Rights Committee (HRC) has with regularity affirmed an understanding of self-determination as applying to indigenous peoples under Article 1 of the ICCPR, as, for example, in its concluding observations on Norway, Canada, and the United States (HRC 1999a, 1999b, 2006a, 2006b, 2006c). Concluding observations contain a committee's opinions on a state party report, and are the main mechanism for monitoring and implementing under the treaties. General comments or recommendations do not refer to specific states, and tend to elaborate on the interpretation of treaty obligations based on the accumulated experience of a committee in reviewing state party reports. General recommendations focused specifically on indigenous concerns have been issued by the Committee on the Elimination of Racial Discrimination (CERD) (CERD 1997), and, more recently, the Committee on the Rights of the Child (CRC) (CRC 2009).[21] CERD's General Recommendation 23 is particularly important in calling upon states 'to recognize and protect the rights of indigenous peoples to own,

21 Other general comments relevant to indigenous peoples include the Committee on the Elimination of Discrimination Against Women (CEDAW) General Recommendation No. 24 on Women and Health (CEDAW 1999, esp. para. 6) and the Committee on Economic, Social, and Cultural Rights (CESRC) General Comments No.13 (CESRC 1999, esp. para. 13), No.14 (CESCR 2000, esp. para. 27), and No.15 (CESCR 2003, esp. para. 7), which deal with the right to adequate food, the right to the highest attainable standard of health, and the right to water, respectively.

develop, control and use their communal lands, territories and resources and, where they have been deprived of their lands and territories traditionally owned or otherwise inhabited or used without their free and informed consent, to take steps to return those lands and territories' (CERD 1997, para. 5). Interpretations issued by CERD are especially influential insofar as the prohibition of racial discrimination is a peremptory norm or *jus cogens* of international law.

A significant amount of normative content on the rights of indigenous peoples can also be found in the declarations and programs of actions arising out of high-level UN summits or issue-specific UN-sponsored world conferences, of which there was a proliferation during the 1990s and beyond the millennium. Taken as opportunities to sow new rights and norms in international law, such conferences generally culminate in the adoption of non-binding instruments that nevertheless reflect an international consensus and from which more explicitly binding rules of international law may eventually emerge. Indigenous peoples' issues have received attention at a range of global *ad hoc* conferences, with indigenous concerns emerging as relevant not only to issues of human rights, but also sustainable development and the environment. Instruments emerging from the 1992 UN Conference on Environment and Development in Rio – the so-called Earth Summit – make extensive references to indigenous peoples. Agenda 21, in particular, contains a chapter (Chapter 26) devoted to 'Recognizing and Strengthening the Role of Indigenous People and their Communities' in which it makes the link between the rights and security of indigenous peoples and environmentally-sound development, as follows (United Nations 1992a, Ch. 26, para. 1):

> In view of the interrelationship between the natural environment and its sustainable development and the cultural, social, economic and physical well-being of indigenous people, national and international efforts to implement environmentally sound and sustainable development should recognize, accommodate, promote and strengthen the role of indigenous people and their communities.

The 'vital role' of traditional indigenous knowledge for sustainable environmental management is also contained in the Rio Declaration on Environment and Development (United Nations 1992b, principle 22) and more obliquely implied in the Statement of Principles for the Sustainable Management of Forests (United Nations 1992c, at 5.a, 12.d). Article 8(j) of the *Convention on Biological Diversity*, which was opened for signature at the Earth Summit, affirms indigenous peoples' rights to their traditional knowledge and recognizes the contribution that traditional knowledge and practices make to conservation and the sustainable use of biological diversity (United Nations 1992d). More recently, the World Summit on Sustainable Development (WSSD) in Johannesburg in 2002 reaffirmed the 'vital role of the indigenous peoples in sustainable development' (United Nations 2002a, 25).

Other UN summits to address indigenous concerns include the 1993 World Conference on Human Rights, the 1994 UN Conference on Population and

Development, and the 1995 Fourth World Conference on Women. The Vienna Declaration and Program of Action devotes a section to indigenous 'people' – terminology reflecting the sensitivities of states on the issue of indigenous self-determination – in which it calls for, amongst other things, the proclamation of an international decade and the establishment of a permanent forum (United Nations 1993a, paras. 28–32). The Programme of Action of the International Conference on Population and Development also earmarked indigenous peoples for special attention, and called on governments to respect the cultures of indigenous peoples, protect and restore their ecosystems and natural resources vital for their survival, and to take indigenous peoples' perspectives into account in the formulation of national population and development strategies (United Nations 1994b, paras. 6.21–6.27). The Beijing Declaration and Platform of Action makes a number of references to indigenous women, principally in relation to issues of cultural diversity, education, media, and development (United Nations 1995b, see e.g. paras. 58.q, 242.d, and 83.n). Finally, the World Conference Against Racism in 2001 also dealt relatively extensively with indigenous peoples' issues, though on the whole indigenous representatives were disappointed with the conference outcomes, not least the qualification attached to the use of the word 'peoples' in the World Conference Against Racism, Racial Discrimination, Xenophobia, and Related Intolerance Declaration. Paragraph 24 of the Declaration states that the use of the term 'indigenous peoples' must be regarded as 'in the context of, and without prejudice to the outcome of, ongoing international negotiations on texts that specifically deal with this issue, and cannot be construed as having any implications as to rights under international law' (United Nations 2001a, para. 24).

Another source of normative content in respect of indigenous rights emerges from the declarations and programmatic guidelines of UN specialized agencies. The United Nations Educational, Scientific, and Cultural Organization (UNESCO) Universal Declaration on Cultural Diversity is broadly relevant to indigenous peoples, especially where it makes the connection between the protection of cultural diversity and respect for human dignity, and in outlining the contribution of traditional knowledge to environmental conservation (UNESCO 2001). The United Nations Development Program's (UNDP) policy on indigenous peoples, UNDP and Indigenous Peoples: A Practice Note on Engagement, is broadly consistent with standards of indigenous rights, and prioritizes the principles of equitable globalization, human rights, participation, poverty reduction, conflict prevention and peace-building, and environment and sustainable development in guiding UNDP practice (United Nations Development Program 2001). The World Health Organization (WHO) adopted the 1999 Geneva Declaration on the Health and Survival of Indigenous Peoples (WHO 1999), and the organization is further mandated through a number of World Health Assembly resolutions to promote the right of indigenous peoples to the highest attainable standard of health, which is linked in WHO approaches to traditional lifestyles and cultural well-being.[22] Other programmatic statements include the Inter-American Development Bank's Operational Policy on Indigenous Peoples (Inter-American Development Bank 2006a) and Strategy for Indigenous Development (Inter-American Development Bank 2006b) and the World Bank's Revised Operational Policy and Bank Procedure on Indigenous Peoples OP/BP 4.10 (World Bank 2005a).

Two UN Decades

An initiative that points to systemic interest in indigenous concerns within the UN system is the calling of two consecutive UN International Decades on the World's Indigenous People from 1995–2004 and 2005–2014, respectively (United Nations 1994a, 2005a). The first Decade was called under the theme of 'partnership in action' and was committed to the goal of strengthening 'international cooperation for the solution of problems faced by indigenous people in such areas as human rights, the environment, education, and health' (United Nations 1994c, para. 2). The program of activities for the Decade identified a number of general, far-reaching objectives, including: the promotion and protection of the rights of indigenous peoples, the education of indigenous and non-indigenous societies concerning the situation, cultures, aspirations, and rights of indigenous peoples, the implementation of resolutions concerning indigenous peoples made at high-level conferences such as the World Conference on Human Rights, and the development by UN specialized agencies and international and national agencies of activities and initiatives benefiting indigenous peoples (United Nations 1996b, Annex). The second Decade commenced in 2005 with the goal of 'further strengthening of international cooperation' (United Nations 2005a, para. 2), and was called in part as a result of the shortcomings of the first decade, including the failure to adopt a declaration on indigenous rights. The first UN Decade was subject to a number of critical evaluations, accused by some of being purely symbolic and a distraction from the lived concerns of indigenous peoples (see e.g. Corntassel 2007; Parisi and Corntassel 2005).

In spite of the manifest disappointments of the first UN Decade, a review of developments during the Decade undoubtedly reveals a number of significant achievements and an overall increase in UN activities in relation to indigenous peoples (see United Nations 2005b, 2004a). The most notable of these include the creation of a UN Permanent Forum on Indigenous Issues (PFII) and a UN Special Rapporteur on the Situation of the Human Rights and Fundamental Freedoms of Indigenous People (Special Rapporteur), both of which are discussed in more detail below. Other concrete institutional developments include the launch by the Office of the High Commissioner of Human Rights (OHCHR) of the Indigenous

22 These resolutions include WHA 54.16, WHA 53.10, WHA 51.24, WHA 50.31, WHA 49.26, WHA 48.24 and WHA 47.27, all of which were passed within the remit of the first International Decade of the World's Indigenous People.

Fellowship Programme, a development intended to support capacity-building in indigenous communities through the provision of human rights training for indigenous fellows (with training offered in English, Spanish, French, and Russian). Diverse specialized agencies have also promoted a whole host of initiatives that reflect the view of the former Secretary General Kofi Annan that 'there is virtually no United Nations activity which does not affect indigenous peoples in some way or another, and in which indigenous peoples do not have a legitimate interest' (cited in IITC 2004, 8). As for raising awareness on the situation, cultures, and rights of indigenous peoples, the first UN Decade saw the holding of a number of workshops and seminars on a range of topics, including: indigenous media (United Nations 1998a); higher education and indigenous peoples (United Nations 1999a); multiculturalism in Africa (United Nations 2002b, 2001b, 2000b); indigenous peoples and the administration of justice (United Nations 2004b); and treaties, agreements and other constructive arrangements between states and indigenous peoples (United Nations 2004c). Additionally, a number of specialist studies were carried out by expert members of the Sub-Commission, notably on the cultural and intellectual property of indigenous peoples (Daes 1993a), the protection of the heritage of indigenous peoples (Daes 1995), treaties, agreements and constructive arrangements between states and indigenous peoples (Alfonso Martínez 1999), indigenous peoples and their relationship to land (Daes 2001a), and indigenous peoples' permanent sovereignty over natural resources (Daes 2004a).

UN Special Rapporteur

The post of UN Special Rapporteur on the Human Rights and Fundamental Freedoms of Indigenous People was created in 2001 with the original mandate to gather communications from relevant sources, including governments and indigenous peoples, regarding violations of the human rights of indigenous peoples, and to formulate recommendations and proposals on measures and activities to remedy and prevent such violations (United Nations 2001c). In this respect, it acts as a kind of non-treaty monitoring procedure, whereby – unlike the former WGIP – the Special Rapporteur is authorized to investigate specific complaints brought to him by indigenous organizations and communities. The role is fulfilled via a number of work methods, involving receiving and responding to communications from indigenous peoples and communities, undertaking country visits and compiling country reports, preparing annual reports, and carrying out thematic studies on issues of particular relevance for indigenous peoples. Past thematic studies have focused on the impact on indigenous peoples of large-scale development projects (United Nations 2003a), indigenous peoples and the administration of justice (United Nations 2004d), and indigenous peoples and education systems (United Nations 2005c). This latter aspect of the work of the Special Rapporteur has been downgraded since the establishment in 2008 of the UN Expert Mechanism on the Rights of Indigenous Peoples (EMRIP), the main role of which is to provide thematic expertise to the Human Rights Council on human rights issues affecting indigenous peoples.[23] Since 2007, the Special Rapporteur has also been mandated to examine the 'ways and means of overcoming existing obstacles to the full and effective protection of the human rights and fundamental freedoms of indigenous people' and to 'identify, exchange, and promote best practices' (United Nations 2007b, Art. 1.a), reflecting an emphasis on implementation. The current Special Rapporteur is Professor S. James Anaya, who succeeded Mexican anthropologist Professor Rodolfo Stavenhagen in 2008. Since his appointment in 2008, Professor Anaya has conducted country visits to Australia, Botswana, Colombia, Chile, Nepal, Brazil, and Bolivia.[24] His latest report to the Council explores the duty of states and private companies to consult with indigenous peoples on decisions affecting them and its implementation (United Nations 2009a).

UN Permanent Forum on Indigenous Issues

Following a decade or so of activity on the part of indigenous campaigners, the UN Permanent Forum on Indigenous Issues (PFII) was established in 2000 as a subsidiary body of ECOSOC (United Nations 2000c). It is comprised of sixteen expert members, eight appointed by governments and eight nominated on the basis of consultations with indigenous organizations. As such, it is the first UN body to be constituted with a membership inclusive of indigenous peoples' representatives, who meet on an equal basis with their governmental counterparts, a development described by Ole Henrik Magga at the opening session in 2002 as 'symbolizing a new kind of partnership between indigenous peoples and governments' (from the author's notes, 13 May 2002). Located at a higher position in the UN hierarchy than other UN bodies dedicated to indigenous concerns, the PFII has a broad mandate that goes beyond human rights to include the wider range of social, economic, and related issues relevant to the ECOSOC. Its mandate is threefold, and involves: providing advice and making recommendations on indigenous issues to ECOSOC, as well as to relevant UN agencies, programmes, and funds; raising awareness and promoting the coordination of indigenous activities within the UN system; and preparing and disseminating information on indigenous issues (United Nations 2000c, para. 2). The establishment of the PFII is widely acknowledged to be a radical development in terms of the structural orientation of the United Nations, and one that goes a significant way towards enacting the international legal personality sought by indigenous peoples.

---

23 At the first session of the UN Expert Mechanism in October 2008, the Special Rapporteur suggested that rather than engaging in thematic studies he complement the Expert Mechanism by providing input to its thematic mandate, thus allowing him to focus primarily on examining specific situations of violations of indigenous peoples' rights (United Nations 2009b, para. 21).

24 Country Reports can be found on the website of the OHCHR at: http://www2.ohchr.org/english/issues/indigenous/rapporteur/countryreports.html.

The PFII meets for two weeks each year at UN headquarters in New York, and has done so since its first session in May 2002. The annual reports of the sessions contain scores of recommendations on wide-ranging issues affecting indigenous peoples, from indigenous children and youth to poverty eradication and the Millennium Development Goals, indigenous women, matters relating to territories and natural resources, and climate change and the stewardship role of indigenous peoples.[25] Other important work carried out by the Forum has involved the preparation of a number of publications, reports, and desk reviews concerning indigenous peoples, including the first edition of *The State of the World's Indigenous Peoples*, a comprehensive assessment of how indigenous peoples are faring in terms of poverty, health, education, cultural wellbeing, environment, and human rights (United Nations, Department of Economic and Social Affairs, 2009). Further achievements of the PFII have been in the area of coordination and harmonization of indigenous activities across the UN system. Notably, the establishment in 2002 of the Inter-Agency Support Group on Indigenous Issues (IASG) to promote and support the mandate of the PFII has created an important space for international dialogue and cooperation among UN agencies on activities aimed at advancing indigenous concerns. As of 2008, some 31 UN agencies and programmes are members.[26]

25 Reports of the annual sessions are available on the official website of the PFII at: http://www.un.org/esa/socdev/unpfii/en/sessions.html.

26 These are: UN Department of Economic and Social Affairs (DESA); UN Department of Public Information (DPI); Secretariat for the Convention on Biological Diversity (SCBD); Food and Agriculture Organization of the United Nations (FAO); International Fund for Agricultural Development (IFAD); International Labour Organization (ILO); International Organization for Migration (IOM); United Nations Office of the Coordination of Humanitarian Affairs (OCHA); Office of the United Nations High Commissioner for Human Rights (OHCHR); United Nations Programme on HIV/AIDS (UNAIDS); United Nations Conference on Trade and Development (UNCTAD); United Nations Development Program (UNDP); United Nations Environment Programme (UNEP); United Nations Educational Scientific and Cultural Organization (UNESCO); United Nations Framework Convention on Climate Change (UNFCCC); United Nations Population Fund (UNFPA); United Nations Human Settlements Programme (UN-HABITAT); United Nations Children's Fund (UNICEF); United Nations Development Fund for Women (UNIFEM); United Nations Industrial Development Organization (UNIDO); United Nations Institute for Training and Research (UNITAR); World Intellectual Property Organization (WIPO); World Health Organization (WHO); World Bank; Inter-American Development Bank (IADB); European Union; Fondo Indígena; Economic Commission for Latin America and the Caribbean (ECLAC); Commonwealth Secretariat; United Nations University, Institute of Advanced Studies; United Nations Non-Governmental Liaison Service (NGLS). Complete list available at: www.un.org/esa/socdev/unpfii/en/iasg.html.

UN Expert Mechanism on the Rights of Indigenous Peoples

Established in 2007 by Human Rights Council Resolution 6/36 (United Nations 2007c), the UN Expert Mechanism on the Rights of Indigenous Peoples (EMRIP) is a relatively recent initiative emerging out of the reform of the UN human rights machinery in 2006, which replaced the Commission on Human Rights – long considered to have become too politicized – with the Human Rights Council, comprised of the representatives of 47 states and charged with 'promoting universal respect for the protection of human rights and fundamental freedoms for all', 'addressing situations of violations of human rights and making recommendations thereon', and 'promoting the effective coordination and mainstreaming of human rights within the UN system' (United Nations 2006b, Arts. 2 and 3). The EMRIP is a subsidiary expert mechanism of the Human Rights Council and was established as the most appropriate mechanism to continue the mandate of the WGIP, which held its final session in 2006. Its mandate assumes some of the work of the former WGIP, and is two-fold: (a) to provide thematic expertise on the rights of indigenous peoples to the Council, focusing mainly on studies and research-based advice; and (b) to suggest proposals to the Council for its consideration and approval (United Nations 2007c, Arts. 1.a and 1.b). In composition, the Expert Mechanism reflects the constitution of the former WGIP in being composed of five expert members, though with one important difference, namely that 'in the selection and appointment process, due regard be given to experts of indigenous origin' (*ibid.*, Art. 4). The current experts are Jannie Lasimbang (Malaysia), President of the Asian Indigenous Peoples' Pact (AIPP), Catherine Odimba Kombe (Democratic Republic of Congo), John Bernhard Henriksen (Norway), a Saami and advisor to the Norwegian Foreign Ministry, José Carlos Morales Morales (Costa Rica), and José Mencio Molintas (Philippines), Ibaloi lawyer and former Chair of the Cordillera Peoples' Alliance.

The EMRIP has held two sessions to date. The first session in October 2008 made a series of proposals to the Human Rights Council, relating to the organization of work, the participation of indigenous peoples, coordination of the EMRIP with other United Nations bodies and mandates, and the right of indigenous peoples to education (United Nations 2009b). It also made a number of recommendations regarding the 2009 Durban Review Conference, including that the Durban Declaration and Programme of Action be revised to take into account the that 'the right of self-determination and the principle of free, prior and informed consent are now universally recognized through the adoption of the Declaration [UNDRIP], making paragraph 24 of the Durban Declaration obsolete' (*ibid.*, 4). Studies commissioned by the EMRIP thus far include a *Study on Lessons Learned and Challenges to Achieve the Implementation of the Right of Indigenous Peoples to Education*, completed in 2009 (United Nations 2009c), and a *Study on Indigenous Peoples and the Right to Participate in Decision-Making*, due for completion in 2011.

1972	Special Rapporteur Martínez-Cobo commissioned by UN Sub-Commission on the Prevention of Discrimination and Protection of Minorities to undertake study on the problem of discrimination against indigenous populations
1977	International NGO Conference on Discrimination against Indigenous Populations held in UN in Geneva
1981	International NGO Conference on Indigenous and the Land held at UN premises, Geneva
1982	Establishment of UN Working Group on Indigenous Populations (WGIP)
1985	WGIP mandate extended to encompass standard-setting
1985	Creation of UN Voluntary Fund for Indigenous Populations
1989	ILO adopts ILO Convention No.169 Concerning Indigenous and Tribal Peoples in Independent Countries
1992	Earth Summit in Rio adopts Agenda 21, including Chapter 26 'Recognizing and Strengthening the Role of Indigenous Peoples and their Communities
1993	UN International Year of the World's Indigenous People
1993	WGIP completes Draft UN Declaration on the Rights of Indigenous Peoples
1993	UN World Conference on Human Rights in Vienna recommends establishment of a permanent forum
1994	UN Sub-Commission adopts Draft UN Declaration as received and transmits to Commission on Human Rights
1995	UN Commission on Human Rights establishes Open-Ended Inter-Sessional Working Group of the CHR to consider Draft Declaration (WGDD)
1995	UN designates 1995–2004 UN Decade of the World's Indigenous People
2001	Post of UN Special Rapporteur on the Human Rights and Fundamental Freedoms of Indigenous People created
2002	Inaugural session of Permanent Forum on Indigenous Issues held in UN Headquarters, New York
2005	UN calls second UN Decade of the World's Indigenous People (2005–2014)
2007	General Assembly adopts United Nations Declaration on the Rights of Indigenous Peoples (UNDRIP)
2007	Establishment of UN Expert Mechanism on the Rights of Indigenous Peoples (EMRIP)

Figure 1.1 Overview of Main UN Initiatives

Chapter 2
Theoretical Framing

This book sets out to examine the emergence and achievements of the global indigenous movement and its role in pressing the UN to take the human rights of indigenous peoples seriously: how does a movement of resource poor and conventionally powerless peoples organize as a global movement, gain extensive and unprecedented access to the UN, and use that access to influence the reshaping of international human rights law and the establishment of mechanisms and spaces geared towards the protection of indigenous rights? How are indigenous peoples' rights and claims being pressed and defended? What can we attribute to the strategies and approach of indigenous advocates? Why do states and the international system respond? What has been the impact of the movement, including at the local, community level? In responding to this task it traverses several literatures in the social sciences, from which it draws diverse analytical devices and perspectives able to cast light on our concerns. This chapter engages in the prior undertaking of elaborating those literatures, which relate to the themes of human rights, social movements, and the role of norms and identities in international relations. First, in order to locate the book in the context of legal and social scientific work on human rights, it offers up a conceptualization of human rights, which are understood in this book not as natural entitlements implied in our humanity, universal and inalienable, but as socially constructed products of struggle between assorted social and political actors with diverse and conflicting interests and means of asserting power. Second, it elaborates on the array of orienting concepts for explaining the timing and impact of social movements, and points to the limits of existing social movement theory for understanding something of the character of indigenous protest and advocacy, as well as the relationship of the global indigenous movement with the UN institution. Third, it considers the way in which norms – broadly understood as sets of values and principles that enter into a political actor's definition of its identity and interests – empower social movements and other non-state actors in world politics, a by now well-established tenet of international relations theory in the realm of transnational collective action that nevertheless carries important explanatory leverage in this particular case.

Human Rights

Approaching Human Rights

While human rights have long been an important subject matter in the disciplines of law and philosophy, the social sciences traditionally neglected the study of human rights. This has its basis in two main, related reasons. First, the origins of the concept of human rights lie in the disciplines of theology and philosophy, which are metaphysical rather than empirical disciplines, whereas practitioners of the social sciences have regarded themselves as committed to the development of objective and empirical knowledge about reality, gleaned through methods analogous to those employed in the natural sciences. Emerging in an era profoundly influenced by the natural sciences, the social sciences were imbued from their inception with scientific positivism, poised 'to "learn" the truth on the basis of empirical findings, not to invent or intuit it' (Wallerstein 1996, 13). Second, the doctrine of human rights as developed in the 17th and 18th centuries is inherently normative, whereas the social sciences – being underpinned by scientific positivism – have traditionally sought to avoid consideration of how things ought or should be in human affairs (McCamant 1981), advocating instead a 'value-free' approach to the study of social reality unhampered by normative evaluations.

Distinct grounds for reticence can also be found in the various social science disciplines. In political science, for instance, we find a discipline influenced on the one hand by positivism and on the other by a body of classical and contemporary political theory critical of human rights (e.g. Bentham, in Waldron 1987; MacIntyre 1984). Sociology, similarly, shares the influence of positivism – particularly evident in the works of Auguste Comte and Emile Durkheim – whilst also inheriting an ingrained scepticism towards rights from the works of Karl Marx (Turner 1993; Waldron 1987). Further, sociology has traditionally rejected a universal human ontology in favour of attention to cultural and social particularity and an emphasis on processes of social construction (Roach Anleu 2001, 1999; Turner 1993), while an identification of society with the nation-state has meant that sociology has, until recently, lacked the theoretical means to explore those rights that are tied to a supranational rather than a societal framework (Woodiwiss 2003). Anthropology, as is well known, championed relativism well into the twentieth century. In 1947, the American Anthropological Association (AAA) submitted a statement to the UN Commission on Human Rights warning against the adoption of a universal declaration of human rights that did not respect cultural particularities, a view built on a static and outdated view of culture and a blanket tolerance of all cultures 'validated by the scientific fact that no technique of qualitatively evaluating cultures has been discovered' (AAA Statement, cited in Dembour 2006, 156). The AAA did not rescind this view until 1999, when it issued a subsequent statement in the form of its *Declaration of Anthropology and Human Rights* (American Anthropological Association 1999; see also Engle 2001).

It can of course no longer be said that social scientists are reticent about tackling human rights. In the last few decades, research on human rights problems has bourgeoned in the social sciences, as a growing community of human rights scholars has produced an expanding body of work based on qualitative, quantitative, and mixed method approaches addressing, amongst other things: the political, economic, social, and cultural conditions that explain both why human rights violations occur and variations in the degree of human rights protection (e.g. Carey and Poe 2004); the origins and development of human rights in both their historical and contemporary manifestations (e.g. Ishay 2008; Plummer 2006); processes of human rights translation from the global to the local (e.g. Merry 2006; Woodiwiss 2003, 1998); politics and interests in the human rights regime, including the inclusions and exclusions of human rights (e.g. Evans 2005, 1996; Stammers 1993); the practices of human rights activism (e.g. Brysk 2000, 1994a, 1994b; Risse, Ropp, and Sikkink 1999; Keck and Sikkink 1998); the legalization of human rights (e.g. Meckled-Garcia and Cali 2006); terrorism and human rights (e.g. Wilson 2005); the impact of globalization on human rights (e.g. Brysk 2002); and more. Suffice to say that in the last fifty years or so, human rights has emerged as an organizing framework of truly global relevance and that, notwithstanding tensions inherent within the social scientific study of human rights, social scientists could not have realistically overlooked so significant a phenomenon.

What this book principally has to offer a burgeoning social science of human rights is an understanding of how rights are constructed, and, more specifically, the role of social movements as agents in the making of international human rights law. At its core is a case study of the global indigenous movement and its efforts to write indigenous rights into international law in the context of the human rights organs of the United Nations, a process involving indigenous representatives, state delegates, and UN bureaucrats in protracted negotiations over the content of indigenous peoples' rights. From this it will be apparent that I do not adhere to a natural law perspective on the nature of human rights, according to which human rights are regarded as innate in all human beings, inalienable, self-evident, and existing regardless of social and legal recognition, but rather to a social constructionist approach. The latter posits that ideas and practices of human rights are generated from political and moral struggles between people located in particular political, social, economic, and cultural circumstances, and riven by diverse and conflicting interests (Plummer 2006, Donnelly 1999; Stammers 1999; Waters 1996). Rather than being intrinsic to individuals, human rights are the outcome of specific social and political struggles through which rights become attached to new bearers, more usually via their institutionalization in legal form.

The idea that human rights are given, innate, and universal is one that is held by many people; we might regard it as the 'human rights orthodoxy' (Dembour 2006, 2). In the West at least, many people 'believe' in human rights, recalling Elie Wiesel's (1999) characterization of human rights as a 'world-wide secular religion'. That this is so is perhaps unsurprising given that the original liberal formulations of human rights that developed in the seventeenth century were of natural rights; the idea that the source of human rights lies in forms of metaphysical abstraction, whether these be God, 'man's moral nature' (Donnelly 1989, 12), reason, or dignity, is 'as old as the idea of human rights itself' (Stammers 1999, 990). As for human rights scholarship, Dembour (2006, 11) argues that 'natural scholars dominate the field'. This might certainly be said to be true of the legal literature, which is generally inclined to treat human rights as 'an article of faith' (Ignatieff 2001) and to accede to some notion of natural rights, a tendency that is slightly at odds with an otherwise technical 'black letter' focus as regard the internal logic, coherence, interpretation, and application of human rights law. Naturalistic allusions can also be found in the works of social scientists of human rights, though by and large the latter are less disposed towards a naturalist account of human rights in favour of recognizing the socially and historically contingent modes of their production. Where, as in Donnelly (e.g. 2003, 1999, 1989), human rights are conceived as 'the rights that one has simply because one is human', the source of rights is acknowledged to be at once natural and social, borne out of 'a social choice of a particular moral vision of human potentiality' (1989, 16).

It is easy to feel the pull of a naturalist conception of human rights, particularly where it is employed by social movements, NGOs, and other proponents of human rights in support of their efforts to relieve forms of human suffering, as is frequently the case. A natural perspective, however, presents a number of serious limitations, turning principally on the lack of agreed upon philosophical and metaphysical foundations justifying their existence, which Conor Gearty (2006) refers to as the 'crisis of authority' at the heart of an otherwise politically dominant and ethically confident doctrine. I will not rehearse the failures of the quest for philosophical foundations in any depth here, but suffice to say that foundational appeals have encountered marked difficulties in the face of the diversity of human societies across times and places, and that a lack of substantive justification as to why human rights are universal leaves natural approaches vulnerable and 'subject to penetrating criticism' (Brown 1999, 103). By contrast, there seem to be clear reasons for social scientists to adopt a social constructionist approach. A social constructionist perspective faces none of the difficult questions as to the source of human rights, whilst benefiting from the ability to describe the social and political origins of particular human rights institutions, to relate their development to social forces in the form of social movements, NGOs, and other social change vehicles, and to explain historical and cultural variation in the making of human rights claims and institutions (Waters 1996). A constructionist approach also benefits from being able to reveal the configurations of interests and power relations that lie behind human rights institutions, thereby exposing the inclusions and exclusions of human rights. Input of this kind is critical to an understanding of human rights as an open concept subject to reworking across different times and places, and for developing an awareness of the potentially 'sustaining' dimensions of human rights in the exercise and holding of power (Stammers 1999).

A constructionist approach might be looked upon as consistent with what has been described as the 'anti-foundational mood of our times' (Gearty 2006), in which many important scholars of human rights have cast off the question of foundations in favour of legal and political arguments justifying the role of human rights as practically important political and legal principles (e.g. Dembour 2006; Ignatieff 2001; Wilson 2001). Adherents of this approach include Michael Ignatieff, who favours a prudential justification for human rights (2001, 54–55):

> It is tempting to relate the idea of human rights to propositions like the following: that human beings have innate or natural dignity, that they have a natural and intrinsic self-worth, that they are sacred. The problem with these propositions is that they are not clear and they are controversial. They are not clear because they confuse what we wish men and women to be with what we empirically know them to be. … They are controversial because each version of them must make metaphysical claims about human nature that are intrinsically contestable. … Far better to forgo these kinds of foundational arguments altogether and seek to build support for human rights on the basis of what such rights actually *do* for human beings. People may not agree why we have rights, but they can agree that we need them. While the foundations for human rights belief may be contestable, the prudential grounds for believing in human rights protection are much more secure.

Constructionist and anti-foundational approaches are of course compatible, but it is worth pointing out that a constructionist perspective need not necessarily be viewed as at odds with the search for foundations, as has sometimes been supposed (e.g. Waters 1996). There is evidently a problem in attaching accounts of the social construction of human rights with an understanding of human rights that views them as metaphysical abstractions existing entirely independently of social or political context and recognition, but it should be emphasized that foundationalist accounts need not be tied to the abstract or transcendental, and that where such abstractions are avoided there is no such antagonism between foundationalist and social constructionist approaches. An example of a foundational claim for the universality of human rights that avoids reification or abstractions of any kind can be found in Turner (2006, 1997, 1993; Turner and Rojek 2001), who argues that a foundationalist conception of human rights might be based upon our ontological vulnerability, a universal condition arising from our bodily frailty and the precariousness of our social and political institutions. This is a foundational approach that avoids the pitfalls of the natural law tradition in being at once material and sociological, and which is not likely to be disputed across times and places.

One reason why it is important to highlight the compatibility between social constructionist and foundationalist accounts is that social constructionist explanations alone do not provide a means to talk about justice or to engage in a defence of human rights. Yet it is the view of this author that social scientific research in the field of human rights is incomplete without normative evaluation, calling for some basis to appeal to moral discourse and to make judgements of a normative and moral nature. This basis is provided for in foundationalist accounts, which present social scientists with a universal basis to justify the existence of human rights, and so with a moral vocabulary to make observations on human rights violations as perpetrated by state and non-state actors. In this respect, far from being incompatible, social constructionist and foundationalist accounts can complement and reinforce one other, for inasmuch as the former benefit from the ability to contextualize particular conceptions of human rights, and indeed to reveal their inclusions and exclusions, the latter offer the means to critique those exclusions. For the purposes of this book and the approach taken within, it should therefore be stressed that a focus on social constructionism does not in any way exclude an interest in justifying the moral authority of human rights, as seen for example in Turner (1993, 1997, 2006).

The Social Construction of Human Rights: Interests, Actors, and Process

In spite of recognition of the constructed nature of human rights amongst social scientists, theoretically and empirically the study of human rights as a social and political project has been relatively neglected. The closest we have to an attempt to theorize the social construction of human rights is offered by Waters (1996), for whom the core assumption of a social constructionist theory of human rights is that 'the institutionalization of rights is a product of the balance of power between political interests' (1999, 595). Drawing on the example of the Universal Declaration of Human Rights (UDHR) of 1948, he accounts for its human rights specifications on the basis of four sets of interests: the interests of the Allies in stigmatizing and penalizing the defeated Axis powers; the interests of Cold Warriors in seeking to undermine each other's legitimacy; the interests of superpowers in justifying intervention in the internal affairs of other states; and the interests of various disadvantaged groups in claiming protection from the abusive actions of states (*ibid.*, 597).

An important contribution, Water's account of the historical origins of the UDHR nevertheless suffers from being both excessively realist and state-centric. It fails to do justice to the normative dimensions of the construction of the UDHR, and makes very little of the role that the recent memory of the Holocaust and other World War II atrocities played in driving many of its key drafters towards the articulation of a clear statement of international ethics. It also privileges powerful states over small or traditionally less powerful states, therefore overlooking the important contribution of less dominant but nevertheless influential states in the writing of the UDHR, including Muslim states (Waltz 2001, 2004). Water's account similarly underestimates the role of ordinary individuals, social movements, and organizations in the drafting process, whose interests and influence he mentions but radically underplays (see e.g. Korey 1998). Women's organizations, in particular, were very active in negotiating textual changes to the UDHR (Morinsk 1999).

Any workable framework for approaching both the historical and present day construction of human rights must foreground the role of social movements and NGOs. Few would object to the view that many of the key developments in the history of human rights were triggered in the context of challenges to power made by revolutionary or social movements, while the authorship of what Baxi (2002) terms 'contemporary' as distinct from 'modern' human rights is regarded as being increasingly diverse and inclusive. In the last thirty years in particular, the United Nations has incrementally deepened the extent of NGO participation in human rights law-making processes, so that NGOs now form an important sector in human rights norm creation. Research shows that NGOs have made significant contributions both in constructing new human rights issues and in negotiating human rights standards, in a number of issue areas: children's rights (e.g. LeBlanc 1995), torture (e.g. Baehr 1989), women's rights (e.g. Elson 2006; Merry 2005), Roma rights (e.g. Klímová-Alexander 2005), Dalit rights (e.g. Bob 2007), indigenous peoples' rights (e.g. Morgan 2004, 2007, this volume), and more.

Evidently, exactly *who* is included in the authorship of human rights is critical to understanding the form in which they emerge. Also important to understanding the content of human rights are the particular rules and procedures informing their construction, which prescribe the modes of intervention and depth of involvement of the various different actors, and therefore the extent of their influence. Formal modes of intervention available to NGOs participating in creating human rights at the United Nations are, in general, fairly limited. NGOs are designated what is termed ECOSOC consultative status, which enables them to make oral statements to meetings within specified time limits and to submit lengthier written statements which may then be distributed as UN documents. Consultative status does not give NGOs the right to participate in the decision-making process, which is reserved for states. Informal modes of intervention are more varied and include lobbying governments over the text of documents, disseminating information to the press, including internal UN media, and holding panel discussions and side events intended to educate about core issues. Lobbying usually takes place in the hallways and coffee lounges of the UN, and is more likely to be successful when NGO delegates make specific suggestions for alternative language. Success is also heavily dependent on the sympathy, flexibility and willingness of individual state delegates, as well as personal relationships and affinities.

Informal modes of input augment the relatively limited formal opportunities available to NGOs operating in the UN arena. Additionally, particular proceedings may be characterized by the adoption of what might be termed 'informal inclusive strategies' (Passy 1999) intended to increase the influence of NGOs. During the drafting of the UNDRIP, indigenous representatives succeeded in pressing for unprecedented levels of inclusiveness and participation, allowing not only for the extensive input of indigenous perspectives as to the content of their rights but also some degree of control over decision-making processes. The WGIP fostered a culture of openness and involvement, while the WGDD – following a great deal of pressure from indigenous organizations and a walkout by the indigenous caucus – adapted its working methods in order to include indigenous delegates in the consensus for the adoption of articles, which is discussed in more detail in

Chapter 4. This latter measure enabled indigenous delegates to prevent dilution of the Draft UN Declaration as negotiated in the WGIP, and was greeted by some observers as revolutionary. In general, the elaboration of a UN declaration addressing indigenous peoples' rights has been characterized by exceptional levels of participation on the part of indigenous peoples' representatives over and above what has been seen in other issue areas.

Human Rights and Emancipation

This book concerns the efforts of the global indigenous movement to reconfigure human rights discourse in order that it might be put to use in redressing the harms borne by indigenous peoples and in protecting them from further encroachments upon their cultures and ways of life. Yet for some writers, human rights discourse occupies an ambiguous status as an emancipatory vocabulary. Critiques of human rights have been around for a long time and are wide-ranging, reflecting different categories of rights challenges that are conceptual, pragmatic, and moral, and which are more or less relevant for our purposes here. Thus, one branch of rights scepticism, emerging particularly from the debate about rights in the United States, finds that rights are excessively individualistic and associated with undesirable characteristics such as selfishness, egoism, self-interest, and indifference to the concerns and welfare of others (e.g. Glendon 1991). Another criticizes the hegemony of human rights discourse and worries that an emphasis on rights crowds out other emancipatory possibilities, for example vocabularies based around responsibilities or faith. A third branch finds that human rights is limited by its origins in and relationship to Western liberalism, with the result that human rights discourse offers limited promise for aspirations framed in terms other than those based on a traditional, liberal conception of politics and rights. This critique contains a number of variations. Thus, feminist critiques point to the androcentrism behind mainstream human rights discourse arising from the public/private dichotomy within the liberal rights logic (e.g. Ashworth 1999; Peterson and Parisi 1998). Another version questions the emphasis on individual rights in the human rights discourse, and the priority of individual over group or collective identity. Additional challenges concern the insulation of the market and the neglect of violations in the non-state, economic domain. Rajagopal (2003, 2006), for instance, argues that human rights discourse is incapable of understanding or acknowledging violations caused by the market, and cautions against a reliance on human rights 'as the next grand discourse of emancipation and liberation' (2003, 173), finding in human rights a discourse 'caught up in the discursive formations of colonialism that makes it blind to many types of violence', particularly 'economic violence' (*ibid.*, 186). Mutua (2002), similarly, cautions against a human rights discourse annexed to the advancement of Western culture, the global free market, and liberal democracy, and points to the 'parallels between Christianity's violent conquest of Africa and the modern human rights crusade' (2002, xi). In a related vein, Brown (2004, 453) warns that:

> It [human rights discourse] ...converges neatly with the requisites of liberal imperialism and global free trade, and legitimates both as well. If the global problem today is defined as terrible human suffering consequent to limited individual rights against abusive state powers, then human rights may be the best tactic against this problem. But if it is diagnosed as the relatively unchecked globalization of capital, postcolonial political deformations, and superpower imperialism combining to disenfranchise peoples in many parts of the first, second, and third worlds from the prospect of self-governance to a degree unparalleled in modernity, other kinds of political projects ... may offer a more appropriate and far-reaching remedy for injustice defined as suffering and as systematic disenfranchisement from collaborative self-governance.

These and related critiques – there are many more (see e.g. Kennedy 2002, 2004) – are evidently important in exposing the shortcomings in the discourse. It is interesting, however, that even many of those most critical of human rights do not dismiss them out of hand, and instead regard critique as contributing to dialogue and evolutionary change within the human rights movement. In part, this may relate to a lack of options; alternative emancipatory projects are 'typically vague' (Dembour 2006, 251), making it very difficult to see what could replace human rights. What, after all, would be the alternatives for contemporary social movements? A social movement framing its claims outside of the human rights framework has little opportunity for legal or institutional resonance, not to mention 'a dubious potential for sustainability' (Hurwitz 2005, 4). Human rights provide social movements with a potent source of legitimation, whereas to frame claims in an 'alien, esoteric, exogenously derived lexicon simply would be "senseless" as a motivation and ineffective as a strategy given the cultural orientations binding activists, their constituents, and their opponents' (McCann 1994, 272). Human rights, further, constitute the 'horizon of justice to which public institutions try to conform' (Coicaud 2003, 178), as well as providing a 'ready legal means to secure redress for violations' (Darrow 2003, 6). As for limitations arising from its origins, moreover, Hunt (1990) reminds us that counter-hegemonic politics is anyhow 'not some purely oppositional project conceived of as if it were constructed elsewhere ... it involves the "reworking", that is, doing "new work" on old materials' (Hunt 1990, 324), while the porosity and flexibility of human rights – a key characteristic of human rights – makes them inherently open to reconfiguration and 'reworking'. The global indigenous movement is just one example of a movement that has grasped the transformative, dynamic potential lodged in the discourse of human rights, drawing on its manipulability and malleability to foster the reform of human rights. The women's movement is another to have successfully reshaped human rights discourse in order that it might effectively address women's needs and concerns (e.g. Robinson 2003; Guzman Bouvard 1996). Evidently human rights can be conservative, not least in their traditional liberal manifestations, but something in their intrinsic mutability enables the emergence of alternative conceptions with the potential to reflect and respond to a diversity of claims and needs, including the survival of communities and peoples.

One need look no further for evidence of this intrinsic flexibility than to the diverse corpus of human rights instruments that has emerged since the adoption of the UDHR in 1948, which encompasses protections for varied categories of persons (e.g. women, ethnic, racial and religious minorities, indigenous peoples, children, the disabled, migrant workers, refugees), prohibitions on an assorted range of practices (e.g. slavery, genocide, torture, apartheid, forced labour, death penalty), and safeguards for various public goods (e.g. the environment, development, distribution of socio-economic resources). The international human rights regime is both extensive in its current reach and, it is clear, open to fresh articulations borne of need, new threats, and evolving identities.

Social Movements

Social Movement Theory: The Timing and Fate of Movements

Analysts within a general social movement framework work with an array of orienting concepts for understanding the emergence and trajectories of social movements. Mobilizing structures, political opportunity structures, cultural framing processes, repertoires of contention, and activist identities are concepts that are routinely used to explain why and when movements emerge, how they mobilize, and, to a lesser extent, how they achieve their impacts. Originating for the most part from American resource mobilization (RM) theories and political process approaches, these conceive of social movements as flourishing to the extent that they can mobilize a diverse pool of resources (McCarthy and Zald 1977, 1973) and in so far as political opportunities exist to act as a spur to and facilitate collective action (Tarrow 1994; McAdam 1982; Tilly 1978). The nature of resources varies, and includes resources of movement organization, bureaucratization and centralization (McCarthy and Zald 1977), cultural resources (Snow et al. 1986; Snow and Benford 1988), and other human resources such as authority, faith, celebrity, or leadership (Morris and Staggenborg 2007). The type of resources available, together with the character and extent of political opportunities, explain movement emergence, the form of movement protest, and the impact of collective action on the relevant political system.

Resource mobilization and political process approaches go a significant way to mapping the context in which the global indigenous peoples' movement emerged. For instance, advocacy organizations such as the International Work Group for Indigenous Affairs (IWGIA) and Cultural Survival, established in the late 1960s and early 1970s, provided technical and organizational advice and financial support to fledgling indigenous organizations, while a number of conferences held in the mid to late 1970s provided occasion and spaces for early indigenous networking and organization. At the same time, charismatic and educated indigenous leaders acted as agents in the process of identifying new political opportunities, which presented themselves in the form of increased institutional openness at the global level, as the UN enhanced access to NGOs from the 1970s onwards (Gaer 1995). The relative openness or closure of the institutionalized political system is characteristically cited as a key dimension of political opportunity structure. Other dimensions suggested by empirical research have included electoral instability (Piven and Cloward 1977), elite fragmentation and conflict (Brockett 1991), the availability of influential allies (Gamson 1990), and the conflict structure as regards a challenger (Rucht 1996). Synthesizing across different approaches, McAdam's (1996, 27) consensual list of key dimensions of political opportunity includes: i) the stability or instability of that broad set of elite alignments that typically undergird a polity; ii) the presence or absence of elite allies; and iii) the state's capacity and propensity for repression.

In focusing primarily on structural, organizational and material variables, political process and RM approaches have been criticized as economistic and, in particular, as lacking in the ideational and normative realm. Certainly, the early development of RM – seeking to distance itself from the functionalist accounts of previous decades in which protest was viewed as irrational, irregular, and uncontrolled (e.g. Kornhauser 1959; Hoffer 1951) – sought to present protestors as rational, purposeful actors, and with the result that the role of culture and social psychology were initially self-consciously minimized.[1] In contrast to the European inspired school of 'new' social movements (Melucci 1989; Cohen 1985), moreover, which focuses chiefly on the role of identity in collective action, RM and political process perspectives must appear to underemphasize the importance of meaning in the analysis of social movements. The most explicit engagement with culture and ideas in the American tradition can be found in the work of Snow and his colleagues (Snow and Benford 1992; Snow and Benford 1988; Snow et al. 1986), who use the concept of 'framing' to capture the ways in which meanings are proposed by movement organizers to potential recruits (Snow and Benford 1988, 198):[2]

1 Both RM and political process approaches developed in opposition to the functionalist accounts of previous decades as represented, for example, in the work of Hoffer (1951) and Kornhauser (1959). These traditional approaches had been influenced by a concern to censure Stalinism and fascism, but by the 1970s, sociologists and political scientists sympathetic to the claims of contemporary social movements such as the peace and environmental movements were eager to give social movements a more positive image (Nash 2000, 115; Tarrow 1998, 15).

2 The work of Snow and his colleagues is the only most comprehensive explication of the ideational dimensions of collective action. At roughly the same time that Snow and his colleagues were developing the framing perspective, McAdam (1982) proposed the term 'cognitive liberation' to signify the transformation of consciousness amongst potential new recruits, which he viewed as a prerequisite for mobilization. Gamson's (1989) discussion of the way in which social movements are increasingly involved in struggles over meaning, in particular through the media, also contributed to emerging discussions on the role of

> We use framing to conceptualize this signifying work, precisely because this is one of the things that movements do. They frame or assign meaning to and interpret, relevant events and conditions in ways that are intended to mobilize potential adherents and constituents, to garner bystander support, and to demobilize antagonists.

Social movements face a number of framing tasks. They must define a situation or condition as unjust and identify causality, imputing blame to culpable agents, 'be they individuals or collective processes or structures' (Snow and Benford 1992, 137). A frame must also propose solutions to stated grievances and suggest a line of action for ameliorating a problematic situation, what Snow and Benford refer to as prognostic attribution (*ibid.*). Finally, a characteristic of collective action frames is that they contain some kind of 'prod to action' or incentive to motivate people (Snow and Benford 1988, 202). These can be inducements of a material, status, moral, or emotional kind. Snow and his colleagues also identify several processes of frame alignment, whereby movement actors relate their ideational work to the predispositions of their target audiences, creating an 'intersection between a target population's culture and the goals and values of the movement' (Tarrow 1994, 123). They propose four types of frame alignment process: (i) frame bridging; (ii) frame amplification; (iii) frame extension; and (iv) frame transformation. Frame bridging describes the 'linkage of two or more ideologically congruent but structurally unconnected frames regarding a particular issue' (Snow et al. 1986, 238). Through frame amplification, movements elucidate or reinvigorate an interpretation of the world that may have become unclear or surrounded with indifference. They distinguish between 'value' and 'belief' amplification, the former meaning the identification and elevation of one or more values that may have atrophied or been suppressed, and the latter meaning the amplification of 'presumptions about the relationship between two things, as exemplified in such presumptions as God is dead, capitalists are exploiters, and black is beautiful' (*ibid.* 240). Frame extension refers to the extension of a movement's interpretative work to encompass interests and perspectives that might not be directly relevant to its main objectives, but which are of considerable importance to relevant targets. Frame transformation involves supplanting existing understandings with new meanings. The success or potency of framing strategies depends upon their internal coherence, empirical credibility, and experiential commensurability, the latter referring to the actual intrusion of a situation into the lives of potential movement participants. Another factor affecting 'frame resonance' concerns the alignment between the goals and values of the movement and the life world and culture of the intended audience.

As we shall see in Chapter 5, the framing perspective is useful for understanding something of the impact of the global indigenous movement, particularly as concerns the development of a new indigenous rights framework within the

---

meaning construction. He introduced the concept of 'ideological packages' to refer to a cluster of frames and ideas.

UN system. Most scholarship on framing tends to apply itself to explanations of movement mobilization and recruitment, but it is also possible to shift the object of alignment from potential recruits to elites in order to explore the role of framing in the achievement of movement impact and outcomes (Morgan 2004). Strategic frames fashioned by leaders in the global indigenous movement have been critical in introducing a fundamental change into international law in the area of indigenous peoples' rights, functioning to attribute blame and causality, to identify a mode of resolution, and to offer moral, material, and legal incentive for the recognition of core rights.

Social movement theory evidently provides a diverse analytical arsenal that goes a long way in explicating aspects of the emergence and development of social movements. Yet it is not quite adequate to fully comprehend the timing, activities, or outcomes of the global indigenous movement. One way in which the global indigenous movement exposes the explanatory limits of existing theory is by forcing us to contemplate the dynamics of interaction between social movements and the law, an area that has otherwise received little theoretical attention from social movement scholars. Inclined until relatively recently – upwards of fifteen years or so – to cast social movements as unconventional outsiders to formal politics, social movement scholarship has not addressed the law in a sustained, theoretically rigorous way (Rubin 2001). This poses a limitation when approaching the global indigenous movement, which, in addition to defining many of its core goals in terms of international law, can be thought of as emerging in tandem with shifts in international legal discourses and as applying a legal consciousness to the pursuit of its goals.

Though law has not been the focus of much theoretical development within social movement scholarship, analysts of specific social movements have time and again demonstrated a critical role for legal institutions, norms, practices, and agents, and across a wide range of social movements, including the civil rights movement (Harding 1984; Morris 1984; McAdam 1983), movements for equal opportunity (Burnstein 1991), the gay and lesbian movement (Werum and Winder 2001), and the women's movement (Pedriana 2004). In the case of the global indigenous movement, legal norms can be seen to have played an important role in its overall emergence and 'externalization' (della Porta and Tarrow 2005, 5), imparting legitimacy to claims for self-determination, raising expectations of political efficacy, and accelerating mobilization efforts. Legal norms can also be credited with lending the movement much of its political efficacy, providing indigenous strategists with discursive resources to engender the emergence of new meanings and new rights.

Attention to the role of legal norms and institutions in social movement trajectories may call for the elaboration of a concept of 'legal opportunity structure'. This may be preferable to subsuming legal factors within the concept of political opportunity, as is sometimes seen (e.g. Pedriana 2004; Werum and Winders 2001). Legal institutions and norms reflect distributions of power and resources and might reasonably be incorporated as variables of political opportunity structure

(Pedriana 2004, 184), but the latter already risks becoming tautological as scholars of specific social movements conflate all kinds of environmental factors within it (McAdam 1996a, 25). As expressed by Gamson and Meyer (1996, 275), political opportunity structure 'threatens to become an all-encompassing fudge factor for all the conditions and circumstances that form the context for collective action'.[3] Law, moreover, potentially manifests as opportunity or constraint in a number of ways, and so we arguably miss an opportunity for the development of a comprehensive and substantive theory when we attach legal factors to the concept of political opportunity structure. At the very least, what is clearly indicated by the case of the global indigenous movement is that law matters for social movements, particularly as a discursive resource.

The global indigenous peoples' movement is in a number of other respects a critical case for social movement theory. One of its distinguishing features is that it operates, though not exclusively, in a highly institutionalized setting in and around the UN and other supranational institutions. As a location for social movement activity, this no longer challenges core premises of social movement scholarship, which for upwards of fifteen years has recognized that social movements have in fact long engaged in both protest and conventional political activities (Goldstone 2003). The accepted picture is now overwhelmingly one of social movements, both in the past and increasingly in the present, complementing 'unusual' tactics with conventional political behaviour, for example in the form of lobbying, legislative politics, and interest representation (e.g. Roth 2004; McAdam et al. 2001; Meyer and Tarrow 1998a, 1998b; Kriesi et al. 1995; Burnstein 1991; Dalton and Kuechler 1990; Rucht 1990). Even so, while the past 15 years or so has seen recognition of the reach of social movements into institutionalized politics, our understanding of what this involves for the form and content of social movement activity continues to be dominated by a singular paradigmatic view. This propounds that social movements accessing institutions experience a more or less predetermined process of 'institutionalization' by which social movements eschew confrontational strategies and claims for more moderate approaches, which can occur in a linear fashion (Michels 1962) or in fits and starts (Jimenez 1999).[4] A

3 Conceptual overreach as regards the concept of political opportunity structure also results from the different ways in which it has been used, that is, both to explain the timing of movements and to account for cross-national differences in the structure, development, and success of comparable movements. Whereas most early work on political opportunity structure employed the concept to explain the emergence of movements (e.g. McAdam 1982), later work, much of it instigated by European scholars, has used political opportunity structure to explain the differential impacts of movements in the context of cross-national comparisons (e.g. Rucht 1990; Kriesi et al. 1995).

4 In much of the literature 'institutionalization' is seen to occur whether or not a movement engages in institutional politics; in such cases, it is regarded as the end-point of political mobilization, which is taken to proceed 'in an almost law like fashion' (Seippel 2001, 123) from spontaneity through to formalization and deradicalization (e.g. Michels 1962).

central factor in the process of moderation, according to this view, is a change in the organizational structures of social movement organizations (SMOs) from informal to professional organizations (Della Port and Diani 1999; Lo 1992), whereby professionalized SMOs turn to political conservatism as a means to ensure their survival. Scholars have noted a number of distinct but complementary processes of institutionalization. Cooptation involves the modification of progressive claims, deradicalization rather than the abandonment of political goals (Meyer and Tarrow 1998a, 21). Cooptation also entails the rejection of disruptive strategies, and closely relates to routinization, whereby movement actors are brought into the realm of established politics. Marginalization is the provision of token spaces purportedly aimed at inclusion, but created to keep activists away from centres of power (Gelb 1989). Fading occurs when, over time and partially as a result of organizational consolidation and formalization, institutionalized contexts 'drain the life out of legitimized spaces' (Roth 2004, 152).

The experience of indigenous activism in and around the UN is not adequately captured by this paradigm. Though considerably enmeshed with the UN system, even to the point of establishing what Katzenstein (1998a, 197) describes as 'habitats of activists' within the UN, for example in the form of the PFII, the global indigenous movement has not been subject to the kind of taming identified as an inevitable consequence of entry into institutional arenas. Of particular note has been a determined refusal on the part of indigenous organizations and their representatives to modify their core claims, in particular for recognition of the right of indigenous peoples to self-determination in international law, and in spite of enduring vehement opposition from some states. As to what might explain a resistance to deradicalization in the indigenous case, a key factor can be found in the creative use of normative resources drawn from within the UN's own legal arsenal, which have provided indigenous claims with authority and legitimacy, a matter that is discussed in detail in Chapter 5. Also of note is the fact that indigenous organizations accessing the UN have not been subject to usual UN rules concerning accreditation, whereby SMOs are required to undergo a number of organizational changes in exchange for access. As a consequence, what Kriesi (1996, 153) terms the 'SMO infrastructure' of the global indigenous movement is constituted by a wide range of organizational types, including both formal, professionalized organizations and informal, loosely structured grassroots organizations. This study highlights the limitations in the dominant paradigm, and suggests the need for a more flexible approach that allows for more variation in terms of what takes place when social movements engage in institutional politics.

Another characteristic sometimes presumed of movements where they engage in institutional politics is that they are not identity-orientated. Evident in part in attempts to classify social movement types, these have distinguished movements on the basis of a linkage between social movements' goals and their logic of action, and according to which movements intent on pursuing concrete, measurable goals employ an instrumental rather than an identity logic of action (e.g. Duyvendak and Guigni 1995). By contrast, identity movements, with their 'internal', cultural goals – the promotion of democratic values, personal empowerment, and cultural change in civil society – follow an identity logic of action, and 'realize their goals, at least partly, in their activities' (*ibid.*, 278). Yet collective identity is an important tool for thinking about the origins, activities, and successes of the global indigenous movement, a movement otherwise focused on pursuing legal and institutional change through various UN forums. Indeed, for some writers, the global indigenous movement is first and foremost an identity movement (e.g. Niezen 2003), whether or not it is framed as a new social movement. Identity figures in an understanding of both the emergence of the global indigenous movement, and, more unusually perhaps, its strategic approach and appeal, what Bernstein (2003) terms 'identity as strategy'.

As yet, this discussion of theoretical approaches to social movements has omitted a definition of 'social movement'. Various definitions exist, including a number based on systematic comparison of existing conceptualizations (e.g. della Porta and Diani 1999, 14–16; Diani 1992). For the purposes of this book, a social movement is defined as an informal interaction network of a plurality of individuals, groups, and organizations, including NGOs, characterized by a collective identity and/or sense of solidarity, and engaged in protest to achieve or prevent social, cultural, political, or legal change. By 'protest', I refer to a range of activities designed to pursue movement goals and not necessarily to demonstrative or unruly forms of behaviour more typically associated with social movements. Thus, 'protest' may include pressure exerted through institutional channels, as when, for example, 'a citizen group litigates against the construction of a nuclear power plant regardless of whether the group's members are present in the courtroom' (Rucht 1998, 30).

Transnational Contention, Norms, and Identities

With the relatively recent publication of a number of works focused on the dynamics of global social movements (e.g. Cohen and Rai 2000; Guidry et al. 2000; della Porta et al. 1999; Smith et al. 1997) it is no longer fair to accuse social movement scholarship of being 'myopically domestic' (Khagram et al. 2002, 6). Over the last decade, social movement scholars have focused increasing attention on trends in the 'transnationalization' of social movements, demonstrating an interest in the structures, tactics, targets and significance of transnational social movements (Rucht 1999). In the process, insights have been drawn from the study of international relations, resulting in an emerging synthesis and a growing body of work characterized by a kind of theoretical convergence (e.g. Khagram et al. 2002; Tarrow 2001; Brysk 2000; Keck and Sikkink 1998). Critical to this convergence has been the turn in IR towards a concern with norms and identities in the international system and the general development of constructivism by international relations scholars (e.g. Finnemore and Sikkink 1998; Finnemore 1996; Katzenstein 1996; Klotz 1995).

'Constructivism' has sought to demonstrate how international norms influence state interests, preferences, and behaviour, and has resulted from the empirical failure of approaches emphasizing material factors as the primary determinants of state behaviour (Risse and Sikkink 1999, 6). Norms are understood as 'collective expectations about proper behaviour for a given identity' (Jepperson, Wendt, and Katzenstein 1996, 54), and are seen to shape states' interests in an international system defined as a social system, in which states organize their conduct not solely according to material interests or the traditional tenets of sovereignty, but because they value the security and legitimacy of a particular identity. In this way, norms are seen, by their constitutive aspects for states' identities, to be relevant during the process by which states define their interests and organize their behaviour, while *principled* ideas and norms, in particular, are understood to mitigate states' self-interested behaviour and to act as a powerful constraint on the established norms of state sovereignty (Robinson 2003, 165–166).

Much of the work within constructivism in IR has focused on norms based on moral principles, in particular norms of human rights (e.g. Thomas 2002, 1999; Clark 2001; Risse et al. 1999; Keck and Sikkink 1998). Human rights norms have a special status in that they are widely accepted as authoritative within the society of states, and can be thought of as having achieved the status of 'settled norms' (Frost 1996, cited in Donnelly 2003, 39). They also contain an inherent challenge to traditional tenets of state sovereignty, whereby international human rights norms limit the ability of states to treat individuals, groups, and increasingly the environment as within their exclusive domestic jurisdiction. For the most part, the literature has shown an interest in what has been referred to as a 'central core of rights' (Risse and Sikkink 1999, 2) promoting the dignity and security of the human person before the law, including the right to life, freedom from torture, the right of protection from arbitrary arrest, and the right to a fair trial (e.g. Hawkins 2002; Clark 2001; Granzer 1999; Smitz 1999; Keck and Sikkink 1998). These rights have been widely institutionalized in international treaties, and are often regarded, though not without contestation, as representing the 'most accepted as universal rights' (Risse and Sikkink 1999, 2). Other rights given focus in the literature include certain rights of democratic citizenship such as freedom of speech and assembly (e.g. Thomas 1999), racial equality (e.g. Black 1999; Klotz 1995), and a range of so-called 'solidarity' rights, including rights to development, environmental protection, and alleviation of poverty (e.g. Donnelly 2002; Khagram 2002; Keck and Sikkink 1998). As a rule, the literature regards human rights as defining the behaviour that constitutes the necessary attributes of the liberal state. Human rights provide the criteria differentiating the normative community of liberal states from illiberal states, whereby good human rights performance signals membership in the former.

A number of scholars have sought to theorize the causal mechanisms of norm socialization. Risse and his colleagues, for example, identify three processes in the socialization of international human rights norms into the domestic practices of states of: i) adaptation and strategic bargaining; ii) moral consciousness-raising, argumentation, dialogue, and persuasion; and iii) institutionalization and habitualization (Risse et al. 1999; Risse and Sikkink 1999; Risse and Ropp 1999). The former occurs when states adjust their human rights practices in order to gain access to the material benefits attached to certain behaviours, for example the receipt of foreign aid or the end to international sanctions. Though this process is instrumentally motivated, where it leads to engagement in argumentative processes it can set in motion a process of identity transformation resulting in turn in the belief of the validity of the norms in question (*ibid.*, 10–12, 16–17). Norm socialization is considered complete when 'human rights norms are incorporated into the "standard operating procedures" of domestic institutions' (*ibid.*, 17).

Critical to this model of norm socialization is the important role of transnational advocacy networks in the internalization and domestic implementation of principled norms. Networks engender socialization by drawing international attention to norm-violating behaviour and by empowering and legitimating the claims of domestic social movements and NGOs in target countries, leading to pressure 'from above' and 'from below' (Risse and Sikkink 1999, 5). The particular methods deployed are diverse, but all involve manipulating norms, which lend networks a kind of 'soft power' that should not be regarded as either weak or superficial (Sikkink 2002, 303–304). Networks are not powerful in any traditional sense of the term – they do not possess military strength or economic power, nor do they control valuable resources – but to the extent that they can exploit the legitimacy inherent in international norms, they may assert considerable influence over states aspiring to certain identities. As explained by Thomas (2002, 71–72):

> Transnational networks of non-state actors gain greater access to and influence over states when they identify their cause with prevailing norms, defined as standards of appropriate behaviour for actors with a given identity in world politics ... International norms enable transnational networks to mobilize and achieve influence beyond their command of traditional power resources because world politics is as much about authority and legitimacy as it is about material resources.

One way that transnational networks exercise influence as 'teachers of norms' (Finnemore 1993)[5] is via a process of moral consciousness-raising, whereby transnational actors draw on what Baehr (1999) refers to as the 'mobilization of shame'. Shaming involves publicizing norm-violating behaviour to embarrass states into conforming to norms, and relies upon states rejecting practices that are inconsistent with a particular identity. Though not all states may be vulnerable to shaming, most value the good opinion of the international community and are susceptible to this form of 'moral leverage' (Keck and Sikkink 1998, 23). Amongst those most susceptible are states aspiring to belong to a normative community of

5 Finnemore's work (1993) discusses the role of international organizations, in particular UNESCO, in the teaching and learning process.

nations and those placing human rights at the heart of national self-conception. The latter are also particularly sensitive to so-called 'accountability politics' (*ibid.*, 24), which involves holding states accountable to their public pronouncements in favour of human rights principles or to their commitments under international human rights treaties. 'Norm entrepreneurship' (Finnemore and Sikkink 1999) or the writing of new norms into international law also depends for its success on the manipulation of the global norm structure, whereby new norms are justified in terms of already existing norms. As explained by Sikkink (2002, 306), 'new norms and discourses don't enter an empty international stage, but rather interact in an already existing terrain of norms and discourses'. Global indigenous activism has relied extensively upon this strategic handling and manipulation of information and norms, which have lent indigenous representatives the ability to influence the creation of new norms otherwise perceived by states as not in their own interests.

Chapter 3

The Development of a Global Movement

This chapter concerns the collective actor that I call the global indigenous movement, but that others have varyingly termed the international indigenous movement (Feldman 2002; Barsh 1991) and the transnational indigenous movement (Maiguascha 1994). The movement has several 'global' dimensions. In composition, it consists of organizations and representatives of indigenous peoples from all continents of the globe, including Asia and also latterly Africa, whose marginalized peoples such as the Khoi, San, Ogoni, and Maasai are increasingly tapping into global sources of support, funding, information, and legitimacy. Global networks are also built into indigenous organizations themselves, while a significant part of the mobilization of the movement takes a global guise, as many of its new recruits come to the movement through the UN. It also casts its goals in universal terms, whilst defining many of its causes as global, particularly those arising from neoliberalism.

This chapter introduces 'indigenous peoples' as subjects of a global movement. First, it discusses the question of definition, taking into account the approaches of international organizations and international legal experts and the perspectives of indigenous peoples. It then charts the emergence of the global indigenous movement, which it locates in the context of the threats and opportunities generated by heterogeneous processes of globalization, before turning to the task of profiling the movement.

Who are Indigenous Peoples? Issues of Definition and Identity

Since the 1970s, and in tandem with the development and expanding activities of the global indigenous movement, the concept of 'indigenous peoples' has been transformed from a marginal category with little significance in international law and politics into a concept increasingly associated with rights and benefits, and with considerable currency with the legal and practical agendas of international institutions (Kingsbury 1998). Against this background, the question of who is indigenous has played out as a contentious issue, with much debate in the past thirty years or so focusing on what a definition of indigenous peoples should look like, and indeed whether a definition is either feasible or desirable. As a rule, demands for precision have tended to reflect interests concerned to restrict the application of the concept and its attendant rights and to exclude certain groups from the protections that they would otherwise enjoy.[1]

Following years of considerable debate, the prevailing view in the international community is that it is preferable to identify rather than define indigenous peoples, and that a single formal definition is neither possible nor desirable. UN agencies and international organizations proceed on the basis of various working definitions, statements of coverage, and descriptive criteria, a number of which exist. Perhaps the most widely accepted is the working definition provided by Special Rapporteur José R. Martínez-Cobo, author of the first comprehensive UN study on the situation of indigenous peoples in the world, the *Study of the Problem of Discrimination against Indigenous Populations* (United Nations 1986a). Martínez-Cobo describes indigenous peoples as (*ibid.*, para. 379):

> Indigenous communities, peoples and nations are those which, having a historical continuity with pre-invasion and pre-colonial societies that developed on their territories consider themselves distinct from other sectors of societies now prevailing in those territories, or parts of them. They form at present non-dominant sectors of society and are determined to preserve, develop and transmit to future generations their ancestral territories, and their ethnic identity, as the basis of their continued existence as peoples, in accordance with their own cultural patterns, social institutions and legal systems.

Martínez-Cobo's working definition has been regarded by some as 'underinclusive' (Weissner 1999, 111) and as 'taking a potentially limited, controversial view of indigenous peoples' (Kingsbury 1998, 345) and, certainly, it does not fit comfortably with all situations where indigenous identity is claimed. Indigenous Fijians, for instance, could not be said to constitute 'non-dominant sectors of society', whereas an emphasis on a determination 'to preserve ancestral territories' risks excluding the many indigenous peoples who have been forcibly or non-forcibly removed from their territories and who now reside in urban settings, frequently on the margins. Whether, however, Martínez-Cobo's definition should be seen as applying primarily to indigenous peoples in the settler states of the Americas and Australasia is less certain (e.g. Weissner 1999; Stamatopoulou 1994). Such a view has been relatively widespread, and finds its basis in the requirement of 'historical continuity with pre-invasion and pre-colonial societies', consisting of 'the continuation for an extended period reaching into the present' of (United Nations 1986a, paras. 379–380):

> (a) occupation of ancestral lands, or part of them; (b) common ancestry with the original occupants of these lands; (c) culture and/or specific manifestations

1 The question of definition was especially manifest in the early sessions of the WGDD, where the necessity of defining the concept of indigenous peoples was forcibly pressed by Asian governments in particular, notably Bangladesh, China, India, Indonesia, Japan, and Malaysia (see e.g. United Nations 1996b, paras. 27 and 28; see also Barsh 1996).

> of culture such as religion, living under a tribal system, membership of an indigenous community, dress, means of livelihood, life-style etc.; (d) language; and (e) other relevant factors.

This requirement has been thought in particular to potentially exclude indigenous or tribal peoples in Africa and Asia, where all might be considered indigenous following the departure of Europeans. Weissner (1999, 111), for example, argues that the Martínez-Cobo definition establishes a 'mandatory link to the phenomena of European colonization and invasion' and potentially leaves out indigenous peoples in Africa and Asia that are 'oppressed by equally "original" inhabitants of neighbouring lands that have now become the dominant groups of their society' (Weissner 1999, 111). Arguably, however, though colonizing processes are referred to, there is no indication that colonizers must come from other parts of the world (Thornberry 2002, 50), whereas an emphasis on historical *continuity* is distinct from historical priority (Xanthaki 2007, 10). The former is evidently a more plausible basis for recognition of groups in the context of post-colonial Africa and Asia, where determining priority over neighbours also present for millennia may be complicated by a number of factors, including complex patterns of migration and displacement and 'genetic exchanges harking back to prehistoric times' (Lam 2000, 3). In such cases, indigenousness *per se* may be less pivotal as a basis for indigenous identity than other cultural or distinctive aspects of community and organization.[2]

Both the World Bank and the ILO have adopted approaches that aim to take historical complexities into account. Until 2005, the World Bank Operational Directive (OD) 4.20 described indigenous peoples without reference to any historical criteria, deploying 'vulnerability' as a key marker (World Bank 1991):

> The terms 'indigenous peoples', 'indigenous ethnic minorities', 'tribal groups', and 'scheduled tribes' describe social groups with a social and cultural identity distinct from dominant society that makes them vulnerable to being disadvantaged by the development process.

Since July 2005, the World Bank has foregone a definition in favour of a statement of coverage recognizing a range of characteristics, which may apply to a greater or lesser degree, and which capture both the original inhabitants of states settled by Europeans and those groups that may or may not constitute 'first peoples' as such but who otherwise possess characteristics of indigenousness, notably a social

2 Martínez-Cobo's first attempt at definition, dating from 1972, evinces a more limited conceptualization evident in particular in the requirement that colonizing forces 'arrive there from other parts of the world' (United Nations 1972, para. 34), thereby linking the concept to the indigenous inhabitants of the Americas and Oceania. In carrying out his study, however, Martínez-Cobo sought information from all UN member states, not solely those created by European settlers.

and cultural distinctiveness accompanied by an experience of vulnerability and subjugation, as follows (World Bank 2005a, paras. 3–4):

> 3. *Identification.* Because of the varied and changing contexts in which Indigenous Peoples live and because there is no universally accepted definition of "Indigenous Peoples," this policy does not define the term. Indigenous Peoples may be referred to in different countries by such terms as "indigenous ethnic minorities," "aboriginals," "hill tribes," "minority nationalities," "scheduled tribes," or "tribal groups."
> 4. For purposes of this policy, the term "Indigenous Peoples" is used in a generic sense to refer to a distinct, vulnerable, social and cultural group possessing the following characteristics in varying degrees:
>   a) self-identification as members of a distinct indigenous cultural group and recognition of this identity by others;
>   b) collective attachment to geographically distinct habitats or ancestral territories in the project area and to the natural resources in these habitats and territories;
>   c) customary cultural, economic, social, or political institutions that are separate from those of the dominant society and culture; and
>   d) an indigenous language, often different from the official language of the country or region.

The ILO, similarly, avoids potential exclusion by applying its terms equally to both 'indigenous' and 'tribal' peoples, which are distinguished in ILO Convention No. 169 as follows (ILO 1989, Arts. 1 and 2):

> 1. This Convention applies to:
>   a) tribal peoples in independent countries whose social, cultural and economic conditions distinguish them from other sections of the national community, and whose status is regulated wholly or partially by their own customs or traditions or by special laws or regulations;
>   b) peoples in independent countries who are regarded as indigenous on account of their descent from the populations which inhabited the country, or a geographical region to which the country belongs, at the time of conquest or colonization or the establishment of present state boundaries and who, irrespective of their legal status, retain some or all of their own social, economic, cultural and political institutions.
> 2. Self-identification as indigenous or tribal shall be regarded as a fundamental criterion for determining the groups to which the provisions of the Convention apply.[3]

3 The description of the beneficiaries of ILO Convention No. 169 reflects a significant advance from ILO Convention No. 107 of 1957, which characterizes its beneficiaries according to the 'vertical, hierarchical narratives' of the time (Thornberry 2002, 44). It

None of the UN bodies or mechanisms most closely involved in indigenous issues has formally defined 'indigenous peoples'. In 1997, having completed an in-depth study into the question of definition, the longstanding Chairperson of the WGIP, Erica-Irene A. Daes concluded that 'no single definition could capture the diversity of indigenous peoples worldwide, and it was not desirable or possible to arrive at a universal definition at the present time' (United Nations 1997a, para. 25). She nevertheless identified a list of factors in common amongst formal attempts at definition, constituting a so-called 'concept of indigenous peoples' distinct from definition in pointing to elements which may or may not all be present for coverage to apply, as follows (Daes 1996a, para. 69):

> c) Priority in time, with respect to occupation and use of a specific territory;
> d) The voluntary perpetuation of cultural distinctiveness, which may include aspects of language, social organization, religion and spiritual values, modes of production, laws and institutions;
> e) Self-identification, as well as recognition by other groups, or by State authorities, as a distinct collectivity; and
> f) An experience of subjugation, marginalization, and dispossession, exclusion or discrimination, whether or not these conditions persist.

As for indigenous peoples' perspectives, these have generally reflected a preference to eschew definition in favour of a set of flexible criteria that may apply to a greater or lesser degree in different regions and contexts.[4] Indigenous representatives have regarded a formal universal definition as both potentially

---

identifies two categories of beneficiary, namely: (a) 'members of tribal and semi-tribal populations in independent countries, whose social and economic conditions are at a less advanced stage than the stage reached by the other sections of the national community' and; (b) 'members of tribal and semi-tribal populations in independent countries which are regarded as indigenous on account of their descent from the population which inhabited the country, or a geographical region to which the country belongs, at the time of conquest or colonization' (ILO 1957, Art. 1). The category of 'indigenous' is therefore subsumed under 'tribal' (all 'indigenous' peoples are 'tribal', though not all 'tribal' people are 'indigenous'). Semi-tribal' refers to those 'groups and persons who, although they are in the process of losing their tribal characteristics, are not yet integrated into the national community' (ibid.). The rights in the Convention apply equally to all beneficiaries, though, reflecting the integrationist aims of the Convention, it is the individual members rather than the populations concerned that are the subjects of the rights recognized within.

4 Early movement documents offer up some attempts at definition, such as that proposed by the World Council of Indigenous Peoples (WCIP) for the purpose of accrediting delegates to its founding conference in 1974. This describes indigenous people as referring to 'people living in countries which have a population composed of differing ethnic or racial groups who are descendants of the earliest populations living in the area and who do not as a group control the national government of the countries within which they live' (in Sanders 1980).

exclusionary and as delimiting the right of indigenous peoples to self-determination by denying them the right to define themselves (see e.g. United Nations 1997, paras. 29–30; Daes 1996, paras. 35–36; United Nations 1996a, paras. 29–31). The right to self-identification is held to be extremely important to indigenous peoples and contains both individual and group elements, involving an individual's right to self-identification as an indigenous person and the right of an indigenous group to define itself as such. Both aspects are contained in the UNDRIP, which states in Article 9 that 'indigenous peoples and individuals have the right to belong to an indigenous community or nation, in accordance with the traditions and customs of the community or nation concerned' (United Nations 2007). Article 33, further, posits that 'indigenous peoples have the right to determine their own identity or membership in accordance with their customs or traditions' (*ibid.*). The UNDRIP otherwise avoids anything akin to either a definition or a statement of coverage, though it inevitably contains a number of descriptors or characteristics of indigenous peoples; notably, Article 25 refers to the 'distinctive spiritual relationship' that indigenous peoples have with their 'traditionally owned or otherwise occupied and used lands, territories, waters and coastal seas and other resources' (*ibid.*), a characteristic that some writers have placed at the core of indigenous identity (e.g. Muehlebach 2003).

The adoption of a flexible approach that avoids fixed definitions is consistent with the nature of international law, which requires a certain level of abstraction in order to take account of the diversity of national practice, and which refrains from precise definitions (Xanthaki 2007, 9; Thornberry 2002, 57). This is particularly true of international law in the area of group rights, which lacks a definition of either 'peoples' or 'minorities'. In spite of a diversity of documents on minority rights, including a UN Declaration on the Rights of Persons Belonging to National, Ethnic, Religious, or Linguistic Minorities (United Nations 1992e), no definitive definition of 'minority' exists in international law. An influential description was presented as early as 1979 by Special Rapporteur F. Capotorti in his *Study on the Rights of Persons Belonging to Ethnic, Religious and Linguistic Minorities*, as follows (United Nations 1991, para. 568):

> A group numerically inferior to the rest of the population of a State, in a non-dominant position, whose members – being nationals of the State – possess ethnic, religious or linguistic characteristics differing from those of the rest of the population and show, if only implicitly, a sense of solidarity, directed towards preserving their culture, traditions, religion or language.

Further efforts to clarify the concept of 'minorities' in the UN Working Group on Minorities – either the working group established to implement the Declaration or the working group that drafted it – have not resulted in a precise definition.

In practice, the lack of a formal definition of 'indigenous peoples' seems not to have encouraged the kind of spurious claims predicted by some states regarding a proliferation of false representations (see e.g. Bangladesh and Indonesia, in

Barsh 1996, 795; see also Sanders 1999; United Nations 1996a, para. 28), even given the open, informal accreditation procedures adopted by many of the UN bodies established to handle indigenous peoples' issues. With few exceptions, those presenting themselves as indigenous at international meetings of indigenous peoples have been accepted as such.[5] Nor has the taking of a fluid approach led to the development of too diffuse a movement, in which an eclectic array of groups struggles to achieve either cohesion of claims or a unified identity. Expanding over time to encompass indigenous groups from all over the world, including Asia and Africa, the diversity of peoples participating in the movement under the label of indigenous has not stifled commonality, as indigenous groups of all kinds cohere around a distinctive indigenous identity. The character of that identity is complex, but at its core is a common experience of historical and ongoing colonialism, state repression and control. Niezen (2003, 87) expresses it as follows:

> When we look for the things that indigenous peoples have in common, for what brings them together and reinforces their common identity, we find patterns that emerge from the logic of conquest and colonialism. They are similarities based largely on the relationship between indigenous peoples and states. Of course, there is great variety in state behaviour towards distinct original peoples within their borders; but whatever the specific arrangement, policy, or action pursued by states, it usually falls into one of three categories that arise from the ways indigenous cultures are perceived within the policy influencing sectors of a dominant society: assimilative state education, loss of subsistence, and state abrogation of treaties.

Indigenous participants also share what Castells (1997, 9–12) terms a 'resistance identity', as well as a 'project identity' based on what they hope to achieve from

5 A notable exception occurred at the twelfth session of the WGIP in 1994, when the indigenous caucus produced a petition signed by 82 indigenous participants opposing the participation of the Afrikaner Volksfront and the Rehoboth Baster Community 'because of alleged racist backgrounds' (United Nations 1994a, para. 28). In another related incident, at the seventeenth session of the WGIP in 1999 much of the audience withdrew from the room in silent protest during a statement read by a representative of the Rehoboth Baster Community. The Rehoboth Basters are descendents of Khoi and Afrikaans settlers who claim since Namibian independence to have been deprived a number of rights, including land and subsistence rights, but who are viewed by a majority of indigenous representatives as a dominant white community pressing illegitimate claims to African homelands. This latter event has been the subject of discussion in a number of journal articles characterizing the global indigenous movement. For example, Kuper (2003) misrepresents the occasion to support his characterization of the indigenous movement as an aggressive movement. Kenrick and Lewis (2004) take issue with Kuper's argument and misrepresentation of events. They make the point that quiet withdrawal is the act of a peaceful rather than an aggressive movement, and also characteristic of indigenous peoples' responses more generally (see also Saugestad 2004).

international society. These elements of an indigenous identity are captured by Mick Dodson, former Aboriginal and Torres Strait Islander Social Justice Commissioner and Chair of the Board of Trustees of the UN Voluntary Fund for Indigenous Populations, who describes his experience of attending the WGIP (Dodson 1998a, 18–19):

> I was sitting in a room, 12,000 miles away from home, but if I'd closed my eyes I could just about have been in Maningrida or Doomadgee or Flinders Island. The people wore different clothes, spoke in different languages or with different accents, and their homes had different names. But the stories and the sufferings were the same. We were all part of a world community of Indigenous peoples spanning the planet; experiencing the same problems and struggling against the same alienation, marginalization, and sense of powerlessness. We had gathered there united by our shared frustration with the dominant systems in our own countries and their consistent failure to deliver justice. We were all looking for, and demanding, justice from a higher authority.

The Emergence of the Global Indigenous Movement: Diverse Globalizations

Incentive, Organization and Alliance

International appeals on behalf of indigenous peoples date back to the 1920s, when the leader of the Six Nations Iroquois Confederacy, Deskaheh, famously sought the assistance of the League of Nations in efforts to prevent Canada from invading their territory, but it is not until the early to mid-1970s that we can trace the emergence of the global indigenous movement. This was a decade in which indigenous communities, both on their own account and on the instigation of North American and European advocacy organizations, and faced with the inherent limitations of working within state-based institutions, came increasingly to foster relationships and networks with each other and to organize into national and international organizations with an international strategy.

Its emergence at this time can be traced to a number of political and legal opportunities deriving in large part from changes in the goals of international politics, but it must also be explained in terms of renewed incentive, 'push' as well as 'pull' factors. What we see in the mid-1970s is not only the entrenching of crises in indigenous communities in terms of health, housing, and education – exemplified for Mick Dodson (1998, 18) in the 'runny eyes, the angry, frustrated faces, the lost knowledge, the desecrated land and the hopelessness' – but also the increasing penetration of the forces of predatory globalization into indigenous lives, lands, and territories. A process well documented elsewhere (e.g. Mander 2006), and accelerating in subsequent decades, globalization as neoliberal globalization has brought a range of assaults upon indigenous peoples the world over, the most pernicious of which have involved the intrusion of indigenous territories by global corporations for purposes of resource extraction. Inhabiting some of the last remaining pristine environments in the world, it is a regrettable fact that indigenous territories often coincide with the location of the most sought-after natural resources, leaving indigenous peoples vulnerable to extractive claims by transnational corporations (TNCs) in hybrid ventures with weakened nation-states, and necessitating the collective mobilization for survival.

The connection between resource ventures on indigenous territories and the emergence of the global indigenous movement is evident in early declarations and manifestos issued by the nascent movement, which highlight the pressures placed on indigenous peoples by the unfettered expansion of the global economy (see e.g. WCIP 1981a, 1981b). The linkage is also well documented in relation to national and regional indigenous movements, which are time and again shown to have formed in response to harmful international interventions, compounding the vulnerability of indigenous peoples already multiply jeopardized by processes of 'simple' modernization from an earlier period (Havemann 2000, 18–19) and catalyzing the mobilization of resistance. In the Latin American context, for instance, Brysk traces the rise of the transnational indigenous movement to the incursion of the 'global triad of modernity – states, markets, and ideology', which are seen to shape the movement's 'trio of core demands: self-determination, land rights, and cultural survival' (2000, 59). Rodríguez-Garavito and Arenas (2005, 244), similarly, explain that, 'the simultaneity of the turn to neoliberalism and the rise of the indigenous movement in Latin America is not accidental. Beginning in the mid-1970s and gaining momentum in the 1980s, these two processes have developed in explicit confrontation with each other, as shown by the massive indigenous protests against neoliberalism since the early 1990s, from those that have driven neoliberal presidents in Bolivia and Ecuador out of office to those of the Zapatistas in Mexico'.

Globalization, it is widely accepted, involves an incredibly varied range of processes spanning economics, politics, and culture, and requiring social scientists to speak in terms of globalization*s* (Guidry et al. 2000, 10). While increased incursions of the global economy provided bitter incentive for indigenous peoples to mobilize internationally, other globalizing processes helped to create the global indigenous movement and to facilitate mobilization. Thus, globalization as the intensification of flows of interaction and communication – the diffusion of global telecommunications and computer networking technology, the information revolution, cheaper and more frequent air travel, and so on – provided crucial opportunities for early networking and organization amongst geographically dispersed indigenous peoples. In the mid-1970s, both the International Indian Treaty Council (IITC) and the World Council of Indigenous Peoples (WCIP) were formed at international gatherings of indigenous representatives in Dakota and Port Alberni respectively, creating new constituencies of indigenous peoples across borders. In 1975, the Port Alberni conference brought together indigenous delegates from North America, the Pacific, South and Central America, Northern Europe and Greenland, and produced a 'Solemn Declaration' vowing to 'control again our own destiny and recover our complete humanity and pride in being Indigenous Peoples' (Sanders 1980, 5). The IITC was established as the international or diplomatic arm to the American Indian Movement (AIM), and played a critical early role in articulating claims and setting an agenda focused on bypassing the state via a so-called 'boomerang strategy' (Keck and Sikkink 1998). In 1977, the IITC was the first indigenous organization to gain ECOSOC consultative status with the UN, followed in 1979 by the WCIP (Minde 2007, 18; Wilmer 1993, 137).

Further conferences provided the context for the expansion of organizational networks, and strengthened a growing sense of solidarity and collective indigenous identity. In the late 1970s and early 1980s, both the Inuit Circumpolar Conference (ICC) and the WCIP held periodic assemblies, with the latter meeting in Sweden, Canberra and Panama between 1977 and 1984. In 1980, the Fourth Russell Tribunal in Rotterdam heard the testimonies of indigenous speakers from the Americas, leading to a 'Declaration of Indigenous Peoples' that called 'upon the people of the world to join in asserting that the genocide and dispossession of indigenous peoples is a matter of rightful concern for the world community'.[6] Testimonies played a role in revealing common patterns of conquest and colonialism and highlighting similarities of experience based primarily on confrontations with states, TNCs, and Western culture. The judgements of the tribunal 'jury' condemned the violation of domestic and international laws and drew considerable publicity to the indigenous cause.[7]

Alliances with principled outsiders such as those involved in the Fourth Russell Tribunal deserve considerable mention in any narrative of the emergence and mobilization of the global indigenous movement, pointing to another international influence that aided movement development. Anthropologists, in particular, can be seen to rally to the indigenous cause in the late 1960s and early 1970s, both organizing conferences and establishing organizations dedicated to exposing threats to the cultural and physical survival of indigenous peoples. Of particular note, two conferences – Barbados I and II – were convened by anthropologists in 1971 and 1977 respectively, reflecting the role of anthropologists in the early development of the movement (Varese 1997). The first Barbados conference issued a 'Declaration of Barbados' that called for the 'termination of colonial relationships, internal and external' and the establishment of 'truly multi-ethnic state[s] in which each ethnic group possesses the right to self-determination and the free selection of available social and cultural alternatives'. The Declaration is signed by eleven prominent anthropologists, and offers both a critique of the

6 This Declaration, along with a number of other documents associated with the early development of the global indigenous movement, is available online from the Fourth World Documentation Project archives at the Centre for World Indigenous Studies at http://www.cwis.org.

7 The archives of the 1980 Fourth Russell Tribunal are available through IDC Publishers at http://www.idc.nl/.

historical role of anthropology in 'colonial domination' and a vision for a new anthropology (*ibid.*):

> Anthropology took form within and became an instrument of colonial domination, openly or surreptitiously; it has often rationalized and justified in scientific language the domination of some people by others. The discipline has continued to supply information and methods of action useful for maintaining, reaffirming and disguising social relations of a colonial nature. … The anthropology now required in Latin America is not that which relates to Indians as objects of study, but rather that which perceives the colonial situation and commits itself to the struggle for liberation.

Indigenist advocacy organizations established by anthropologists and human rights activists during this period still exist today, and include the International Work Group for Indigenous Affairs (IWGIA), set up in 1968 in Copenhagen in response to the genocide of Amazonian Indians in Brazil and Paraguay, the London-based Survival International, established in 1969 also in response to atrocities, land thefts, and genocide taking place in the Brazilian Amazon, and Cultural Survival, founded in 1972 by anthropologists at Harvard University. These and a number of other NGOs not exclusively focused on indigenous issues – in particular the World Council of Churches (WCC) – played an important early role in funding indigenous organizing; IWGIA, for example, advised the WCIP during its formation, and provided financial support for its founding conference in Port Alberini (Sanders 1980, 5). They also contributed experience, resources, and expertise, which is not to suggest that expertise could not be found in indigenous communities. One of the ironies of international indigenous mobilization in the 1970s is that it owed a great deal to assimilative education policies imposed upon indigenous peoples as a means of eradicating indigenous and tribal identities, which, failing in that aim, contributed instead to the training of educated indigenous leaders versed in the language, laws, and ways of the societies that impinged upon them.

The United Nations and International Law

The above account shows that strong transnational networks and shared claims already existed between differently situated indigenous peoples prior to UN engagement with indigenous issues, as did an emerging collective indigenous identity. It would therefore be wrong to claim too great a role for the UN in the early emergence of the movement, as is sometimes seen (e.g. Passy 1999). Yet it is clear that the evolution of the movement is to a significant extent intertwined with the UN and international law, which provided physical spaces for processes of horizontal networking and solidarity building and discursive resources for mobilization, respectively. Importantly, these were not spaces that were bestowed or 'offered' by the UN (Passy 1999, 159) but rather *fought for* by indigenous peoples, as we see from various accounts of the nascent movement and its early development (see e.g. Minde 2007; Dunbar-Oritz 2006; Ziegler 1985).[8]

Two UN conferences provided early opportunities to consolidate, extend, and deepen contacts, and to rehearse the framing of claims and grievances. In 1977, the International NGO Conference on Discrimination Against Indigenous Populations in the Americas was organized within the remit of the 1973–1982 UN Decade for Action to Combat Racism and Racial Discrimination,[9] assembling more than 100 indigenous representatives together with the representatives of 38 states and 50 international NGOs (Dunbar-Oritz 2006, 64; Report of the International NGO Conference on Discrimination against Indigenous Populations 1977). The conference is said to have dramatically inaugurated indigenous peoples' entry into the UN institution, with demonstrations and traditional ceremonies drawing substantial media and public attention. It issued a number of recommendations, including a recommendation for the UN Sub-Commission to establish a working group for the consideration of indigenous issues. Indigenous delegates to the conference produced a 'Draft Declaration of Principles for the Defence of the Indigenous Nations and Peoples of the Western Hemisphere' which, together with a number of other important political declarations from this time, can be thought of as forming the basis of the movement's political and legal platform and as laying out its fundamental claims upon the international community, starting with the recognition of indigenous peoples as nations and subjects of international law.[10] A second conference, the International NGO Conference on Indigenous Peoples and the Land, also held in Geneva and attended by unprecedented numbers of indigenous leaders as well as state and UN bureaucrats, followed in

8 The film *Indian Summer in Geneva,* produced by Volkmar Ziegler, recounts very early efforts to press indigenous interests at the UN, and focuses particularly on the testimony of Jimmie Durham. It is available in CD-ROM format from the Geneva-based Indigenous Peoples' Centre for Documentation, Research, and Information (DoCip), 14, av. Trembley, CH-1209, Genève.

9 The final declaration of the 1978 World Conference to Combat Racism and Racial Discrimination 'endorses the right of indigenous peoples to maintain their traditional structure of economy and culture, including their own language, and also recognizes the special relationship of indigenous peoples to their land and stresses that their land, land rights, and natural resources should not be taken away from them'. See United Nations Declaration and Program of Action to Combat Racism and Racial Discrimination, printed in Bodley (1990), 217–218.

10 The 'Draft Declaration of Principles' is reprinted in Anaya (1996), pp. 185–187. See also the list of principles produced at the fourth WCIP General Assembly in Panama in 1984 and the declaration authored by the Indian Law Resource Centre, the Four Directions Council, the National Aboriginal and Islander Legal Service, the National Indian Youth Council, the International Indian Treaty Council and the Inuit Circumpolar Conference and adopted by indigenous peoples at the fourth session of the WGIP in 1985. Both of these are reproduced in the *Report of the Working Group on Indigenous Populations at its Fourth Session* (United Nations 1985a, Annex I, II, and III).

1981, invigorating indigenous mobilization further. The conference heard the testimonies of indigenous spokespersons first hand and called for a number of actions to protect indigenous peoples from abuses at the hands of nation-states, including recognition of a range of rights to land ownership and use (United Nations 1981).

The impetus from these conferences led to the establishment in 1982 of the WGIP, which provided a more enduring institutional space for the development of global indigenism. Comprised of five independent human rights experts sympathetic to the claims of indigenous peoples, and faced with a dual mandate that depended for its achievement on extensive input from indigenous peoples, one of the first acts of the newly constituted WGIP was to break with UN convention by opening its doors to indigenous organizations regardless of whether or not they possessed ECOSOC consultative status, the formal status normally required of NGOs seeking to participate in UN proceedings. The former Chair of the WGIP, Asbjorn Eide, describes the decision and its effects (Eide 2007, 45):

> At that time, almost no indigenous organizations had consultative status with ECOSOC, and it was difficult to get. In the role as Chairman, however, the present author took the decision that in order to fulfill the mandate to review developments concerning indigenous populations and to work towards the development of corresponding standards, there would be a need to have the best possible experts present, and the best experts would be the indigenous representatives themselves. While this was a complete break with tradition and was met by some objections, it was supported by the then director of the UN Centre for Human Rights, Theo van Boven from the Netherlands. The WGIP was opened up for the indigenous representatives, and over the years they joined in large numbers from all over the world. In hindsight, it is clear that this laid the ground for the emergence of a global indigenous movement which came to leave its imprint on much of the United Nations human rights work in the years to follow.

As indicated by Eide, the implications of this opening in opportunity structure were dramatic. It led, first and foremost, to a rapid increase in the number and type of indigenous organizations taking their claims to the UN from 1982 onwards; fifteen indigenous representatives attended the first session of the WGIP in 1982, increasing by 1993 to over 400 indigenous delegates representing diverse constituencies of indigenous peoples (Stamatopoulou 1994, 69). It also opened up a regular and reliable space for the activities of movement mobilization, networking and strategizing, creating a connective location – a 'focal point of our coming together as the world's Indigenous peoples' (Dodson 1998b, 63) – where indigenous representatives could meet on a regular basis, caucus, extend and deepen contacts, coordinate campaigns, and so on.[11] To adopt the language

11 The WGIP met annually for one to two weeks until the reform of the UN human rights machinery in 2006–2007, with the exception of 1986, when a financial crisis facing

of social movement scholars, it created a 'mobilizing structure' (McCarthy and Zald 1973, 1977), and one with enormous importance for the initial and ongoing business of movement mobilization, organization, and coordination. By its twentieth anniversary in 2002, the WGIP had become, as Kenneth Deer of the Mohawk Nation of Kahnawake put it in a speech to the anniversary session, 'almost like an alternative UN for indigenous peoples, the indigenous caucus of the WGIP is the largest gathering of indigenous representatives ever to gather on a regular basis; it is a strategic triumph' (author recording).

Key to the success of the WGIP as a 'space that difference makes' (Feldman 2002) were a number of UN experts and bureaucrats involved in its workings, whose flexibility, expertise, and enthusiasm brought attention and momentum to the indigenous cause. Key individuals in this respect include Professor Asjborn Eide, the first Chairperson of the WGIP and later Chair of the United Nations Working Group on the Rights of Minorities (1995–2004), whose initial handling of the newly created WGIP served to open a space for the claims of indigenous peoples, as discussed above, and Professor Erica-Irene Daes, Chair of the WGIP from 1984–2002. No narrative of the history and achievements of the global indigenous movement in the last thirty years or so would be complete without recognition of the important role of Erica-Irene Daes, who has worked tirelessly promoting the cause of indigenous peoples' rights. A driving force behind the creation of the UNDRIP and one of the principal drafters of the Draft UN Declaration prepared by the WGIP, Erica-Irene Daes was made an honorary life member of the WGIP in 2001 in recognition of her work. Since retiring as Chairperson of the WGIP, she has remained an advocate for indigenous peoples' rights through her widespread public speaking and publishing (see e.g. Daes 2002, 2004, 2008). Other important individuals in this respect include Dr Julian Burger, former Secretary of the WGIP and Coordinator of the Indigenous and Minorities Unit at the OHCHR and author of numerous books and articles highlighting the indigenous cause (see esp. Burger 1987, 1990), and Elsa Stamatopoulou, Chief of the Secretariat of the PFII from 2003–2010. An esteemed figure with a history of longstanding service to a number of UN human rights bodies, including the Commission on Human Rights and the OHCHR, Elsa Stamatopoulou has promoted the rights of indigenous peoples through her various UN offices and was honoured in 2005 with the award of the NGO Committee on the Decade of the World's Indigenous Peoples.

By the time the WGIP was established in 1982, the incipient indigenous movement was already in a position to influence its agenda and to articulate core claims. These drew substantially upon international law, which, having undergone fundamental changes in the post-World War II period, offered a reformed normative context for the pursuit of claims. Traditionally conceived in its Westphalian form as the law of and for the regulation of relations among states, what we see in the post-war period is an extension of the scope of international law to incorporate individuals as subjects of international norms, as, focused by the horrors of the

---

the UN led to the cancellation of the Sub-Commission and its subsidiary bodies.

Holocaust and its central lesson – that states could not always be trusted to respect the rights of their citizens – states moved to elaborate an international human rights regime. The regime is built around an international bill of rights comprising three core documents: the Universal Declaration of Human Rights (UDHR) of 1948; the International Covenant on Civil and Political Rights (ICCPR) of 1966; and the International Covenant on Economic, Social, and Cultural Rights (ICESCR), also of 1966. The latter covenants entered into force in 1976, and reflect the complications of the Cold War context in which a single treaty envisioned in 1948 proved unrealizable. The elaboration of seven further treaties in subsequent years has extended the number of human rights treaties to nine.[12]

Though the concept of human rights has a long history in Western thought and normative philosophy, the development of a human rights regime in the second half of the twentieth century represents the first attempt to establish a global political and legal framework for promoting human rights. At the beginning of the 21st century, the regime is characterized by much breadth and depth, both in terms of the diversity of subjects of rights, which include women, children, disabled people, ethnic minorities, and refugees, and the range of specific human rights concerns addressed, which can be classified according to categories of civil and political rights, economic, social, and cultural rights, and solidarity rights.[13] Developments in the area of implementation have not measured up to those in standard-setting, as a proliferation of norms has not translated into significant restrictions on the principle of state sovereignty through strong enforcement practices. Implementation mechanisms centred on the human rights treaties are generally weak, while developments in international criminal justice have been criticized for various shortcomings (Forsythe 2006; Falk 2002). At the same time, sovereignty *is* conditioned and states do find themselves subject to pressure to conform to human rights standards, while the importance of human rights increases. Human rights have become a 'world-level organizing concept' (Soysal 1994, 43), central to the legal, political, and institutional arrangements of the contemporary world order, and bound up with states' identities (e.g. Risse et al.

12 There are nine core international human rights treaties. These are: International Convention on All Forms of Racial Discrimination (1965); International Covenant on Civil and Political Rights (1966); International Covenant on Economic, Social, and Cultural Rights (1966); Convention on the Elimination of All Forms of Discrimination Against Women (1979); Convention against Torture and other Cruel, Inhuman, or Degrading Treatment or Punishment (1984); Convention on the Rights of the Child (1989); International Convention on the Protection of the Rights of All Migrant Workers and Members of their Families (1990); International Convention for the Protection of All Persons from Enforced Disappearance (2006); and Convention on the Rights of Persons with Disabilities (2006). With the exception of the International Convention for the Protection of All Persons from Enforced Disappearance, which has at the time of writing not yet entered into force, all of the core treaties are overseen by supervisory bodies that monitor their implementation.

13 For a list of human rights protected under international law see Landman 2005, 16; see also Donnnelly 2003, 24).

1999). Human rights constitute the preeminent discourse of normative evaluation, mobilization, and social justice in the contemporary world, and in a way that seems little threatened by alternative emancipatory projects or vocabularies.

Almost without exception, NGOs and social movements voice their challenges using the moral, legal, and political language of human rights. A vocabulary of rights has powerful resonance in global and national politics, providing social movements with a source of legitimation for claims articulated through its framework (Walby 2003). A characteristic of rights discourse is also that it can be adopted in support of a variety of interests, that is, it is politically agnostic (Roach Anleu 1999, 202), which, according to Hunt (1990, 322), 'is not to condemn them, but to praise them'. Another related feature of rights discourse is that it is flexible and fluid, enabling transnational social movements and other social forces to call for the reconstruction of human rights, often via analogy or extension to other rights or rights-holders. Indigenous rights claims challenge legal meanings that attribute rights to individuals rather than collectives, and are a dramatic example of the way in which new rights claims call into question long established understandings of the nature of rights, while contributing to the evolution of what is a pluralized, flexible, and responsive system (Messer 1997, 295).

A significant evolution of the international human rights agenda – and one presenting critical discursive opportunities to the nascent indigenous movement – occurred not long into the post-war period under the influence of the decolonization movement, and what Rajagopal (2003, 73) describes as 'Third World engagement with (what was still then) a European international law'. As is well known, the dismantling of European colonies that started with India and Indonesia in 1947 and accelerated during the 1950s and 1960s led to a quantitative and qualitative change in UN membership, as the number of UN members in this period swelled by more than half, with a majority of new states constituting newly independent Third World states. These were concerned to see the formal endorsement of a decolonization regime in international law, and had, by 1960, promoted recognition of a right to self-determination. Contained in the UN Declaration on the Granting of Independence to Colonial Countries (Declaration on Colonial Countries), the right of self-determination became attached to 'all peoples' (United Nations 1960a, Art. 2), an otherwise undefined category in international law. The adoption of the International Human Rights Covenants followed in 1966, giving the right of self-determination even greater prominence in international law (United Nations 1966a, United Nations 1966b, Common Art. 1; see Chapter 4 for a more detailed discussion of the development of self-determination in international law).

Despite the universality implied by the language of 'all peoples', these developments were not in fact intended to extend the right of self-determination to all kinds of cultural or ethnic groupings defined by historical patterns of association and sovereignty, and particularly not to those existing within the borders of sovereign states. A corresponding resolution to the Declaration on Colonial Countries, GA Resolution 1541 (XV), delimits the scope of application of the right of self-determination by applying the 'salt-water' thesis to claims for qualification, that is, the requirement that territories qualifying for self-determination be at once 'geographically separate' and 'distinct ethnically and/or culturally from the country administering it' (United Nations 1960b;). Amounting to a limit on the application of self-determination to those territories typifying what Wilmer (1993, 96) terms the second wave of colonization, namely those governed by colonial authorities overseas – frequently through 'deculturized and reculturized' indigenous elites (Wilmer 1996, 362) – but not settled by colonizing immigrant populations, this formulation ignored indigenous peoples otherwise living under conditions of colonial subjugation inside the borders of sovereign states.

This construction of self-determination and decolonization in international law is evidently contradictory at a fundamental level, and reflects the multiple agendas of states in preserving colonial borders intact and in protecting their territorial integrity and resource sovereignty. Yet it is precisely the contradictions entailed in promoting some peoples for self-determination and not others that suggested to indigenous activists that they could articulate a challenge to their exclusion from decolonization, and particularly by drawing on the universalizing logic inherent in human rights discourse. As Sanders (1980, 1) put it three decades ago, 'the contradictions between theory and practice suggested to indigenous populations that they could influence the European powers by political and legal agitation'. The nebulous, contradictory character of the law can be regarded as key to the legal opportunity presenting itself to indigenous peoples, combining with a context characterized by the international delegitimation of colonialism to offer a robust basis for contest and the construction of new meanings.

1966	Adoption of International Human Rights Covenants (ICCPR, ICESCR)
1968	International Work Group for Indigenous Affairs (IWGIA) founded in Copenhagen
1971	UN Sub-Commission commissions Study on the Problem of Discrimination Against Indigenous Populations (Martínez-Cobo Report)
1971	Barbados I
1974	International Indian Treaty Council (IITC) established at Standing Rock, South Dakota
1975	World Council of Indigenous Peoples (WCIP) constituted at founding conference, Port Alberni, Canada
1977	International NGO Conference on Discrimination against Indigenous Populations held at Palais des Nations in Geneva, inaugurating indigenous peoples' entry to the UN
1977	Barbados II
1977	IITC gains ECOSOC consultative status
1978	Robert Tim Coulter establishes Indian Law Resource Centre (ILRC)
1980	Fourth Russell Tribunal hears the testimony of indigenous peoples in Rotterdam
1981	International NGO Conference on Indigenous Peoples and the Land held at the Palais des Nations in Geneva
1982	Establishment of WGIP

Figure 3.1 Key Events in the Emergence of the Global Indigenous Movement

Guide to the Global Indigenous Movement

Social movements, as defined in Chapter 2, comprise relatively amorphous networks of interaction between a plurality of organizations, groups, and individuals characterized by shared beliefs and identity and motivated towards some form of social or political change, with *global* social movements taking this form 'on the transworld plane' (O'Brien 2000, 13). In profiling the composition of the global indigenous movement, we find a plethora of organizations and actors – indigenous organizations, non-indigenous advocacy and support organizations, volunteer activists, academics – bound by strong ties and identity and engaged in various campaigns to promote the rights and status of indigenous peoples at and through the UN. At its core are the indigenous organizations that constitute the structural framework of the movement, of which there is a striking volume and diversity. That diversity is reflected in activist composition as indigenous lawyers and attorneys steeped in what Merry (2006) terms the 'culture of transnational modernity' engage in shared purpose with ethnicized campesinos and local tribal leaders and elders.

Indigenous Organizations

Within the plethora of indigenous organizations that constitute the main organizational layer of the global indigenous movement, very different organizations interact. In the first instance, indigenous NGOs differ according to their formal relations with the UN. Many have some form of ECOSOC consultative status. Many more have no formal accreditation, but have gained access to the UN as a result of exceptional, informal inclusive strategies put in place by the various different bodies dealing with indigenous issues. Indigenous organizations also diverge as to their geographical coverage or networked constitution. As shown in Figure 3.3, the movement is comprised of indigenous organizations constituted transnationally, regionally, nationally, and sub-nationally. The World Council of Indigenous Peoples (WCIP) was dissolved in 1996, which means that there are no longer any truly global indigenous organizations. A distinction is made between transnational and regional organizations to the extent that the movement contains transnational organizations – referring to organizations with constituencies in two or more countries – whose organizing rationale is thematic rather than geographical. Transnational confederations of indigenous peoples exist, for example, around issues of environmental justice, biocolonialism, and the protection of tropical forests and forest peoples. Finally, variations exists between indigenous organizations in relation to their primary functional purpose, mode of operation, or organizational form, with highly professionalized and formal NGOs coexisting alongside grassroots groups and local associations typified by weak structure.

Relationship with the United Nations

The usual rules governing access of NGOs to the UN system dictate that NGOs wishing to participate in UN activities must have formal accreditation in the form of ECOSOC consultative status, which is the basis for gaining access to UN meetings and events. In accrediting indigenous organizations, however, the UN has adopted a flexible approach to allow for the accreditation of indigenous NGOs not in consultative status. Accordingly, the indigenous organizations that operate in the UN context have a range of different relations with the UN, while the movement as a whole presents a more diverse profile than many other NGO sectors pressing their interests at the UN.

As seen in Figure 3.2, a growing number of indigenous organizations have obtained ECOSOC consultative status, which can be regarded as testament to the high levels of professionalism and organization that characterize many indigenous organizations today. In order to acquire consultative status, NGOs must meet a number of formal criteria as per ECOSOC Resolution 1996/31 governing access arrangements (United Nations 1996c). They must 'conform with the spirit, principles, and purposes of the Charter of the United Nations', and their work must come within the competence of ECOSOC, an authoritative structure with a broad remit in relation to issues of human rights and social and economic affairs (*ibid.*, Arts 1 and 2). They must have an established headquarters, a democratically adopted constitution, authority to speak for its members, a representative structure, mechanisms of accountability, and transparent decision-making processes (United Nations 1996c, Arts 8, 9, 10, 11, 12).). They may be international, regional, sub-regional, or national in scope. Resolution 1996/31 identifies three categories of consultative status with different statuses: general, special, and roster. 'General' status is conferred on large, international NGOs whose work covers most of the issues on the ECOSOC agenda, and is the most privileged category. 'Special' status refers to NGOs that have a specific competence and are concerned with only a few of the fields of activity covered by ECOSOC. 'Roster' status applies to NGOs with a narrow or technical focus but whose competence enables them to make occasional and useful contributions (*ibid.*, Arts 22, 23, 24). Amongst those indigenous organizations with ECOSOC consultative status, a majority have 'special' status, a handful have 'roster' status; none have the more privileged 'general' status.

The current rules are a reform of General Assembly Resolution 1296 (XLIV) of 1968 (United Nations 1968a), and were introduced in 1996 following a three year review that identified new criteria and principles for establishing consultative status. The review was initiated in the light of changing expectations about the role of NGOs and their increasing visibility in post-Cold War international processes, and in particular to update the rules to reflect the expanding participation and procedural repertoire of NGOs in UN world conferences (Otto 1996). Important changes include the introduction of the tiered system allowing for a first, second, and third track to accreditation, with the second and third tracks applying slightly

Special

Aboriginal and Torres Strait Islander Commission (1995)
American Indian Law Alliance (1999)
Asian Indigenous and Tribal Peoples Network (2002)
Assembly of First Nations –National Indian Brotherhood (2002)
Association of Indigenous Peoples of the North, Siberia and Far East of Russia (RAIPON) (2001)
Centre d'Accompagnement des Autochtones Pygmées et Minoritaires Vulnérables (2003)
Comision Juridica para el Autodesarrollo de los Pueblos Originarios Andinos "Capaj" (1999)
Congress of Aboriginal Peoples (2004)
Coordinating Body of the Indigenous Organizations of the Amazon Basin (2003)
Cultural Survival (2005)
Foundation for Aboriginal and Islander Research Action and Aboriginal Corporation (2003)
Foundation for the American Indian Special (2005)
Four Directions Council (1983)
Fundación de Ayuda y Promoción de las Culturas Indígenas Rosa Collelldevall (2009)
Indian Movement 'Tupaj Amaru' (1997)
Indigenous and Peasant Coordinator of Communal Agroforestry (2003)
Indigenous Peoples of Africa Coordinating Committee (2006)
Indigenous Peoples Centre for Policy Research and Education (Tebtebba) (2001)
Indigenous Peoples Survival Foundation (Special 2004)
Indigenous World Association (1985)
Innu Council of Nitassinan (1997)
International Commission for the Indians of the Americas (INCOMINDIOS) (2003)
International Indian Treaty Council (1977)
International Native Tradition Interchange (2004)
International Organization of Indigenous Resource Development (1989)
International Work Group for Indigenous Affairs (IWGIA) (1989)
Inuit Circumpolar Conference (1983)
Métis National Council of Women (1999)
National Aboriginal and Islanders Legal Services Secretariat (1985)
National Aboriginal Forestry Association (2005)
National Congress of American Indians (2002)
Native American Rights Fund (2002)
Native Women's Association of Canada (2005)
Netherlands Centre for Indigenous Peoples (2002)
New South Wales Aboriginal Land Council (1998)
Partnership for Indigenous Peoples Environment (2004)
Pauktuutit Inuit Women's Association of Canada (1998)
Rigoberta Menchu Tum Foundation (2003)
Shimin Gaikou Centre (1999)
Society for Threatened Peoples (1993)

Tribal Link Foundation (2007)
Union of British Columbia Indian Chiefs (2003)
Yachay Wasi (2008)

Roster

Asociación Kunas Unidos por Nabguana (1996)
Cherokee Nation of New Jersey (2000)
Grand Council of the Crees (1987)
Indian Committee of Youth Organizations (1996)
Indian Council of South America (1983)
Indian Law Resource Centre (1981)
Indigenous Tourism Rights International (2002)
Métis National Council (1997)
National Indian Youth Council (1984)
Saami Council (no date)
Survival International (1981)

Figure 3.2 Indigenous Organizations and Non-Indigenous Advocacy/Support Organizations with Consultative Status with ECOSOC as of 1 September 2009, with date granted (United Nations 2009)

more liberal criteria to the granting of consultative status, and the removal of the requirement that NGOs have 'international standing', both positive outcomes that have evidently made the process of obtaining consultative status more accessible to a wider range of NGOs, including many indigenous NGOs. In spite of modifications, however, the route to formal accreditation remains a difficult one, and is particularly daunting for community or grassroots organizations. Such organizations are less able to demonstrate formal modes of governance and organization, but they also lack the resources necessary to implement a process of what social movement scholars call 'internal structuration' (Kriesi 1996), making informal flexible measures the only route into the spaces of the UN.

The number of indigenous organizations lacking consultative status but accredited through flexible measures to participate in relevant UN activities far outweighs the number of indigenous organizations with some form of ECOSOC status, though the latter category increases every year as new applications are accepted. In general, organizations lacking consultative status demonstrate lower levels of formalization than those with formal status, and many are community or grassroots organizations whose attendance at UN meetings is dependent on various sources of UN funding. The UN Voluntary Fund for Indigenous Populations is an important source of funding in this respect, not least because its funding allocations demonstrate a preference for informal community organizations particularly in need of financial support. The Voluntary Fund was established in 1985 to provide financial assistance to indigenous representatives wishing to attend the WGIP and has since seen its mandate extended to facilitate the participation of indigenous representatives in sessions of the WGDD, the PFII, and the Expert Mechanism (United Nations 1985b).

Geography of Movement Organizations

Indigenous organizations are constituted on different levels from the transnational to the local. All are internationalized in the sense of having relations with the UN. The layers of movement organization are represented with examples in Figure 3.3 below.

Decade	Transnational	Regional	National/Sub-National
1950s		Saami Council	
1970s		IITC	ILRC
		Inuit Circumpolar Conference (ICC)	Naga Peoples Movement for Human Rights
1980s		Consejo Indio de SudAmerica (CISA)	Assembly of First Nations (AFN)
		Comisión Jurídica para el Desarrollo de los Pueblos Originarios Andinos (CAPAJ)	Grand Council of the Crees
		Asian Indigenous and Tribal Peoples Network	Cordillera Peoples Alliance
		Asia Indigenous Peoples Pact (AIPC)	
1990s	International Alliance of Indigenous and Tribal Peoples of the Tropical Forests	Indigenous Peoples of Africa Coordinating Committee	Russian Association of Indigenous Peoples of the North
2000+	Indigenous Peoples' Biodiversity Network		

Figure 3.3 Indigenous Organizations by Geographical Scope/Networked Constitution: Examples

Types of Indigenous Organization

Organizational differences between indigenous organizations relate chiefly to levels of formalization and professionalization and overarching mandate or functional purpose. Allowing for some overlap between organizations, six broad types define the spectrum: advocacy organizations, tribal administrations, national representative organizations, research and education foundations, issue-specific organizations, and grassroots groups. Figure 3.4 organizes these types with examples.

- *Advocacy/legal service*: while all the indigenous organizations participating in the global indigenous movement are to some extent involved in advocating for the rights and status of indigenous peoples, this category of organizations employ advocacy as their core or characteristic activity. Advocacy includes lobbying around particular issues and campaigns, and is heavily informed by legal activity and expertise. Advocacy organizations tend to be well integrated into established modes of interest mediation and to maintain diverse alliance relationships, including amongst state representatives. Most of their staff are highly trained and educated and have backgrounds in law, education, or other related professions providing legal and political skills. These groups tend to have a much longer history of access to the UN and many have consultative status with ECOSOC. Structurally, they tend to follow relatively formal forms of organization, with clear modes of decision-making, boards of directors, functional commissions, clearly defined and organizationally approved mandates, and structures of accountability to members or beneficiaries. An archetypal organization in this category is the Indian Law Resource Centre (ILRC). The Indian Law Resource Centre (ILRC) was founded in 1978 by Citizen Potawatomi Nation member and Colombia law graduate Robert T. Coulter, and defines itself as an advocacy organization providing legal assistance to indigenous peoples seeking to protect their lands, resources, cultural heritage, and human rights in the United States and throughout the Americas. The ILRC has played a critical role in advocating for the rights and status of indigenous peoples at the United Nations. It led efforts to establish the WGIP in 1982 and in the resulting years was at the forefront of efforts to write the Draft UN Declaration. Many of the articles in the UNDRIP reflect wording suggested by the ILRC. In addition to standard-setting at the UN, the Centre is heavily involved in monitoring under the UN treaty-based system. In 2006, together with the Western Shoshone Defence project and a number of other organizations, it successfully brought an early warning and urgent action procedure against the United States under the Convention on the Elimination of All Forms of Racial Discrimination. The ILRC and others claimed persistent violations of the human rights of the Western Shoshone peoples, a claim that was supported in strong terms by the Committee on the Elimination of Racial Discrimination, which called for the United States to 'freeze' plans to privatize Western Shoshone lands for transfer to extractive and energy industries, 'desist from' extractive activities on the ancestral lands of the Western Shoshone, and 'stop' imposing a range of restrictions and accompanying fines intended to hinder the Western Shoshone in the use of their traditional hunting and fishing grounds (CERD 2006, para. 10).

- *Tribal administrations*: self-governing administrations operating zones of local autonomy. Examples include Greenland Home Rule and the Torres Strait Regional Authority.
- *National representative organizations*: referring to: (a) national organizations representing the shared interests of member indigenous nations within the territory of individual states; and (b) national organizations representing the interests of individual indigenous nations. Examples of the former include the Assembly of First Nations, a national organization representing 630 First Nation communities in Canada and with a role in advocating First Nation interests in a number of relevant policy areas (AFN 2010), and the National Congress of American Indians, a national organization of tribal governments in the United States. Examples of the latter include the Kuna General Congress, the Métis National Council, and the Grand Council of the Crees.
- *Research, education, and resource foundations*: these organizations play a valuable role in building and supporting the capacities of indigenous organizations for international advocacy and networking through education, training and research. A model organization in this mould is the Tebtebba Foundation, a research, education, and resource centre based in the Philippines undertaking and supporting research on a range of concerns relevant to indigenous peoples, including self-determined development, climate change, indigenous knowledge, biodiversity, and much more. Tebtebba also runs a publication and information programme that disseminates indigenous issues through a number of magazines and briefing series, as well as a training and education institute that offers training and 'community exposure programmes' on diverse issues from international human rights law and multilateral environmental treaties to community organizing and the use of information and communication technologies (Tebtebba 2010).
- *Issue-specific organizations*: issue-specific organizations are established around a range of concerns and subjects, including the environment, tropical forests, indigenous youth, and indigenous women. Examples include the National Inuit Youth Council, the Movimiento Juventud Kuna, the Asian Indigenous Women's Network, the International Indigenous Women's Network, the African Indigenous Women Association, and the International Alliance of Indigenous and Tribal Peoples of the Tropical Forests. Issue-specific organizations reflect different degrees of formalization and professionalization; they also diverge in their geographical reach. Many constitute small, community organizations while others are national-level organizations or confederations with constituencies in two or more countries.
- *Grassroots organizations*: grassroots organizations tend be very rooted in the local community and established with the aim of benefiting local concerns. They are often characterized by informal structures and forms

of organization, involving horizontal, informal, and spontaneous modes of decision-making, relatively loose governance arrangements, and lower levels of professionalization, understood as the number of paid personnel. They tend to demonstrate lower levels of integration into established modes of interest mediation at both national and international levels than many of the other types of organizations outlined above. Lower levels of both professionalization and formalization correlate to limited resources; participation in UN processes is frequently driven by the need to secure funding for local projects and programmes. Characteristic examples include the Pokot Community and Yois Nigeria.

Advocacy	Tribal Administration	National Rep.	Research/ Info	Issue-Specific	Grassroots
ILRC	Torres Strait Regional Authority	AFN	Tebtebba Foundation	Asian Indigenous Women's Network	Dene Sulene Nation of Cold Lake
Native American Rights Fund	Greenland Home Rule	National Congress of American Indians	Shimin Gaikou Centre	Juventud Kuna	Pokot Community
Inuit Circumpolar Conference		Ainu National Congress	Core Manipur	Pauktuuit Inuit Women of Canada	Tana Uma Amee
IITC	Samson Cree Nation		Indigenous Information Network	Africa Indigenous Women's Association	Dapangu Community of Ali-Shan
	Navajo Nation				

Figure 3.4 Types of Indigenous Organization: Examples

Non-Indigenous Advocacy Organizations

In addition to indigenous organizations, non-indigenous support and advocacy organizations play a central role in the movement, both in advocating for recognition of the rights of indigenous peoples at national and international levels and providing services and resources to indigenous groups and organizations. Diverse organizations exist, including NGOs set up specifically to promote the indigenous cause and NGOs for which indigenous issues constitute one strand of their overall focus. Examples of the latter include the International Commission of Jurists, Minority Rights Group (MRG), and the World Council of Churches (WCC), the latter of which hosts regular preparatory meetings prior to UN meetings on indigenous issues at its premises in Geneva. Support organizations designating indigenous issues as their specific focus include the International Work Group for Indigenous Affairs (IWGIA), the Netherlands Centre for Indigenous Peoples (NCIV), and Cultural Survival. The Copenhagen-based IWGIA is particularly visible at international meetings of indigenous peoples and encompasses both advocacy and service roles that include lobbying to 'enhance respect for indigenous peoples' human rights' (IWGIA 2009) and providing grants to support the participation of indigenous representatives in various UN meetings, which it finances through its Human Rights Fund. IWGIA also reaches a wide audience through its publications – a quarterly journal, *Indigenous Affairs*, and its yearbook, *The Indigenous World* – which are produced in both English and Spanish. Additionally, IWGIA supports a number of projects with indigenous communities across the world, focusing in the main on capacity-building, education, and legal assistance in asserting human rights (IWGIA 2009a). Other organizations offer purely logistical or technical support. The Geneva-based Mandat International, for example, is an interesting organization that supports the participation of indigenous representatives at UN meetings by offering budget accommodation in a former mansion, free transport, and a work infrastructure for the preparation of statements, the holding of seminars, and so on (Mandat International 2010). Also Geneva-based, the Indigenous Peoples' Centre for Documentation, Research, and Information (doCip) is a documentation centre that monitors international meetings of indigenous peoples and collects interventions for storage in its archives, while also providing photocopying equipment and technical services such as translation.

Cultural Survival
Forest Peoples Programme
Indigenous Peoples Documentation and Information Centre (doCip)
International Movement Against All Forms of Discrimination and Racism (IMADR)
International Work Group for Indigenous Affairs (IWGIA)
International Committee for the Indians of the Americas (INCOMINDIOS)
International Commission of Jurists
Mandat International
Minority Rights Group
Netherlands Centre for Human Rights (NCIV)
Rainforest Action Network
Rainforest Foundation
Shimin Gaikou Centre
Society for Threatened Peoples
Survival International
Unrepresented Nations and Peoples Organization (UNPO)
World Council of Churches (WCC)

Figure 3.5 Non-Indigenous Advocacy and Support Organizations

Activist Composition

At the level of activist composition, the global indigenous movement is comprised of a relatively heterogeneous set of individuals. In addition to the representatives of indigenous organizations and communities, UN meetings on indigenous issues see the participation of academics, scholar lawyers, environmentalists, student interns, volunteers, journalists, and what we might think of as an eclectic array of non-indigenous transnational activists drawn to the indigenous cause for a variety of reasons, whether an identification with the indigenous worldview, its rejection of neoliberalism and its embracing of environmental and social harmony, or some form of ethnic identification inspired by their own ethnic marginality; Brysk describes this latter type as 'panethnic fellow travellers' (2000, 93).

Regarding the core of the movement – the indigenous activists representing indigenous organizations and communities – these present two main kinds of profile, with clusters of activists broadly falling into two types personifying different characteristics. On the one hand, there are the lobbyists and articulators, skilled at processes of document negotiation and consensus-building, literate with international law, and adept in the distinctive procedural repertoires that characterize the spaces and routines of human rights norm creation and monitoring. I refer to this group of activists as the *negotiators*. On the other hand, there are those indigenous participants who go to the UN principally to denounce their governments, and whose testimony and presence serve to bring the suffering of indigenous peoples to light in a vivid and experiential way. This group of activists I term *testifiers*. Making a similar observation, Niezen maintains that 'there are basically two kinds of leader who travel to international meetings: elders and statesmen' (2003, 157). In many respects a pertinent characterization, the category of 'elders' – whilst it is clear what Niezen is aiming to render – is arguably too narrow in that testifiers may or may not be traditional elders. I would also reject the apparent oversight of women, who participate widely in the global indigenous movement. Indigenous women have been extremely prominent in the process of drafting the UNDRIP, playing a highly visible and important role as leaders and strategists steering the evolution of international human rights law. Indigenous women have also been elected to key positions within a number of UN bodies relevant to the rights of indigenous peoples, including the PFII, where indigenous women also have their own active caucus focused on the multiple forms of discrimination experienced by indigenous women. Notable women to have served as members of the PFII include the formidable Mililani Trask, leader of the Hawaiian sovereignty movement and founder of Na Koa Ikaika o Ka Lahui Hawaii, who was expert member of the forum from 2002–2004, Igorot activist Victoria Tauli-Corpuz, founder of the Tebtebba Foundation and member of the PFII from 2008–2010, and Dalee Sambo Dorough, human rights advisor to the Inuit Circumpolar Council (ICC) and a current member of the forum (2011–2013.)

Negotiators and testifiers might be thought of as having quite different roles. Testifiers perform an important function in expanding state and institutional imaginations as to the real and concrete experience of human rights abuse. Their interventions to UN forums offer listeners vicarious experiential knowledge and understanding, and have the potential to awaken empathy and arouse the impetus to act. Negotiators, in contrast, engage chiefly on the basis of argumentation and reasoning, applying an argumentative and frequently legal logic to the framing of claims. Negotiators are typically highly educated, with higher degrees in law or other relevant disciplines, and draw on their educational capital in performing the myriad intellectual tasks involved in their role: constructing legal arguments in support of claims, dialoguing with elites, making speeches, interfacing with the media, finding consensus between conflicting positions, debating, and so on. The notion of an epistemic community seems relevant to an understanding of these movement activists (Haas 1992, 3):

> An epistemic community is a network of professionals with recognized expertise and competence in a particular domain and an authoritative claim to policy-relevant knowledge within that domain or issue-area. ... they have (1) a shared set of normative and principled beliefs, which provide a value-based rationale for the social action of community members; (2) shared causal beliefs, which are derived from their analysis of practices leading or contributing to a central set of problems in their domain ... ; (3) shared notions of validity ... ; (4) a common policy enterprise.

Notwithstanding the non-hierarchical culture of the global indigenous movement, we might think of negotiators as sharing a kind of distributed leadership. Negotiators take primary responsibility for core movement tasks, identifying and mobilizing resources, creating and exploiting opportunities, and influencing strategies. They also drive the framing process, identifying effective frames that resonate with different targets and contexts, and managing framing disputes as they arise. These tasks depend upon intellectual, organizational, and political skills, as well as a range of personal qualities such as diplomacy, patience, resolution, and determination. They also demand – framing work in particular – expertise in international legal discourse, which is embedded in core movement frames and which is critical to their legitimacy and resonance.

Socially and professionally, negotiators are at one with the transnational world of UN conferencing, and are not unlike the UN experts and governmental representatives who share that world. They are realistic about what can be achieved from international forums, adept at the routines of international law-making, and are not – in the main – themselves personally vulnerable, which allows them to care about and invest time in negotiating the 'infinity within the brackets'. In this respect they are different from many of the testifiers who attend the UN, who come to the UN to relate the lived experience of human rights violations, and indeed the vast majority of indigenous peoples, whose ongoing experience is one of deprivation and discrimination. As expressed by Mililani Trask (2005, 16):

> There's a handful of us who are privileged enough to engage in this debate. We come every year to Geneva – air-conditioned buildings, nice computers, wear our suits. The vast majority of Indigenous Peoples really have no concern about the words on the paper. The vast majority of Indigenous Peoples, hundreds of millions, live and die in poverty every day. Children are without food, without hope of education. Millions of Indigenous Peoples are still without the hope of receiving medical treatment. Millions are homeless – they have no shelter. Those are the people. Those are the faces of the Indigenous Peoples. … If I took away your clothes, and the food off your table, if I pulled your children out of school, and had them to sleep in the rain, how concerned would you be about preambular paragraph 15 bis. My guess is not very concerned. We cannot forget the reality of our peoples, that commitment, that deprivation is what we have to keep ahead of us, to drive us, and to give us the incentive to stop the interminable debate, come to consensus, and bring this document out to the world. That's an obligation that we all have.

The observation that there are basically two kinds of indigenous activist participating in the global movement is a useful one, but it is not my intention to draw too sharp a distinction between negotiators and testifiers. Activists involved in the global indigenous movement engage in myriad roles that overlap and shift. Moreover, testifiers attending UN meetings year upon year become socialized in the skills of international conferencing and come to share what we might regard as a 'set of informational practices [that] include … the ubiquitous coordination tasks, the endless cataloguing and discussion of documents, and the numerous exercises of drafting and redrafting' (Stiles 2001, xvi). These skills are gathered through observation and practice, plus there is significant guidance to hand from more experienced attendees. They are also assimilated in key spaces such as the indigenous caucus, where to a significant extent the organizational practices reflect intergovernmental forms. A process that Smith (2004, 325) refers to as the 'modelling of organizational forms', the application of intergovernmental templates of organization and procedure in non-governmental spaces allows new activists to quickly assimilate the practices and methods of UN spaces, where 'form generates consensus' in a way that 'content and doctrine' do not (Stiles 2001, 182).

A Note on Intramovement Dispute

Some form of intramovement dissention is the norm for social movements, which may find themselves conflicted along a number of different lines, including membership, leadership, framing, ideology, objectives, and strategies. To the extent that dissention has been present in the global indigenous movement, this has been most evident with respect to negotiating tactics in the WGDD, specifically regarding the so-called 'no change' strategy. The 'no-change' strategy refers to the unified position of the indigenous caucus, adopted at the beginning of negotiations in the WGDD in 1995, to defend verbatim the Draft UN Declaration as adopted by the Sub-Commission and to admit no amendments to any of its provisions. A strategy intended to preserve the integrity of the Draft Declaration, by mid-way through the mandated timeframe for the adoption of the UNDRIP and with very little progress made towards that goal, the 'no change' position was increasingly coming into question, creating discordance within the indigenous caucus between those in favour of the strategy and those regarding it as threatening to the entire declaration process. Amongst proponents of the latter view, concern was expressed that the categorical rejection of any changes to the Sub-Commission text had created a deadlock within the WGDD that made progress impossible and which was delusional given states' evident need to see certain amendments and assurances incorporated into the text.[14] The view was also voiced that certain minor amendments would actually clarify and improve the Sub-Commission text; for example, where its provisions conferred rights inappropriately on 'peoples' rather than individuals.[15] Proponents of the original position, on the other hand, argued that the strategy was essential to uphold the minimum standards as laid out in the Sub-Commission text, and to avoid a so-called 'slippery slope' whereby the demonstration of good will and the acceptance of minor amendments would encourage states to press for more drastic changes that would undermine fundamental principles.[16]

Dissent in social movements is not insignificant and may have important consequences for the direction that movements take, and accordingly, their outcomes and impact. In the case of the 'no change' strategy, subsequent years witnessed its gradual rejection by increasing numbers of indigenous delegates, such that, by the 10th session of the WGDD in 2004, those objecting to any amendments found themselves in 'a clear minority' (Ahren 2007, 96). We can only speculate as to what might have been the outcome of the process had a 'no change' position prevailed. One view, however, is that rather than reaching a kind of consensus around a negotiated text of the Declaration (the Chair's text), the WGDD would have arrived at its mandated deadline still in a deadlock, and that the Commission on Human Rights, encountering an impasse, would have elected not to renew the WGDD mandate, thereby leaving the declaration process dead in the water.

---

14 This view is represented, for example, in a briefing paper by Suhas Chakma of the Asian Indigenous and Tribal Peoples Network, (2002) 'Draft Declaration on the Rights of Indigenous Peoples: The Damp Squib of an International Decade' (on file with author).

15 See e.g. Ahren (2007, 87), who describes the Sub-Commission text as 'far from perfect' and 'positively confusing to the extent of being harmful to indigenous peoples' rights'.

16 For a detailed justification of the 'no change' position, see the rejoinder to Suhas Chakma prepared by the IITC. International Indian Treaty Council (2003) 'Another Perspective on the Process toward the Adoption of the Declaration for the Rights of Indigenous Peoples' [website]. At: http://www.treatycouncil/PDF/Support_for_the_Declaration_paper.pdf. Accessed 1 March 2011.

Chapter 4
Claims of the Global Indigenous Movement

This chapter discusses the main claims pressed by the global indigenous movement and objections raised to them. Drawing on Tennant's (1994) distinction between substantive and procedural 'claims of the resistance', it distinguishes between demands of a *substantive* and *institutional* nature, though evidently the two sets of claims are interlinked. The success of institutional claims, broadly understood as claims pressing for greater openness and inclusiveness in institutional processes and systems, is frequently a precursor to issue creation and the voicing of demands of a substantive nature. In the particular case of indigenous peoples, moreover, institutional claims focusing on meaningful participation and inclusion reflect the movement's core substantive claims in being central to the enactment of self-determination.

Substantive claims pressed by the global indigenous movement coalesce around the right of indigenous peoples to self-determination, which incorporates a universe of claims of a political, economic, cultural, social, legal and territorial nature. Institutional claims include both procedural claims relating to struggles for increased access and participation and claims for more radical institutional reform, such as those focused on establishing a Permanent Forum on Indigenous Issues, embedding what we might think of as 'organizational habitats of [indigenous] activists' (Katzenstein 1998a) within the UN institution consistent with a recognition of indigenous peoples' special status in international society.

'Substantive Claims of the Resistance'

The Historical and Contemporary Roots of Indigenous Peoples' Rights

As anyone who has attended sessions of the WGIP or the PFII will be acutely aware, indigenous peoples the world over experience an appalling and sweeping array of human rights abuses and assaults on their dignity and identity. They face a context of extreme marginalization, discrimination and dispossession, which result from a history of colonization and a present characterized by continuing attempts to dispossess them of their lands and resources. It is no accident that the UNDRIP is one of the longest human rights declarations prepared by the UN, in that its articles reflect the extensive and in many cases particular range of privations and abuses experienced by indigenous peoples. Amongst the issues of greatest concern are threats to their physical and cultural survival as a result of various forms of outside encroachment, forced relocations, land invasions, loss of subsistence, and environmental despoilment, threats that have intensified with the latest global phase of the capitalist economy (Mander and Tauli-Corpuz 2006). Added to this are the countless forms of social trauma experienced in indigenous communities, including alcoholism, substance abuse, domestic violence, physical and sexual abuse, welfare dependency, and high levels of incarceration. Suicide, previously unknown in indigenous societies, now disproportionately affects some indigenous communities, and is reported to be particularly high amongst indigenous youth (Cunningham 2009, Tatz 2006, Samson 2003, Grand Council of the Crees 2001). Extreme poverty is pervasive, while on key indicators of social and economic welfare such as health, life expectancy, housing, education, and employment, indigenous peoples consistently take their place at the bottom rung of the ladder (see e.g. Cunningham 2009).

The historical trajectory leading to this state of affairs is well known, but it bears repeating that historically indigenous peoples have been victims of genocide and ethnocide carried out by various means, more or less violent but nevertheless consistently catastrophic. The early colonial encounter saw indigenous societies drastically reduced through wars and wholesale killing, which, coupled with the spread of diseases carried by European colonists from the Old World, brought about dramatic population decline. The Spanish use of the sword is sometimes contrasted with the Anglo-American tradition of dispossessing indigenous peoples with the pen, but mass killing is as much a feature of expansion and settlement in North America and the Antipodes. White settlers to Tasmania exterminated all but 123 of the indigenous inhabitants in little more than a quarter of a century, while elsewhere in Australia population losses from smallpox and influenza were compounded by widespread massacres and 'dispersals' of Aboriginal people (Tatz 1999, 14–15). In the United States, similarly, colonists carried out massacres of entire Indian villages, as in California, where cold-blooded genocide accompanied Anglo-American expansion and settlement in the West (Wilson 1998). Extermination of indigenous peoples was made possible by a deep rooted racism, which legitimated the dispossession and decimation of peoples classified as inferior, savage, and sub-human.

In addition to wholesale slaughter, which we might properly call genocide, dominant governments have practiced a range of strategies for pacifying and controlling indigenous peoples, and for ridding themselves of the 'indigenous problem'. Common elements in this narrative include the confiscation of indigenous lands and territories, the wrecking of indigenous economies, displacement of indigenous communities from productive areas, segregation on mission lands and reservations, usurpation of traditional forms of government and law, Christianization, legislation prohibiting traditional spiritual and cultural practices, control of marriage and reproduction, and other means of fragmenting indigenous family and collective community structures. The terms 'ethnocide' or 'cultural genocide' apply to many such strategies where the aim is the destruction of indigenous ways of life and distinctiveness, whether or not accompanied by a belief in the 'best interests' of those concerned. Much of what has been most pivotal in instigating crises in indigenous communities has been framed in protectionist language – 'for their own good' (Haebich 1998) – including the forcible separation of indigenous children from their families and their placement in private homes and residential schools, which constituted the lynchpin of assimilationist Aboriginal policy in Australia and Canada until the 1960s. It is now widely accepted that such policies subjected indigenous children to untold suffering, including physical and sexual abuse, not to mention psychological trauma and dislocation experienced as a result of efforts on the part of teachers and clergy to discipline minds and to undermine indigenous epistemologies and cosmologies (Stewart-Harawira 2005).[1]

Current threats to indigenous peoples stem chiefly from the escalation of resource extraction and other activities linked to neoliberal globalization, which indigenous communities everywhere experience as the 'latest iteration of an historic colonial advance – the highly accelerated drive by global corporations seeking access to land and resources' (Mander 2006, 4). The last four decades have seen indigenous lands and resources from the Amazon to the Arctic imposed upon by extractive industries, infrastructure and development projects, representing what is frequently described as yet another wave of colonialism, and posing a serious threat to the survival of indigenous peoples. Maybury-Lewis, speaking of the Amazonian context, captures this new wave as follows (1984: 129):

> The first conquest virtually annihilated the coastal Indians, decimated and enslaved the highland Indians, and drove the remainder into the interior. It is in the interior – the last refuge of the Indian peoples – that the second conquest is now taking place. It is powered by a worldwide quest for resources in which all the Amazonian nations find themselves engaged. The new conquest, unlike the first one, is not particularly interested in Indian labour. It is very interested in Indian land. The threat to the Indians is not this time one of slavery, but of expropriation of their lands and total destruction of their way of life, if not their persons as well.

Amongst the most pernicious of activities threatening indigenous peoples' traditional territories, lifestyles, and cultures are mining, logging, and oil exploration and drilling, activities which have intensified in recent decades, particularly in areas inhabited by indigenous peoples, whose territories often coincide with the sites of the world's last remaining natural resources. Examples abound, ranging from gold mining on Western Shoshone lands in Idaho, Nevada, and California, to oil prospecting in U'wa territories in Colombia, to destructive forestry and logging

1 In 1997, the Australian Human Rights and Equal Opportunities Commission (HREOC) published *Bringing Them Home*, which estimated that between one in three and one in ten indigenous children were forcibly removed from their families between 1910 and 1970. The report also conveyed a finding of genocide, based on evidence of an intention to 'absorb', 'merge', and 'assimilate' indigenous children so that 'Aborigines as a distinct group would disappear' (Human Rights and Equal Opportunities Commission 1997).

on the lands of the James Bay Cree in Canada. It is not possible to do justice here to the widespread nature of the problem, but abundant evidence can be found in the NGO and academic literature (see, among others, e.g. International Forum on Globalization 2009; Tebtebba 2009; Forest Peoples Programme 2007, 2003; Miranda 2007; Mander and Tauli-Corpus 2006; World Rainforest Movement 2005, 2002; Downing et al. 2002; Colchester 2001, 1997; Macklem 2001; Howitt et al. 1996), UN expert reports (e.g. United Nations 2003a, 2002c, 1994d), and the jurisprudence of the UN treaty bodies (see e.g. CERD 2008, 2007; for a compilation of recent treaty body jurisprudence regarding indigenous peoples, including concluding observations in connection with the effects of extractive and other industries on indigenous peoples, see Mackay 2009, 2005, 2006).

Suffice to say that the human rights consequences of resource extraction operations for indigenous peoples are in a majority of cases severe. Mining, logging, and other projects endanger the livelihoods, cultures, and even the survival of affected indigenous communities, forcing indigenous peoples into relocations with devastating impacts on traditional lifestyles and cultures and resulting in spiritual uncertainty, homelessness, impoverishment, and food insecurity, not to mention a host of health problems associated with the contamination of the environment and the toxic pollution that attends extractive industries (Downing et al. 2002; Behera 1998). Such operations also generally require a supportive infrastructure, meaning that road and canal building and the construction of pipelines and power lines precede resource extraction, opening up previously inaccessible and pristine environments to exploitation and giving rise to land invasions and the influx of economic migrants and associated disease epidemics, conflicts, and militarization. In numerous instances concessions are granted without the free and informed consent of indigenous communities (Lloyd et al. 2006), while projects are justified by reference to the overriding 'national interest'. Racism against indigenous peoples makes it possible for elites to contemplate sacrificing indigenous peoples to such operations, and, in certain cases, to justify the use of violence to crush opposition (United Nations 2001b, para.4). The role played by unaccountable multinational corporations and private interests compounds the difficulties faced by indigenous peoples, calling for the application of human rights obligations to TNCs.

Collective Rights

The underlying basis of indigenous claims, arising from historical and contemporary threats to their group survival, is that they are collective in character. The essence of the UNDRIP is the recognition of collective rights, which are described in the preamble as 'indispensable for their existence, well-being, and integral development as peoples' (United Nations 2007a). Yet while the collective rights of indigenous peoples are now widely accepted, the question of collective rights proved highly controversial in negotiations towards the development of specific indigenous rights, involving debates that go to the heart of the nature and character of human rights. Collective rights offend the traditional liberal paradigm whereby rights are entitlements held by individuals and individuals alone. According to liberal human rights approaches, individual rights are capable of accommodating the claims of oppressed or disadvantaged groups.

For indigenous peoples, collective rights have been regarded as of paramount importance, as critical to the protection and affirmation of their cultural integrity and ways of life. They have been described as 'an inherent and essential element of indigenous rights' (United Nations 1988, para. 68), 'critical to indigenous spirituality [and] to maintaining the intergenerational nature of our social, cultural, political, and economic rights' (United Nations 2002d, annex 2). At the same time, indigenous peoples' representatives have strongly argued that individual rights alone are insufficient to protect them from human rights violations, a result of the fact that those violations are themselves so frequently of a collective nature; to the extent that individuals suffer attacks on their human rights, they do so because they are perceived by their attackers as belonging to a particular group. Accordingly, the recognition of collective rights is necessary for the protection of individual rights, as explained by the representative of the Aboriginal and Torres Strait Islander Commission (ATSIC) to the eleventh session of the WGIP in 1993 (statement on file with author):

> It is precisely because the collective rights have not been acknowledged that the individual rights of indigenous persons, for example the right to equality of opportunity in the provision of education, employment and health care – have not been realised in any nation in the world. Only when our collective identities have been recognized will the appalling disadvantage that we suffer as individuals be redressed.

Opposition to collective rights on the part of state delegates was evident throughout most of the UNDRIP drafting process, and was only finally resolved in the end stages of the WGDD negotiations, though by this stage the objecting states were few in number. Objections raised to collective rights during the course of negotiations took a number of different forms, moral, conceptual, and legal. One persistent objection focused on the relationship between collective rights and individual rights, the main concern being that the recognition of collective rights could lead to the erosion or restriction of individual rights. This view was expressed by a number of state delegations, in particular the United Kingdom and Sweden, and probably represents the most serious objection, reflecting as it does longstanding debates in political theory regarding the possible conflicts between collective and individual rights arising from either over-inclusiveness or exclusiveness of group identities (Jones 1994, 186; see e.g. Kukathus 2003; Kymlicka 1996, 1991). Another objection, heard by Japan, the United States, and France in particular, was that contemporary international law did not extend to the protection of collective rights and entities (see e.g. United Nations 1999b, para. 40; United Nations 1997b, para. 108; United Nations 1996a). In actual fact, there are a number of collective rights and collective rights instruments in international law, a number of which precede the adoption of the UNDRIP by some years. The UN Genocide Convention of 1948 protects 'national, ethnic, racial or religious groups' from the crime of genocide (United Nations 1948, Article II). The collective right of 'peoples' to self-determination is recognized in the International Human Rights Covenants (United Nations 1966a; United Nations 1966b), while the African Charter on Human and Peoples' Rights (African Charter) recognizes a range of peoples' rights, noting in its preamble that 'respect of peoples' rights should necessarily guarantee human rights' (African Charter 1981, Arts. 19–24). The ILO Conventions No. 107 and No.169, further, both recognize collective indigenous rights, the latter being in essence a collective rights instrument. The right to development is both an individual right and a collective right of peoples (United Nations 1986b), while other solidarity rights such as the right to a clean environment are also recognized as having significant collective dimensions. These rights are generally interpreted, moreover, as constituting not solely collective rights but collective *human* rights, though this perspective is not universally accepted amongst practitioners and academics (see e.g. Donnelly 2003).

An accommodation regarding collective rights was slow to emerge amongst particularly intransigent states, but was eventually arrived at through a key textual adaptation allowing for interpretive variations as to the nature of collective rights, as contained in preambular paragraph 22 (United Nations 2007a):

> *Recognizing and reaffirming* that indigenous individuals are entitled without discrimination to all human rights recognized in international law, and that indigenous peoples possess collective rights which are indispensable for their existence, well-being and integral development as peoples,

While recognizing that individual rights are human rights, this text avoids stating that collective rights are human rights. At the same time, it does not state that collective rights are *not* human rights. As such, it is an example of what is termed in UN parlance 'constructive ambiguity', referring to deliberately indeterminate language allowing for the emergence of consensus between parties to negotiations. In the event, this language satisfied the UK, which, as the last state delegation to oppose collective rights, finally agreed to their acceptance at the 11th session of the WGDD (United Nations 2006a). In its interpretive statement on the UNDRIP, the UK stated that, with the exception of the right to self-determination, it did not accept the concept of collective human rights in international law, and that it strongly endorsed preambular paragraph 22, which it understood to distinguish between individual rights in international law and collective rights bestowed at national level through constitutional reforms and domestic legislation (United Nations, Department of Public Information, 2007). Other interpretative statements regarding collective rights included that of Sweden, which expressed a similar view to the UK, adding also the firm opinion that individual human rights prevailed over collective rights (*ibid.*). This latter interpretation does not cohere with international law perspectives that – non-dirigible rights such as the right to life and the prohibition of torture aside – do not recognize a predetermined hierarchy between individual and collective or cultural rights, but call for an *ad hoc* approach whereby, in cases where different human rights are simultaneously at issue, the conflicting rights and interests are weighed up in order to assess how and to what extent both can be accommodated, for example through adjustments that respect the 'core' of fundamental rights (Xanthaki 2010), and, in instances where there is no workable accommodation, which right prevails in the relevant case. Such an approach draws on a number of criteria, which have been elaborated in the context of international adjudication in particular. Criteria include consistency with international human rights law, the existence of reasonable and objective justification, necessity, and proportionality (see e.g. HRC 1981, 1988, 1994; see also Article 46(2) of the UNDRIP, which restates a number of these principles). Added to this, it has been argued that 'in any assessment of whether a particular cultural practice is prohibited rather than protected, the cultural group concerned should be accorded a certain deference for its own interpretative and decision-making process in the application of human rights norms' (Anaya 2004a, 26).

An *ad hoc* approach is particularly evident in the jurisprudence of the UN Human Rights Committee (HRC), notably in the cases of *Lovelace v. Canada* and *Kitok v. Sweden*, in which the Committee gave priority to the rights of individual and the rights of the group, respectively. In *Lovelace*, the HRC was called to consider the case of Sandra Lovelace, a woman born and registered as a Maliseet Indian who, as per section 12(1)(b) of Canada's Indian Act, had lost her status and associated rights as an Indian as a result of marriage to a non-Indian, including the right to reside on the Tobique Reserve. The Act not applying to an Indian man marrying a non-Indian woman, Lovelace alleged gender-based discrimination (Articles 2(1), 3, and 26), as well as violations of rights aimed at protecting family life (Article 23(1) and (4)) and the right to culture (Article 27). In the event, the Committee declined to comment on sex discrimination on the basis that the marriage occurred at a time when Canada was not bound by the Covenant, but found Article 27 recognizing the right of 'persons belonging to ethnic, religious or linguistic minorities … in community with the other members of their group, to enjoy their own culture, to profess and practice their own religion, or to use their own language' (United Nations 1966a, Art. 27) to be 'most directly applicable' to her complaint. Ruling that Canada was in violation of Article 27, the Committee concluded that 'the right of Sandra Lovelace to access to her native culture and language "in community with the other members of her group", has in fact been, and continues to be interfered with, because there is no place outside the Tobique Reserve where such a community exists' (HRC 1981, para.15). In coming to its conclusions, the Committee recognized the 'need to define the category of persons entitled to live on a reserve, for such purposes as those explained by the Government regarding protection of its resources and preservation of the identity of its people' (*ibid.*), but did not consider that 'to deny Sandra Lovelace the right to reside on the reserve is reasonable, or necessary to preserve the identity of the tribe' (*ibid.*, para. 17).

Where the Committee's decision in *Lovelace* emphasized the rights of the individual, in *Kitok v. Sweden* the rights of the community were seen to prevail. The case concerned Ivan Kitok, an ethnic Saami who had lost membership in his ancestral village, and who alleged that he was denied his inherited rights to reindeer breeding under Swedish legislation that reserved reindeer herding rights exclusively for members of Saami villages. According to the state party, the 1971 *Reindeer Husbandry Act* sought to restrict the number of reindeer breeders for 'economic and ecological reasons and to secure the preservation and well-being of the Sami minority' (HRC 1988, para. 9.5) and could not be regarded as in violation of Article 27 (*ibid.*, para. 4.3):[2]

> As is evident from the legislation, the Reindeer Husbandry Act aims at protecting and preserving the Sami culture and reindeer husbandry as such … A special circumstance here is that reindeer husbandry is so closely connected to the Sami culture that is must be considered part of the Sami culture itself. In this case the legislation can be said to favour the Sami community in order to make reindeer husbandry economically viable now and in the future. The pasture areas for reindeer husbandry are limited, and it is simply not possible to let all Sami exercise reindeer husbandry without jeopardizing this objective and running the risk of endangering the existence of reindeer husbandry as such … In view of the interests underlying the reindeer husbandry legislation and its very limited impact on Ivan Kitok's possibility of 'enjoying his culture', the Government submits that under all circumstances the present case does not indicate the existence of a violation of Article 27.

The Committee concluded with the state party that the law was justified as 'reasonable and consistent with Article 27 of the Covenant' (*ibid.*, para 9.5).[3] In considering the balance of rights and interests, the HRC considered that (*ibid.*, para. 9.8):

2 It needs emphasizing that Article 27 of the ICCPR confers rights on individuals belonging to 'ethnic, religious, or linguistic minorities … to enjoy their own culture', and is not to be thought of as conferring rights on peoples or groups (i.e. a collective right). However, though the rights protected under Article 27 are individual rights, they 'depend in turn on the ability of the minority group to maintain its culture, language or religion', and therefore bring about obligations on the part of states to the cultural group as a whole. See HRC (1994) *General Comment No.23: The Rights of Minorities (Article 27): 08/04/1994*, U.N. Doc. CCPR/C/21/Rev.1/Add.5.

3 Though accepting the rationale behind the law as protecting Sami culture, the Committee nevertheless registered some concerns vis-à-vis its operation, particularly as regards the 'ignoring of objective ethnic criteria in determining membership of a minority' (HRC 1988, para. 9.7) in favour of its own, more limited, terms. As cited by the Committee (para. 9.6), Section 11 of the *Reindeer Husbandry Act* restricts membership to: i) those engaged in reindeer husbandry within the pasture area of the community; ii) persons who have engaged in reindeer husbandry as their main occupation and who have 'not gone over to any other main economic activity'; and iii) relatives of qualified persons. The concern

> In resolving this problem, in which there is an apparent conflict between the legislation, which seems to protect the rights of the minority as a whole, and its application to a single member of that minority, the Committee has been guided by the *ratio decidendi* in the *Lovelace* case, namely, that a restriction upon the right of an individual member of a minority must be shown to have a reasonable and objective justification and to be necessary for the continued viability and welfare of the minority as a whole. After a careful review of all the elements involved in the case, the Committee is of the view that there is no violation of Article 27 by the State party.

Self-Determination

Self-Determination: A Brief History in International Law

Self-determination is an ambiguous and complex subject matter in international law. In part, its indeterminacies arise from the fact that it is both a general concept and a right, but they are also a consequence of the fact that international legal texts have never fully declared its meaning, which has, moreover, undergone a process of substantial evolution as regards both its scope of application and what it entails. International practice, furthermore, has added to the uncertainty, 'straining conceptual boundaries and creating an increasingly awkward gap between doctrinal and experiential accounts of self-determination, resulting in controversy and confusion' (Falk 2000, 98).

Self-determination can be regarded as a concept with an ancient lineage, but histories of self-determination in modern international law and political discourse begin after World War I, when the principle of self-determination animated attempts by the League of Nations to create regimes of protection for a number of European minorities within the former German, Austro-Hungarian, and Ottoman empires. Closely associated with Woodrow Wilson, whose 'Fourteen Points' – together with free trade, democracy, and open agreements – dealt with self-determination and the grant of national independence to 'nations' within the territory of vanquished empires, the principle of self-determination did not appear in the League of Nations Covenant despite Wilson's recommendations. In 1945, it is given some visibility in the UN Charter, not as a right or even an operative principle but as a principle *desiderata* associated with international stability and

---

with such criteria is that they favour a defined core within the Sami community whilst neglecting the wider community. As noted by the Committee (para. 9.7) 'it can thus be seen that the Act provides certain criteria for participation in the life of an ethnic minority whereby a person who is ethnically Sami can be held not to be a Sami for the purposes of the Act. The Committee has been concerned that the ignoring of objective ethnic criteria in determining membership of a minority … may have been disproportionate to the legitimate ends sought be the legislation' (see also Thornberry 2002, 159–160).

'developing friendly relations among nations'. It is referred to twice in Articles 1(2) and 55 (United Nations 1945). Article 1(2) lists amongst the purposes of the UN the development of 'friendly relations among nations based on respect for the principle of equal rights and self-determination of peoples' (*ibid.*). Article 55 reiterates this aim in the context of the promotion of international economic and social cooperation (*ibid.*). The consensus amongst scholars is that this does not constitute a robust statement on self-determination, a consequence of the fact that, at the time the Charter was drafted, the principle was regarded with disapprobation arising from Hitler's manipulation of the scheme of minority protection put in place by the League.

In spite of a preambular reference to 'developing friendly relations among nations', there is no mention of self-determination in the UDHR of 1948, either as a principle or right; nor does it receive mention in international agreements of the 1950s. In 1960, however, transformed by the decolonization movement from a principle aimed at promoting friendly relations among nations into a revolutionary vehicle for liberation from colonial rule and alien subjugation, self-determination appears as a right in international law. Adopted with the decolonization project in view, GA Resolution 1514 (XV), or the Declaration on Colonial Countries, proclaims that 'the subjection of peoples to alien subjugation, domination and exploitation constitutes a denial of fundamental human rights, is contrary to the Charter of the United Nations and is an impediment to the promotion of world peace and co-operation' (United Nations 1960a, Art. 1). It affirms that 'all peoples have the right to self-determination; by virtue of that right they feely determine their political status and freely pursue their social, economic, and cultural development' (*ibid.*, Art. 2).

As discussed briefly in Chapter 3, though the language of subject application in the Declaration on Colonial Countries is universal, it should not in fact be read as extending a right of self-determination to 'all peoples'. A companion resolution to the Declaration adopted the following day, GA Resolution 1541 (XV), limits, in one step, the beneficiaries of the Declaration to whole peoples of non-self-governing territories administered by European colonial powers, which it achieves by applying the so-called 'blue water' or 'salt water' test to ascertain whether a people qualify for recognition of the right to self-determination. Principle IV, which is generally regarded as identifying the holders of the right to self-determination, states that a duty to submit information exists 'in respect of any territory which is geographically separate and distinct ethnically and/or culturally from the country administering it' (United Nations 1960b).[4] Amounting to a restriction of the right

4 Resolution 1541 (XV) established an obligation that administering states transmit information about non-self-governing territories determined on the basis of both separateness and subordination. Principle V states that 'once it has been established that such a *prima facie* case of geographical and ethnical or cultural distinctness of a territory exists, other elements may then be *inter alia* of an administrative, political, juridical, economic or historical nature. If they affect the relationship between the metropolitan state

of self-determination to the limited universe of non-self-governing territories separated from their colonial oppressors by sea, the 'salt water' thesis was advanced by a coalition of Third World and Socialist states and was patently not based on a principled approach but on an arguably justified fear of instability and a wish to maintain colonial borders intact. It was opposed by a number of Western states, in particular Belgium, whose representatives at the drafting process argued that forms of colonial domination occurring within multi-ethnic states were as pernicious as overseas colonial subjugation, and that self-determination should be made available to all subjugated peoples, not simply the whole populations of overseas colonial territories. Apparently representing an ethical line of reasoning, it is widely recognized that the 'Belgian thesis' was in fact motivated by an attempt to derail the decolonization process, and specifically from the Belgian perspective by a desire to paint itself in a better light in the context of criticism of Belgian activities in the Congo (Lam 2000; Iorns 1992). In addition to the limits imposed by Resolution 1541 (XV) references to territorial integrity in the text of the Declaration establish a limit on universality. Article 6, which describes the relationship between self-determination and territorial integrity, precludes claims for independence on the part of groups within states. It states that 'any attempt aimed at the partial or total disruption of the national unity and territorial integrity of a country is incompatible with the purposes and principles of the Charter of the United Nations' (United Nations 1960a, Art. 6). The seventh paragraph reiterates 'the sovereign rights of all peoples and their territorial integrity' (*ibid.*, Art. 7)

Resolution 1541 (XV) outlines three modalities for exercising the right to self-determination. Principle VI finds that a non-self-governing territory can be said to have reached a 'full measure of self-government' by: (a) emergence as a sovereign independent state; (b) free association with an independent state; or (c) integration with an independent state (United Nations 1960b). Evidently, however, the emphasis is on independence, which is given prominence in the title of the Declaration. Moreover, whereas there are complex procedural requirements involved in attaining the status of either free association or integration, no such conditions are in place for non-self-governing territories seeking to emerge as sovereign independent states. Outlined in Principles VII, VIII, and IX, the conditions state that free association should be the result of 'a free and voluntary choice by the peoples of the territory concerned expressed through informed and democratic processes' (United Nations 1960b, Principle VII). Integration must be on the basis of 'complete equality' between the peoples of the territory and the independent state with which they are integrating, and is only allowable where a territory has achieved an 'advanced stage of self-government with free political institutions' (United Nations 1960b, Principles VIII and IX).

---

and the territory concerned in a manner which arbitrarily places the latter in a position or status of subordination, they support the presumption that an obligation exists to transmit information under Article 73(e) of the Charter' (United Nations 1960b).

The connection between self-determination and human rights was cemented further in 1966, as self-determination was given prominence in common Article 1 of the International Human Rights Covenants (entered into force in 1976). The Covenants posit that 'all peoples have the right to self-determination. By virtue of that right they feely determine their political status and freely pursue their social, economic, and cultural development' (United Nations 1966a, United Nations 1966b, common Art. 1). They are apparently unencumbered by any qualification regarding scope of application, but as a number of legal scholars have pointed out, the *travaux préparatoires* indicate that there was no intention to add anything to the right of self-determination that existed in 1960 (e.g. Daes 2000, 1993b; Cassese 1995; Iorns 1992). The texts themselves offer no guidance regarding a definition of 'peoples'; common Article 1(3) refers to the role of states 'having responsibility for the administration of Non-Self-Governing and Trust Territories', although this reference need not suggest exclusivity. Nor do they elaborate on the content of self-determination, though they do stipulate one of the requisites of its meaningful exercise. Common Article 1(2) states that 'all peoples, may, for their own ends, freely dispose of their natural wealth and resources without prejudice to any obligations arising from international economic cooperation, based upon the principle of mutual benefit, and international law. In no case may a people be deprived of its own means of subsistence' (United Nations 1966a, United Nations 1966b, common Art. 1.2). As to the tension that exists in the Declaration on Colonial Countries between the right of self-determination and the principle of territorial integrity of states, there is no reference in the Covenants to the latter.

From 1968 onwards, the adoption of a series of international documents can be seen to take the right of self-determination beyond the post-war colonial context. In 1968, Resolution 2396 (XXIII) on the Policies of Apartheid of the Government of South Africa affirmed 'the urgent necessity of eliminating the policies of apartheid so that the people of South Africa as a whole can exercise their right to self-determination and obtain majority rule based on universal suffrage' (United Nations 1968b, Art. 3). Linking the right to self-determination with the right to representative and democratic government, this provision at once expands the beneficiaries of self-determination to peoples under racist regimes and develops on the 'nationalist' understanding of self-determination whereby self-determination is akin to decolonization through political independence. A democratic understanding of self-determination is also in evidence in the 1975 Final Act of the Conference on Security and Cooperation in Europe (Helsinki Declaration), which addresses the right to self-determination of the peoples of Europe, that is, 'entire populations living in and identifying with sovereign States (for example, Italian or French citizens)' (Cassese 1995, 289). Principle VIII of the Declaration entitled 'Equal Rights and Self-Determination' finds that (Conference on Security and Cooperation in Europe 1975):

> By virtue of the principle of equal rights and self-determination of peoples, all peoples always have the right, in full freedom to determine, when and as they

> wish, their internal and external status, without external interference, and to pursue as they wish their political, economic, social and cultural development.

Cassese (1995, 286) describes the Declaration as 'breaking new ground in international relations', particularly in that it distinguishes between 'external' and '*internal*' self-determination, with the latter widely interpreted as involving the right of the governed to select and influence the system of government under which it lives, and in a way that is *ongoing*. A view of self-determination as an ongoing or continuous right is markedly different from the General Assembly's 1960 formulation identifying self-determination narrowly with independence, which conceived of self-determination as exercised only once, to be 'consumed in the act' (Stavenhagen 1996, 5). As Kingsbury (2000, 24) has put it, 'the focus was on the realization of an end-state: usually independence', rather than a continuing, participatory process. As for the reference to external self-determination, Cassese cautions against a broad reading, suggesting only that it means that the whole population of a state are entitled to be heard in the event of a possible change in the external status of the state (1988, 287). The Declaration is not thought of as extending a right of external self-determination to national minorities or particular groups within the state; Principle IV concerns the territorial integrity of states – though to be sure the duty here is incumbent upon states and not sub-state groups – while Principle VII enjoins states to respect the rights of persons belonging to national minorities to equality before the law.

The idea of self-determination as a continuing right with strong democratic aspects is also implied in the 1970 Declaration on Friendly Relations. This upholds the principle of 'equal rights and self-determination of peoples' as necessary 'to promote friendly relations and cooperation among States' and 'to bring a speedy end to colonialism' (United Nations 1970, Art. 1, Principle V, para. 1):

> By virtue of the principle of equal rights and self-determination of peoples enshrined in the Charter, all peoples have the right freely to determine, without external interference, their political status and to pursue their economic, social and cultural development, and every State has the duty to respect this right in accordance with the provisions of the Charter.

Cassese (1995, 110) argues that above all the Declaration envisages the right of external self-determination, understood as applying to colonial peoples and peoples under alien domination or foreign occupation; the right of external self-determination in the latter sense forming the counterpart of the prohibition of force in international relations (Cassese 1995, 99).[5] The Declaration does also clearly

5 The legislative history supports this view, as discussed by Cassese (1995). The debates reflect a division between Western States, who were in favour of extending the right of self-determination to the peoples of independent states, and socialist states, who, together with authoritarian governments in the developing world, were eager to restrict its

contemplate internal self-determination, however, referring to the right of the people of independent and sovereign states to representative government, if only as a secondary element. This is most evident in the so-called 'safeguard clause', which states that (United Nations 1970, Art. 1, Principle V, para. 7, my emphasis):

> Nothing in the forgoing paragraphs [proclaiming the principle of self-determination] shall be construed as authorizing or encouraging any action which would dismember or impair, totally or in part, the territorial integrity or political unity of States conducting themselves in compliance with the principle of equal rights and self-determination of peoples as described above and thus possessed of a *government representing the whole people belonging to the territory without distinction as to race, creed or colour.*

The above provision manifestly envisages a concept of internal self-determination as fully representative government. It also raises the question of racial groups denied access to representative government and their right to self-determination, placing it at the centre of debates on secession, and whether and under what circumstances a racial group may be entitled to pursue a secessionist agenda. On the one hand, it affirms in strong terms that the right to self-determination may not violate the principle of territorial integrity, and might be regarded as establishing a strong presumption in favour of the territorial integrity of states. On the other, if we 'frame in positive terms what is couched in a negative manner' (Cassese 1995, 112), it opens the door to the option of secession in remedial cases by making an exception to the principle of the territorial integrity of states in cases where racial or religious groups within the state are unrepresented in government or their human rights consistently and flagrantly violated. As expressed by Cassese (*ibid.*, 120) 'the contention can be made that the Declaration on Friendly Relations *links external self-determination to internal self-determination in exceptional circumstances*. A racial or religious group may attempt secession, a form of external self-determination, when it is apparent that internal self-determination is absolutely beyond reach. Extreme and unremitting persecution and the lack of any reasonable prospect for peaceful challenge may make secession legitimate'.

The view that from 1970 international law accepts the possibility of secession for remedial reasons is one that is shared by increasing numbers of scholars (see e.g. Weller 2008a, 2008b; Raic 2002; Knop 2002; Sharma 1997; Kirgis 1994; Buchheit 1978).[6] Weller (2008b, 86) comments that 'where a defined segment of

---

extension. In the event, Cassese (1995, 109) comments, 'the view of the socialist States prevailed'.

6 Normative theories of secession support a growing legal consensus. Notably, the work of Allen Buchanan (2004, esp. Ch. 8) proposes a justice-based 'Remedial Right Only Theory' justifying secession as a remedy of last resort in cases of genocide and massive violations of human rights, unjust annexation, and persistent violation by a state of intrastate autonomy arrangements.

the state population has been persistently oppressed, excluded from governance of its own area of compact habitation and from the central state, ..., the doctrine of territorial unity may lose its persuasive force'. Kirgis (1994, 306), describing self-determination as a 'variable right' involving a continuum of remedies appropriate to the form and degree of denial of self-determination, comments that 'if a government is quite unrepresentative, the international community may recognize even a seriously destabilizing self-determination claim as legitimate'. Raic (2002, 365) finds a 'strong presumption in favour of the existence of a qualified or remedial secession for minority-peoples within existing States' and describes widespread and serious violations of fundamental human rights as the 'catalytic agent' (*ibid.*, 372) that 'leads to both the fulfilment of the condition of the violation of the right of internal self-determination and the exhaustion of judicial remedies and political arrangements', the latter also being deemed necessary to justify a claim.

Recent judicial decisions also point to a growing consensus that certain circumstances may call for the exercise of remedial secession. For example, in *Loizidou v. Turkey* before the European Court of Human Rights, Judge Wildhaber commented that:

> Until recently in international practice the right to self-determination was in practical terms identical to, and indeed restricted to, a right to decolonization. In recent years a consensus has seemed to emerge that peoples may also exercise a right to self-determination if their human rights are consistently and flagrantly violated or if they are without representation at all or are massively underrepresented in an undemocratic and discriminatory way.[7]

Also at the regional level, in the case of the *Katangese Peoples' Congress v. Zaire* involving a request by the Katangese Peoples' Congress for the African Commission on Human and Peoples' Rights to recognize the Congress as a liberation movement entitled to support the achievement of independence for Katanga, to recognize the independence of Katanga, and to help secure the evacuation of Zaire from Katanga, the Commission concluded that:

> In the absence of concrete evidence of violations of human rights to the extent that the territorial integrity of Zaire should be called into question and in the absence of evidence that the people of Katanga are denied the right to participate in Government as guaranteed by Article 13(1) of the African Charter, the Commission holds the view that Katanga is obliged to exercise a variant of self-determination that is compatible with the sovereignty and territorial integrity of Zaire.[8]

7 *Loizidou v. Turkey* (Merits), European Court of Human Rights, 18 December 1996, (1997) 18 *Human Rights Law Journal* 50, 59.

8 *Katangese Peoples' Congress v. Zaire*, African Commission on Human and Peoples' Rights, Communication No.75/92, para.6.

Further evidence that the African Commission has accepted the notion of remedial secession can be found in the Commission's jurisprudence in the 2009 case of *Kevin Mgwanga Gunme v. Cameroon.*[9] Concerning the case of Kevin Mgwanga Gunme on behalf of the people of Southern Cameroon, the complainants alleged violation of many articles of the African Charter, including Article 20 on the right to self-determination, which the complainants claimed had been violated by the government's failure to address grievances – specifically issues of constitutional, political, and economic marginalization – raised through the constitutional conferences of 1993 and 1994 and the signature referendum of independence of 1995, which endorsed separation. The Commission recognized the claim of the people of Southern Cameroon to be a 'people', but, as in the Katanga case mentioned above, it found against the complainants on the matter of external self-determination (para. 197):

> The Commission holds the view that when a Complainant seeks to invoke Article 20 of the African Charter, it must satisfy the Commission that the two conditions under 20(2) namely oppression and domination have been met.[10]

Without expressly referring to the doctrine of remedial secession, the Commission's reasoning is evidently guided by the need to establish remedial reasons sufficient to warrant the exercise of the right to self-determination through secession and independence. The conditions set by the Commission are equivalent to the 'extremely exceptional circumstances' (Shaw 2000, 138) generally called for by scholars; though finding the government in contravention of Articles 2, 4, 5, 6, 7, 11, and 19 – recognizing the right to equality and freedom from discrimination, the right to life, freedom from torture, the right to liberty, the right to a fair trial, the right to freedom of assembly, and the collective right of all peoples to equality and non-domination, respectively – the Commission does not accept a violation sufficient to call into question the territorial integrity of the state (para. 194), requiring 'proof of massive violation of human rights under the Charter' (para. 199).

Further evidence of a growing consensus regarding remedial secession can be found in judgements at the national level, notably in the Supreme Court of Canada 1998 Québec Opinion:[11]

> The international law of self-determination only generates, at best, a right to external self-determination in situations of former colonies; where a people is

9 *Kevin Mgwanga Gunme v. Cameroon*, African Commission on Human and Peoples' Rights, No. 266/2003, 27 May 2009.

10 Article 20(2) states that 'colonized or oppressed peoples shall have the right to free themselves from the bonds of domination by resorting to any means recognized by the international community'.

11 *Re: Secession of Québec* [1998] 2 S.C.R 217, Supreme Court of Canada.

> oppressed, as for example under foreign military occupation; or where a definable group is denied meaningful access to government to pursue their political, economic, social, and cultural development. In all three situations, the people in question are entitled to a right to external self-determination because they have been denied the ability to exert internally their right to self-determination.[12]

Remedial secession proved a contested notion in the recent International Court of Justice (ICJ) Kosovo proceedings assessing Kosovo's declaration of independence,[13] which revealed considerable differences in the written submissions of states. Disputed by Argentina, Cyprus, Iran, Romania, Russia, Serbia, Slovakia, and Spain, in its written submission Serbia (Republic of Serbia 2009, 215) argued that 'an *a contrario* reading of the "safeguard clause" in order to admit a right to "remedial secession" is not supported by the terms of the paragraph, its context, its object and purpose, the *travaux préparatoires* and subsequent state practice.'[14] Finland, Ireland, Poland, and the United Kingdom supported the doctrine. In its submission, the United Kingdom offered a 'no right, no prohibition' version of secession in international law and practice (United Kingdom 2009, 101):

> International law does not accord to entities within a State any *right* to separate, whether by way of a declaration of independence or otherwise. But neither does it guarantee the territorial integrity of the State against internal developments which may lead to separation or even dissolution.

As for the Court, it declined in its Advisory Opinion to throw light on remedial secession and the circumstances that might legitimate it, finding it was unnecessary to do so in order to respond to the narrow question posed by the General Assembly, namely whether or not Kosovo's declaration of independence was in accordance with international law. Nor did it seek to clarify the differences of opinion as regards the related question of 'whether, outside the context of non-self-governing territories and peoples subject to alien subjugation, domination, and exploitation, the international law of self-determination confers upon part of the population of an existing State the right to separate from that State' (ICJ 2010, para.82). The Court's modest response, moreover, that there was no prohibition of unilateral declarations of independence in either general international law or the practice

12 The Court concluded that 'such exceptional circumstances are manifestly inapplicable to Québec under existing conditions. Accordingly, neither the population of the province of Québec, even if characterized in terms of 'people' or 'peoples', nor its representative institutions, the National Assembly, the legislature or government of Québec, possess a right, under international law, to secede unilaterally from Canada'. See *Re: Secession of Québec* [1998] 2 S.C.R 217, Supreme Court of Canada, para. 138.

13 *Accordance with International Law of the Unilateral Declaration of Independence in Respect of Kosovo, Advisory Opinion* (International Court of Justice, 22 July 2010).

14 Written submissions are available on the website of the ICJ at http://www.icj-cji.org.

of the Security Council, and that 'accordingly, the declaration of independence of 17 February 2008 did not *violate* general international law' (ICJ 2010, para. 84, my emphasis), might be regarded as involving a degree of evasion in that it does not expressly tell us whether Kosovo's declaration was acceptable under international law, only that it did not violate it. [15] An approach intended perhaps to dispose of a highly politically charged case through the shortest possible route of legal argument (Weller 2011, 133–134), or to avoid an endorsement of Kosovo's declaration in the language of international law that might be seen to provide succour to various secessionist movements 'waiting in the wings of the global political stage' (Falk 2010, 51), the narrow opinion nevertheless allows for some broad conclusions – though interpretations vary considerably (see e.g. Hannum 2011) – as regards a post-colonial law of self-determination and secession. Falk (2010, 58), for example, describes 'this approval of Kosovo's march to sovereignty, even if not so described' as amounting to a 'greatly enlarged view of the right to self-determination', and 'an example of self-determination in the third degree':

> The first degree is at the level of a sovereign state, as when a society manages to achieve political independence and end colonial rule. The second degree is a domestically sovereign unit of the sort that constitutes federal states, such as the sovereign states that emerged after the collapse of the Soviet Union and Yugoslavia. The third degree is an ethnic/geographic fragment of a federal substate unit, such as the claimant movements in Chechnya, South Ossetia, and Abkhazia.

To be sure, what the Advisory Opinion does not do is state that Kosovo has a right to self-determination giving it a right to secede, or that sub-state groups in general have such a right. Certain implications, however, can be gathered from the text. Of particular interest is the Court's reading that the principle of territorial integrity, though of fundamental importance in international law, applies only on an inter-state basis, and therefore furnishes no legal bar to the claims of non-state entities (ICJ 2010, para. 80):

> Several participants in the proceedings before the Court have contended that a prohibition of unilateral declarations of independence is implicit in the principle of territorial integrity.

---

15 The Court might have implicitly relied upon the *Lotus* principle, namely that what a state is not expressly prohibited from doing is allowed. In the Lotus judgement, the Permanent Court of International Justice commented that, 'the rules of law binding upon States … emanate from their own free will … Restrictions upon the independence of States cannot therefore be presumed'. 'Far from laying down a general prohibition, it leaves them in this respect a wide measure of discretion which is only limited in certain cases by prohibitive rules'. Permanent Court of International Justice, SS Lotus (*France v. Turkey*), 1927 PCIJ (ser. A, No.10), 18–19.

> The Court recalls that the principle of territorial integrity is an important part of the international legal order and is enshrined in the Charter of the United Nations, in particular in Article 2, paragraph 4, which provides that: 'All members shall refrain in their international relations from the threat or use of force against the territorial integrity or political independence of any State, or in any other manner inconsistent with the Purposes of the United Nations.' In General Assembly resolution 2625, entitled 'Declaration on Principles of International Law concerning Friendly Relations and Co-operation among States in Accordance with the Charter of the United Nations', which reflects customary international law, the General Assembly reiterated '[t]he principle that *States* shall refrain in their international relations from the threat or use of force against the territorial integrity or political independence of any *State'*. This resolution then enumerated various obligations incumbent upon *States* to refrain from violating the territorial integrity of other *sovereign States*. In the same vein, the Final Act of the Helsinki Conference on Security and Co-operation in Europe of 1 August 1975 (the Helsinki Conference) stipulated that '[t]he participating States will respect the territorial integrity of each of the participating *States'* (Art. IV). Thus, the scope of the principle of territorial integrity is confined to the sphere of relations between States.

Much can be made of this when considering the right of sub-state groups aspiring to independence. To the extent that the obligation to respect the territorial integrity of states is not applicable to groups, the conclusion can be drawn that a declaration of independence by a group within an existing state would not be contrary to international law. As expressed by Wilde (2011, 152), 'the Court, in effect, sanctions as lawful what would be a violation of a state's territorial integrity were it conducted by another state rather than a non-state actor. All sub-state groups in the world are now on notice that, according to this view, there would not appear to be a general international law rule barring them from declaring independence.'

An earlier development emerging from the jurisprudence of the ICJ also deserves highlighting in this summary of the development of the international law of self-determination, which is the Advisory Opinion in the case of *Western Sahara*.[16] Called upon by the General Assembly to consider the claims of Morocco and Mauritania to sovereignty over the territory following Spain's withdrawal, the case involved consideration of two questions put to the Court: i) Was Western Sahara at the time of colonization by Spain a territory belonging to no-one (*terra nullius*)?; and ii) What were the legal ties between this territory and the Kingdom of Morocco and the Mauritanian entity? (United Nations 1974, para.1). Answering in the negative to the first question,[17] the Court concluded the question of sovereignty could not be decided without reference to the nomadic tribes living

16 *Western Sahara, Advisory Opinion, I.C.J. Reports 1975.*

17 The proceedings also saw the concept of *terra nullius* declared invalid. As expressed by Justice Ammoun, 'the concept of terra nullius, employed at all periods, to the

in the territory, who had also declared their intention to establish their own state. The Court resolved that although both Mauritania and Morocco had historical ties to the Western Sahara (ICJ 1975, para.162):

> [It] has not found legal ties of such a nature as might affect the application of General Assembly resolution 1541 (XV) in the decolonization of Western Sahara and, in particular, of the principle of self-determination through the free and genuine expression of the will of the peoples of the Territory.

To date, the Western Sahara remains a disputed territory, claimed now by the Kingdom of Morocco and the Polisario Front, an organization recognized by the United Nations as representing the people of the Western Sahara. The territory is controlled by Morocco, and in the light of a stalled referendum on independence and failed negotiations leading up to the present, the people of the Western Sahara have not been able to exercise their right to self-determination recognized by the Court. The ICJ decision is nevertheless highly significant from a normative perspective in establishing that a nomadic people, absent formal modes of political and social organization, permanent settlement, or demarcated territory, may qualify for the right to self-determination.

State Sovereignty and the 'Ancient Fears of States'

The above account describes an evolving international law of self-determination with a number of points of relevance for indigenous claims to self-determination, and is included here as the canvas or backdrop from which indigenous peoples' representatives drew essential framing resources, to be discussed in the following chapter. The picture is, however, as yet incomplete to the extent that the scope and application of the right to self-determination in international law cannot be fully understood without consideration of the norm of state sovereignty, which is a key concept in international law, a 'basic constitutional doctrine of the law of nations' (Brownlie 1979, 287), and a counter-norm in the context of claims to self-determination. Equally, the political doctrine of state sovereignty is critical to understanding the extent and nature of opposition faced by indigenous peoples in their pursuit of self-determination.

Sovereignty and all that flows from it constitutes a fundamental doctrine in international law and international relations. A concept with a long lineage that can be traced to the Peace of Westphalia (1648) and the consolidation of a system of sovereign states in Europe, sovereignty has figured as a signature feature of states in modernity, and has been described as the 'cornerstone of international rhetoric about state independence and freedom of action' (Hannum 1990, 14). As an international legal concept, sovereignty assumed importance in the post-World

brink of the twentieth century, to justify conquest and colonization, stands condemned' (at 78). See *Separate Opinion of Vice-President* at http:///www.icj_cij.org.

War II period as an operative principle of the UN Charter. The 'sovereign equality of Members' constitutes one of the fundamental tenets of the Charter, as stated in Article 2(1), while Article 2(4) imposes an obligation on states to 'refrain from the threat or use of force against the territorial integrity or political independence of any state'. Article 2(7), further, states that:

> Nothing contained in the present Charter shall authorize the United Nations to intervene in matters which are essentially within the domestic jurisdiction of any state or shall require the Members to submit such matters to settlement under the present Charter.

Reflecting a preoccupation with the development and upholding of 'friendly relations' among states, these provisions of the UN Charter principally manifest an understanding of sovereignty in its *external* – Westphalian – rather than internal guise. Westphalian sovereignty is the idea that one sovereign state should not interfere in the domestic authority structures of another. The Charter provisions also reflect what is termed international legal sovereignty, which refers to the 'practices associated with mutual recognition, usually between territorial entities that have formal juridicial independence' (Krasner 1999, 3). Other forms of sovereignty include interdependence sovereignty, which refers to the capacity to control flows of goods, people, pollutants, disease, and capital in and out of a state, and which is closely associated with the idea of globalization eroding state sovereignty. A sovereign state may also be thought of as having *internal* sovereignty, referring to domestic authority structures and how effective they are in wielding authority over all political and legal affairs within a defined territory (*ibid.*, 3–4).

As stated above, sovereignty is commonly thought of as the principal defining feature or attribute of states. At the same time, commentators speak of a 'transformed' or 'reconfigured' state sovereignty, as diverse processes of globalization have created conditions for the diffusion of sovereignty away from states to a range of institutions, actors, and organizations outside and inside the state. At the global governance level, sovereignty is now located in a multiplicity of political, economic, and legal institutions, in which states, by their own consent, find themselves enmeshed. International arrangements concerning human rights are an important factor in this trend (Forsythe 2006, 20–25). Notwithstanding the state-based system of human rights implementation, the generally accepted view of the relationship between human rights and state sovereignty is that the latter is compromised by the existence of higher human rights norms (e.g. Forsythe 2006; Schwab and Pollis 2000; Krasner 1999; Henkin 1999). Even in the absence of strong, effective enforcement mechanisms, most commentators regard state sovereignty as being at least modestly transformed by the existence of an international human rights regime. Other issue areas subject to international regulation include peace and security, trade and finance, communications and transportation, migration, and the environment; the latter are closely associated with the notion of interdependence sovereignty in concerning the ability of states to control transborder flows. Internal challenges to state sovereignty come from a number of different types of 'unit' within the state, from cities and regions to national, ethnic, religious, or cultural groups.

The indigenous pursuit of a right to self-determination of indigenous peoples in international law can be regarded as challenging state sovereignty in two main ways. First, if we view international human rights norms as compelling states to treat those within their territories in a certain way, it can be viewed as compromising sovereignty in the Westphalian sense of the term. Second, and more substantively, the right of indigenous peoples to self-determination can be regarded as reshaping state sovereignty in the internal, domestic sense of the term. Taking different, context-specific forms in practice, the paradigmatic exercise of the right to self-determination on the part of indigenous peoples involves the realization of a set of arrangements allowing for indigenous jurisdiction over spheres of political, cultural, and administrative autonomy, in conjunction with meaningful participation in wider decision-making arenas, together with control over a territorial space and associated lands and resources. It therefore calls upon the state to share or indeed transfer a degree of authority to the appropriate indigenous authorities, circumscribing state sovereignty in the domestic arena and creating a challenge for representatives of governments accustomed to seeing states as the exclusive holders of domestic jurisdiction. A particular concern for states is the loss or transference of *internal* territorial integrity accompanying claims for indigenous self-determination, the exercise of which is made meaningful in demarcated, bounded indigenous territories. In many respects the heart of the contest between states and indigenous peoples, states are particularly jealous of their territorial integrity, which is the foremost corollary of state sovereignty (Brownlie 1990, 287).[18] As Hannum (1990, 463) has put it, states attach a 'mythical status' to their territorial integrity, which forms the 'literal and figurative foundation of the state'. Territory is also constitutive of statehood in international law, which requires in Article 1 of the Montevideo Convention on the Rights and Duties of States of 1933 that a state possess the following characteristics: i) a permanent population; ii) a defined territory; iii) government; and iv) capacity to enter into relations with other states.[19]

To be clear, though internal state sovereignty is to a certain extent infringed by the meaningful exercise of indigenous peoples' right to self-determination, what is not threatened by the indigenous assertion of self-determination is states' *external* territorial integrity. For a number of reasons pursued in the following section, indigenous peoples are not looking to secede from existing states but seek simply

18 Brownlie (1990) describes the principal corollaries of state sovereignty as: i) a jurisdiction, prima facie exclusive, over a territory and the permanent population living there; ii) a duty of non-intervention in the area of exclusive jurisdiction of other states; and iii) the dependence of obligation arising from customary law and treaties on the consent of the obligor.

19 28 AJIL, Supp., 75 (1934).

to control their own territories, institutions, cultures, resources and social orders without undue interference, while negotiating the terms of their relationship with wider society on the basis of consent, mutual recognition and respect. Almost without exception, however, the invocation by states of the principal of territorial integrity as a limitation on the right of self-determination of indigenous peoples has focused on threats to external territorial integrity, manifesting at times in a seeming fascination with secession that has been construed by some observers as effecting a delaying strategy in negotiations over the content of indigenous rights.

Self-Determination and Indigenous Peoples: A Relational and Processual Understanding

In spite of the manifest difficulties raised by indigenous peoples' claims for self-determination, there has never been much suggestion amongst movement actors, if any, of abandoning self-determination. Self-determination has been and continues to be 'the central tenet and main claim' of the indigenous peoples' movement (Daes 2000b, 303). Indigenous delegates have offered a wide range of reasons for their insistence on self-determination. One of the most forceful involves an outright rejection of the state's authority to define the needs and futures of indigenous peoples, whereby self-determination stands for a people's freedom to control its own destiny without undue interference from others. As stated – in reverse – by the former ATSIC Commissioner Mick Dodson at the first session of the WGDD in 1995 (statement on file with author):

> It could be said that at the heart of all the violations of our human rights has been the failure to respect our integrity, and the insistence in speaking for us, defining our needs and controlling our lives. Self-determination is the river in which all other rights swim.

Much of the appeal of self-determination lies in its status as a general principle, from which flows a wide range of potential claims, which may be at once political, economic, social, and cultural. As Niezen (2003, 146) has put it, 'the term "self-determination" encompasses every conceivable aspiration of politically organized societies'. Ted Moses of the Grand Council of the Crees describes self-determination as a 'concept of sweeping scope' (2000, 156), as follows:

> Self-determination is a concept of sweeping scope that encompasses all aspects of human development and interaction, cultural, social, political, and economic. It is not simply a political right as it is characterized. … It is a complex of woven and inextricably related rights which are interdependent, where no aspect is paramount over any other. It is a right that forms the basis of all other rights.

The idea of self-determination as an 'umbrella right' has been criticized by a number of legal scholars. Higgins (1994, 122–123), for example, argues that concepts should be employed carefully so as not to distort their meaning, and rejects the idea that self-determination can be 'all things to all men'. Xanthaki (2007, 154) warns against regarding self-determination as an umbrella right from a tactical perspective, and argues that 'claims that are justified by loose links with established rights, and even more so with a right as controversial as self-determination, are not very convincing'. Yet a so-called 'maximalist approach' seems to be supported by the Covenants, which articulate a right of peoples to self-determination that involves political, economic, social, and cultural elements (United Nations 1966a; United Nations 1966b, common Art. 1), and which also link the right to self-determination with permanent sovereignty over natural wealth and resources (*ibid.*, common Art. 1.2). Such an approach is also flexible enough to encompass the wide range of indigenous conceptions of self-determination. Consistent with the diversity of historical, political, social, economic, cultural, geographic and demographic characteristics of indigenous peoples, the ways that indigenous peoples envision self-determination vary enormously. Many have described self-determination in terms of regional autonomy arrangements, while for others self-determination represents a basis for cultural claims for the protection of cultural or linguistic identity. For others still, it represents control of ancestral lands and territories, and the right to own, use, and develop their resources.

As for secession, few, if any, indigenous peoples' representatives participating in UN debates have described a desire for full political independence as a means of exercising their self-determination. For most indigenous peoples, the political, demographic, and economic realities make the establishment of viable states an unlikely option (Henriksen 2008; Eide 2007; Niezen 2003; Sambo Dorough 2002), which is clearly one reason for a reluctance to invoke secession as a core political goal. Another is that indigenous peoples do not simply wish to replicate the state, which has been repeated often enough at drafting meetings on the UNDRIP. Most palpable, however, is a disinclination to break away from existing states in favour of a so-called 'relational' (Kingsbury 2000; see also Henriksen 2008; Young 2007) approach to self-determination, whereby self-determination is understood not as putting an end to but as restructuring the terms and dynamics of the relationship between indigenous peoples and states. Most of the groups active in the global indigenous peoples' movement need and expect to maintain a continuing association with their surrounding states, but they simultaneously desire to redefine the terms of that association or relationship to enable them to make the choices about their ways of life free from arbitrary interference. Young (2007, 50–51) defines this approach to self-determination as 'a quest for an institutional context of non-domination', allowing for indigenous peoples to pursue their own goals and interpret their own ways of life and forms of development without undue domination or constraint, whilst maintaining enduring relationships with the state, whether these be territorial, economic, political or otherwise.

Understanding self-determination in relational terms is surely convincing, particularly where, as in the Antipodes and the Americas, a long history of settlement, exchange, treaty-making, removal, and integration have resulted in webs and relations of interdependence and interrelation between indigenous and non-indigenous peoples (Young 2007, 49). Equally, self-determination understood as separation is unrealistic in ignoring the relations of interdependence that indigenous and non-indigenous peoples inevitably have with each another. A relational understanding of self-determination is also consistent with an understanding of self-determination as an ongoing, dynamic process, requiring continual reconsideration in the light of varying political, social, and economic conditions and the changing aspirations of the peoples concerned. Indigenous peoples regard this as extremely important to any meaningful exercise of the right to self-determination, which cannot be implemented through a 'one-time choice' (Henriksen 2008, 39). The exercise and implementation of self-determination must be 'endless' (Daes 2000, 79) and 'without point of closure' (Stavenhagen 1996, 5), allowing for a continual and ongoing process of renegotiation between indigenous peoples and states over the terms of their relationships. As expressed by Henriksen (2008, 39), 'the implementation [of self-determination] must be viewed as a dynamic process ... because such an approach makes it possible for incremental changes to be implemented rather than forcing parties to agree on definite changes that can be too radical for some and insufficient for others'.

Autonomy

Although the vast majority of indigenous groups presenting their claims at the UN reject secession in favour of a freely negotiated and ongoing association with the states in which they live, indigenous representatives participating in negotiations over the content of their rights have consistently opposed attempts to impose a limit on indigenous peoples' right to self-determination akin to suggestions of 'internal self-determination' or autonomy. Autonomy is, in effect, the way in which most applications of indigenous self-determination would operate in practice, but there are important reasons why it has been steadfastly opposed. One key reason is that autonomy does not automatically suggest a territorial entitlement, whereas permanent sovereignty over land and resources is generally interpreted as presupposing a right to self-determination in international law and practice (e.g. United Nations 1966a; United Nations 1966b, common Art. 1.2). A territorialized notion of self-determination is particularly important for indigenous peoples, whose cultures depend fundamentally on their relationships with their lands, territories, and resources (Lam 2004; Daes 2002). As Daes (2002, 13; see also Daes 2001a) has put it:

> Land is not only an economic resource for indigenous peoples. It is also the peoples' library, laboratory and university; land is the repository of all history and scientific knowledge. All that indigenous peoples have been, and all that they know about living well and humanly, is embedded in their land and in the stories associated with every feature of the landscape.

Another concern with autonomy is that it does not confer international legal personality, whereas indigenous delegates have sought recognition as legitimate actors in international society, which is in principle conferred by the recognition of a right of indigenous peoples to self-determination (Lam 2000, 59). As an alternative to self-determination, moreover, autonomy offends indigenous identities as self-determining peoples, whereby self-determination is viewed as inherent and inalienable; 'rather than providing self-determination, states can only recognise it' (Xanthaki 2007, 132). More fundamental still, autonomy is not a right in international law, which does not concern itself with internal political subdivisions within states (Lam 2004, 141). Autonomy is 'essentially a gift by the state (grudgingly offered, ungratefully accepted)...' (Thornberry 2000, 56). Lacking any kind of technical meaning in international law, it is a concept 'whose content is filled in by enclosing states according to their domestic laws, good or bad will, and whim' (Lam 2004, 143).

Institutional 'Claims of the Resistance'

One of the recognized successes of the first and second – currently at its midway point – UN decades is the extent to which indigenous peoples have evidently carved out a niche for themselves within the UN and its specialized agencies, with the global indigenous movement becoming one of the most active and visible civil society sectors across the UN system. Indigenous peoples' representatives are visible interlocutors in diverse policy areas, having left their imprint in UN processes relating to human rights, sustainable development, the environment, climate change, and more. The establishment of the PFII, moreover, can be taken as recognition by the international community of the special status of indigenous peoples. The PFII is the first permanent UN body to have a membership that extends beyond state representatives and independent experts to include indigenous representatives, and is a unique space in the UN system.

Access and Participation in the Making of the UN Declaration: The WGIP and the WGDD

Over and above other UN human rights norm writing processes to date, the production of the UNDRIP can be regarded as having seen unprecedented levels of self-representation on the part of those seeking new specifications of rights appropriate to their particular forms of suffering. In both the WGIP were work was initiated and the WGDD where negotiations was resumed with governmental delegations, indigenous representatives played a significant role in the construction of their human rights.

As discussed in Chapter 3, the establishment of the WGIP in 1982 transformed the landscape of access and participation for activists in the nascent indigenous movement. One of the first decisions made by the WGIP experts, and encouraged by indigenous leaders, was to take the unprecedented move of opening its doors to the representatives of a wide range of indigenous organizations and communities otherwise lacking formal accreditation at the UN. A move considered necessary if the WGIP were to succeed in its two-fold mandate to review developments relating to the rights of indigenous peoples and to formulate new standards, the decision overlooked contemporaneous UN rules restricting rights of access to a limited set of NGOs, but was nevertheless made possible by both the flexibility of the WGIP experts, who showed excellent judgement in breaking with UN protocol, and the location of the WGIP at the bottom of the UN hierarchy. As a working group of the former UN Sub-Commission, the WGIP experts were relatively invulnerable to political pressure and were able to go ahead with their work without the restrictions of close state supervision. Wilmer has described the WGIP as a 'marginal site in world politics', whose 'marginalization has both material and ethical implications' (Wilmer 1993, 33).

It is difficult to imagine how the WGIP could have properly undertaken its work without the full participation of indigenous peoples' representatives. Objections were initially raised by some states, notably Brazil and Peru, concerned that the airing of indigenous grievances would embarrass states and that the relaxation of accreditation procedures would set a dangerous precedent. Certainly, the move was somewhat revolutionary and might well be thought of as introducing a pioneering process into the UN system. As for the Draft Declaration composed by the WGIP, the participation of indigenous peoples markedly shaped its content, as indigenous representatives' interventions under the two distinct agenda items – the review of developments and the evolution of standards, often taking the form of testimonial and rule-oriented interventions, respectively – asserted an increasing influence on the WGIP experts, who alone detained the authority to make final decisions over the substance and language. That influence is particularly apparent as regard the eventual inclusion in the text of a right of indigenous peoples to self-determination, which, to begin with, was resolutely opposed by the WGIP experts. As one indigenous delegate put it to me, 'when we first talked about self-determination, I think they thought the sky would fall in' (author interview, January 2003). Dodson has described the effects of indigenous participation as follows (1998b, 63–64):

> The presence of Indigenous peoples at the UN [WGIP] has some very direct effects. In the first years of the Working Group, Indigenous peoples argued that any declaration of Indigenous peoples' rights must include the recognition of the right to self-determination. The members of the Working Group thought we were crazy. The Chairperson made it clear that there was no way that the Working Group could support recognition of such a politically contentious right. An examination of the texts from year to year reveals that our perspectives were eventually accepted. When the final draft left the Working Group it contained the unqualified right to self-determination as one of its articles.

The passage of the Draft Declaration from the WGIP to the WGDD in 1995 raised a number of concerns with indigenous representatives regarding the stricter rules of accreditation and participation characterizing the former Commission on Human Rights – comprised of the representatives of 53 states – and its working groups. Even at the level of the Commission, however, where rules of access only admitted NGOs with ECOSOC status and where NGO input was limited to the most restrictive of interventions, indigenous lobbyists were able to gain access for a wide range of indigenous organizations and to achieve a strong culture of participation. Increasing access was an immediate concern in that, in 1995, only 12 indigenous organizations had ECOSOC consultative status. It was achieved by way of CHR Resolution 1995/32 establishing a procedure authorizing 'the participation of organizations of indigenous people not in consultative status' (United Nations 1995a, Annex). In the first year, 31 indigenous organizations were admitted to participate through this procedure, rising to over 100 in the subsequent 10 years. Beyond gaining access, indigenous representatives also pressed for appropriately inclusive working methods, transforming them incrementally in a way that excited some onlookers (e.g. Feldman 2002). Thus, by the end of the second session in 1996, and on the back of a walkout by the indigenous caucus, the WGDD Chair, José Urrutia of Peru, agreed to consult with the indigenous caucus on the preparation of the agenda. By the end of the third session in 1997, the Chair agreed to a new working approach; dividing the meeting into 'formal' and 'informal' sessions, the Chair proposed to restrict formal sessions to general debate and the adoption of articles agreed upon by the consensus of *all* the participants in informal sessions, including indigenous participants (United Nations 1998b, para. 18). Amounting to an agreement to include indigenous advocates in the consensus for the adoption of articles, the decision effectively allowed for the inscribing of indigenous resistance into the decision-making, and can be regarded as radically transforming or 'decolonizing' the space of the WGDD (Feldman 2002).

Indigenous representatives have regarded struggles to secure their participation in the drafting of the UNDRIP as critical to influencing its content and preventing dilution of fundamental rights sought by the movement. Procedural struggles are also an expression of self-determination on the part of sovereign peoples with historically rooted cultures and identities, whereby participation is both entitlement and due recognition of that status. Equal rights of participation are also critical not to lend legitimacy where it does not belong, a lesson that indigenous representatives learned during the process of revision of ILO Convention No.107 in 1988, when indigenous peoples' representatives had very little direct input other than that allowable through the worker caucus, one of the three constituencies in the ILO's tripartite structure. In the event, some indigenous delegates withdrew from the process, fearing that the ILO and member states would use the indigenous presence to claim legitimate process and outcome, and in spite of the fact that the revisions ultimately failed to produce the document that indigenous representatives wanted (Berman 1988).

Norms and Praxis of Participation

Today, meaningful participation on the part of indigenous representatives might, with few exceptions, be thought of as a standard of UN meetings and decision-making processes concerning indigenous peoples. There is an ethos of indigenous peoples' participation in UN parlance and practice, not solely in the context of indigenous specific organs such as the PFII and the EMRIP but also in mechanisms with a wider relevance to multiple 'stakeholder' interests, such as those focused on issues of biological diversity, intellectual property, and sustainable development. Thus, under the Convention on Biological Diversity (CBD), diverse mechanisms exist for the full and effective participation of indigenous peoples in the various meetings held under the Convention, including the Conference of the Parties (COP), the governing body of the Convention, and the Working Group on Article 8j and Related Provisions, which facilitates the participation of indigenous representatives through its Voluntary Fund. The World Intellectual Property Organization (WIPO), similarly, operates a Voluntary Contribution Fund for Accredited Indigenous and Local Communities as one mechanism to enhance the participation of indigenous peoples in its Intergovernmental Committee. Indigenous peoples also constitute a 'Major Group' in the Commission on Sustainable Development (CSD) and indigenous peoples' representatives participate in the various official sessions of the Commission.

As for the right of indigenous peoples to participate in decision-making concerning them, this is now a relatively well-established norm in international law. It finds textual expression in ILO Convention No.169, which relates the principles of consultation to a range of policy, governance and development decisions and processes affecting indigenous peoples (ILO 1989, Arts. 2.1, 5.c, 6.1.a, 6.1.b, 6.2, 7.1, 7.2, 15.2, 17.2, 22.2, and 23.1). It is also highlighted in Article 18 of the UNDRIP, which maintains that (United Nations 2007a):

> Indigenous peoples have the right to participate in decision-making in matters which would affect their rights, through representatives chosen by themselves in accordance with their own procedures, as well as to maintain and develop their own indigenous decision-making institutions.

The corollary state duty to consult is highlighted in Article 19, as is the principle of free, prior, and informed consent, whereby consent must be obtained without pressure or coercion, prior to authorization or implementation of an initiative, and on the basis of a full understanding of any and all of its implications (United Nations 2007a):

> States shall consult and cooperate in good faith with the indigenous peoples concerned through their own representative institutions in order to obtain their free, prior and informed consent before adopting and implementing legislative or administrative measures that may affect them.

The right of indigenous peoples to participate in decision-making concerning them is also recognized in the jurisprudence of a number of the human rights treaty bodies, including the HRC and the CERD. CERD General Recommendation No. 23 requires states to 'ensure that members of indigenous peoples have equal rights in respect of effective participation in public life and that no decisions directly relating to their rights and interests are taken without their informed consent' (CERD 1997, Art. 4.d). CERD has also emphasized the importance of meaningful consultation; in its concluding observations on Nigeria issued in 2007, for example, it criticized the state's failure to 'engage in meaningful consultation' with ethnic communities experiencing the adverse effects of oil exploration and drilling in the Delta Region and in the River States (CERD 2007b, para. 19). The HRC, similarly, has highlighted the importance of '*effective* participation of members of minority communities in decisions which affect them' (HRC 1994, para. 7, my emphasis).

Institutional Habitat: The PFII

The global indigenous movement is just one of several global social movements to have developed close relations to the UN. According to Keck and Sikkink (1998, 168), chronologies of the international women's movement are largely a litany of UN conferences. The broader human rights movement, moreover, has successfully used UN conferences and meetings to gain momentum. Perhaps distinctively, however, the global indigenous movement has come to *nest* within the UN institution in the sense of having established a permanent space, a 'space that is more than a just a moment' (Menchu in Nelson 1999, 23), within the UN system; Xanthaki (2007, 175) notes that no other vulnerable group has received such treatment from the United Nations or indeed any other intergovernmental organization. The PFII is in this respect a unique forum, and arguably one of the movement's most outstanding achievements.

An idea of indigenous representatives dating back to the 1980s, the indigenous campaign to establish a permanent, ongoing mechanism for indigenous peoples within the UN system grew out of a resolve for recognition of the unique status of indigenous peoples in international society, that is, not solely as one sector of global civil society, but as sovereign nations and peoples with distinctive cultures and identities manifesting in distinct social, cultural, and political institutions, and justifying the acquisition of some kind of international personality beyond that accorded to NGOs and other 'stakeholders'. The idea for a permanent space to address the concerns of indigenous peoples also arose from recognition of certain failings within the UN system regarding its treatment of indigenous concerns, which were highlighted in the many reports and reviews produced in the run up to the establishment of the PFII. Poor coordination and an inconsistency of approach across different UN bodies and agencies dealing with indigenous issues, a lack of mechanisms to prevent duplication of programmes, and the absence of measures allowing for the nominated representatives of indigenous peoples to provide expert advice and to take part in decision-making were identified as particular problems (see e.g. United Nations 1996d).

A number of key developments mark the progression towards the establishment of the PFII. In 1993, responding to the lobbying efforts of indigenous delegates at the World Conference on Human Rights, the recommendation to establish a permanent forum was included in the Vienna Declaration and Programme of Action (United Nations 1993a, para.B.2.32). Then in June 1995, a first workshop to discuss the establishment of a permanent forum was held in Copenhagen, involving independent experts and state and indigenous representatives in a discussion over the mandate, scope, membership, and reporting level of a potential forum.[20] Following shortly after this, the Programme of Activities for the International Decade of the World's Indigenous People adopted by the General Assembly recognized the establishment of a forum as a primary objective of the decade (United Nations 1996b, para. 7), and recommended the convening of a second workshop (*ibid.*, para. 9). This was held in July 1997 in Santiago de Chile, at which participants considered the possible role of the permanent forum and its relationship to existing UN mandates and structures in the light of the Secretary-General's review of existing mechanisms, procedures and programmes concerning indigenous peoples (United Nations 1996d).[21] In 1998, the Commission on Human Rights decided to establish an *ad hoc* working group to consider proposals for a permanent forum. This group met in 1999 and 2000. Finally, in April 2000, the Commission adopted a resolution recommending the establishment of a 'Permanent Forum on Indigenous Issues' (United Nations 2000d). This was endorsed by ECOSOC some three months later (2000c).

20 The *Report of the First Workshop on the Establishment of a Permanent Forum Held in Accordance with Commission Resolution 1995/31* (Copenhagen 26–28 June 1995) is reproduced in García-Alix (ed.) (1999). See also U.N. Doc. E/CN.4/Sub.2/AC.4/1995/7.

21 The *Report of the Second Workshop on the Establishment of a Permanent Forum Held in Accordance with Commission Resolution 1997/30* (Santiago de Chile, 30 June–2 July1997) is contained in García-Alix (ed.) (1999).

Chapter 5
Reconfiguring Human Rights

Emerging at a historical juncture characterized by political turbulence and disruptive protest in public settings, early studies of social movements regarded unconventional and disruptive forms of protest as emblematic of social movement activity, 'the *sine qua non* of the form' (McAdam et al. 2005, 9). Indeed, unorthodox and disruptive tactics have been looked upon as inherent characteristics of social movement activity, the result also of a persistent tendency to view social movements as 'outsiders' (Gamson 1990) marginalized in the political order. Increasingly, however, it is recognized that contemporary social movements employ a diverse set of tactics, which include both unconventional and conventional activities, and that a close association between social movements and disruption may in fact be more pertinent to an earlier period, more particularly the 1960s (Goldstone 2003; Katzenstein 1998). Accordingly, protest is now understood to encompass a wide variety of actions, ranging from confrontational tactics such as marches, demonstrations, strikes, building occupations, and physical violence, to more conventional strategies of political behaviour such as lobbying, litigation, or interest representation, to cultural or symbolic forms of political expression, for example, the use of street performances, song, art, and poetry to shape public opinion and to influence power-holders (Taylor and Van Dyke 2007, 263). Scholars explore the particular tactics used by social movements in relation to a number of factors, including internal factors such as social movement culture and movement framing (McAdam 1996) and external factors such as the nature of political opportunities confronting movements or the wider 'repertoire of contention', understood as a constellation of tactics that a given population recognizes as possible means of asserting influence (Tilly 1978).

The global indigenous movement employs a diverse action repertoire, which we might identify as constituting three basic forms of action: *integrated*, *performative*, and *demonstrative*. Of these types of action, by far the most characteristic of the movement's activities are integrated forms, understood as those activities that engage the processes and procedures of intergovernmental organizations. These activities tend to be modelled after intergovernmental forms, and would include making statements before deliberative bodies such as the the WGIP or the WGDD, lobbying state delegates and UN officials, facilitating consensus between parties to negotiations, documenting and submitting information regarding human rights violations, and bearing witness to the latter in statements before UN bodies. These constitute the core of the movement's activities, and should not be looked upon as accommodative but as critical to accomplishing movement goals, allowing for substantial input into the reinterpretation, reformulation, and rewriting of norms. Performative tactics refer to the expressive dimensions of protest that infuse indigenous protest at the UN, and include identity performances such as those involving prayer and the giving of thanks. By 'demonstrative' actions I refer not to unruly or disruptive forms of protest as such, but rather tactics intended to visibly demonstrate collective conviction and strength of commitment, which may or may not be considered unruly. Thus, an example of a demonstrative tactic employed by indigenous representatives is collective withdrawal, which indigenous delegates have employed on a number of occasions to effect a change of direction or to register strongly held positions, as in 1996, when the indigenous caucus staged a walkout from the second session of the WGDD in protest at their effective exclusion from the resumed drafting process, and in 1999, when hundreds of indigenous delegates withdrew from the plenary of the WGIP as a way of protesting the participation of representatives of the Rehoboth Baster Community. Other forms of demonstrative protest employed by the global indigenous movement include processions and, less frequently, demonstrations and marches. The latter make less sense in the UN political arena in which the global indigenous movement predominantly operates, where it is more difficult to muster many of the key routines of the classical social movement repertoire, and where organizations and activists valuing ongoing access and participation are wiser to adhere to institutional rules and routines, which may be highly prescribed, and eschew activities likely to be looked upon as disruptive or falling outside the 'rules of the game'. In such a context, opportunities for various forms of discursive activism have proved far more convincing.

Discursive Activism as Disruption

Standard social movement thinking that has tended to associate social movements with unconventional and disruptive forms of activity such as marches, strikes, sit-ins, and demonstrations has also frequently associated such forms with social movements' impact and success. Much empirical work on social movements in national contexts has found that movements employing disruptive and disorderly tactics are more successful that those preferring more conventional forms of political activism such as lobbying. Early studies establishing this view include Gamson (1990 [1975]), whose study of the tactics of 53 challenging groups in the United States found that those employing violence were more likely to achieve both policy gains and access to political power. Similarly in their study of four poor peoples' movements in the United States – the unemployed workers and the industrial union movements of the 1930s and the civil rights and welfare movements of the 1960s – Piven and Cloward (1977) found that all four movements achieved their greatest influence before they became more formally organized and as a result of disruptive forms of protest, namely strikes, sit-ins, and demonstrations. More recent work in this vein includes McAdam and Su (2002), whose analysis of antiwar protests and their impact on Congressional voting on US involvement in the Vietnam War concluded that disruptive protest was particularly effective in contributing to favourable voting outcomes.

There may be a variety of reasons why such methods have proved to be successful. Disruption, as Tarrow (1998, 98) points out, obstructs the routine activities of authorities and forces them to attend to movement grievances. Where it takes the form of large-scale demonstrations or strikes, moreover, disruption reflects a 'logic of numbers' that serves to draw attention to the numerical strength behind a movement (della Porta and Diani 1999, 174–177). Yet while there may be compelling reasons for the efficacy of disruption, we also know from empirical studies that other, more conventional tactics may be more influential with respect to political authorities, and that in fact success may stem from the ability not to disrupt as such but to access and input discursively into the policy process. Soule et al. (1999), for example, find that women's groups have been more likely to win Congressional support when engaged in so-called insider tactics, while a host of studies show that disruption must be supplemented with conventional forms of action (e.g. McCann 1994; Morris 1993; Staggenborg 1991).

This latter view of social movements' efficacy has much more to say towards explaining the success of movements, like the global indigenous movement, constrained by their institutional location and perhaps also identity choice from mounting unruly tactics. The global indigenous movement has rarely drawn on unruly forms of protest yet has achieved notable impacts, predominantly through a discursive politics aimed at transforming meanings. It also suggests that the meaning of 'disruptive' may be different for social movements operating predominantly within institutions and organizations, and that in fact integrated activities modelled after intergovernmental forms, which are neither confrontational nor unruly but which allow for discursive input into policy debates, may be as disruptive as anything aimed at interrupting the order of the day. A similar point is made by Katzenstein (1998, 196) in the context of her research into feminist movement activism in the US military and Catholic Church, as follows:

> But what does 'disruption' really mean? Is a demonstration outside the White House or a snake dance around the Pentagon that causes security to be deployed and that may temporarily interrupt traffic and block the entry of people trying to reach their place of employment more disruptive then the presence of self-acknowledged feminists at the workplace who make known their expectations about changes in language, sexual behaviour, and office hierarchies? Disruption needs to be distinguished from 'interruption'.

But what do I understand by discursive activism, and how has it worked in the context of reconstituting human rights to accommodate the claims of indigenous peoples? By discursive activism, I refer to activism drawing principally on words, language, and symbols aimed at disrupting and reformulating accepted understandings, definitions, and assumptions, and involving the justification and promotion of alternative meanings leading to shifts in discursive positions and the ways in which issues are perceived. It 'is largely about questioning, criticizing, and publicizing ... these actions can change the terms of discourse, and the balance of different components in the international constellation of discourses' (Dryzek 2000, 131). It may take the form of information politics, symbolic politics, leverage politics, or accountability politics (Keck and Sikkink 1998). It may involve the elaboration of frames of meaning (Snow and Benford 1992; Snow and Benford 1988), or the strategic use of identity (Bernstein 2003). It may draw on argumentative processes, whereby authorities or opponents defending norm-violating behaviour 'become entangled in arguments and the logic of argumentative rationality slowly but surely takes over' (Risse and Sikkink 1999, 16), resulting in 'argumentative self-entrapment' and change (Risse 199, 531). It may also involve moral consciousness-raising, whether through testimony and storytelling or 'reporting facts'. All of these activities lend social movements or transnational activists what Habermas (1996) and Dryzek (1999, 2000) have termed 'communicative power', a form of power drawing its currency not from conventional, coercive sources such as economic resources or military capacity, but from credible information, the force of argument, and an overall 'communicative competence' (Dryzek 2000, 134). As Dryzek (2000, 131) explains:

> This capacity to affect the terms of discourse and change the balance of competing discourses is widely distributed. One does not need an army, control over governmental bureaucracies, massive wealth, or even large numbers of activists to be effective. One does need a certain minimum of conventional political resources: money, personnel, access to the media, and credibility. More importantly, actors need to be astute enough to recognize the importance of the discursive realm, and to figure out how to act effectively within this realm.

Indigenous activism focused on reshaping the contours of human rights at the UN provides a very convincing example of social movement actors acting effectively in the discursive realm. Pressing their case in a variety of UN forums, and drawing on the inherent flexibility of human rights, indigenous representatives have successfully worked to transform orthodox understandings and assumptions in conventional human rights discourse, overcoming the narrow individualistic premises of its liberal origins in favour of a reformed concept of human rights capable of embracing group claims based on a collective notion of human flourishing. Central to this process, and as the core modality for indigenous peoples to achieve appropriate control over their own destinies, indigenous representatives have been involved in the discursive reconfiguration of the right to self-determination of peoples, diminishing if not entirely surmounting its association with the model of nation-state sovereignty and supplanting it with a more pliable and much less threatening vision of self-determination allowing for mutual respect and recognition within a context of non-domination.

Indigenous Discursive Politics and the Law

In some accounts of discursive activism, discursive approaches are presented as providing an alternative when recourse to the law is not available. Discussing feminist movement activism within the Church, for example, Katzenstein describes feminists as turning to 'language in lieu of law' (1995, 49). No doubt there are institutional contexts where legal language fails to hold much sway, the church being a prime example; after all, 'those whose speech has been silenced by clerical decree cannot turn to the courts for protection' (*ibid.*). The trouble with such framing, however, is that is could be suggestive of an antagonism between discursive politics and legal language and forms, whereas evidently there are contexts where meaning work demands extensive engagement with the law. The United Nations is one such context where law affirms the legitimacy and validity of claims, calling for a discursive politics infused with legal and normative reasoning and argument.

Much of indigenous discursive activism is underpinned by an intricate knowledge of what Thornberry (2002, 9) terms the 'dense undergrowth of concept and instrument'. Frames deployed by the movement invoke a range of legal resources drawn from the terrain of international human rights law and associated jurisprudence, and reflect the high level of legal and technical expertise possessed by core movement activists. They also reflect a sound appreciation of the logic of legal argumentation in legal mobilization, whereby ambiguities, indeterminacies, and contradictions in the legal landscape are directed towards the development of new meanings and the recognition of new claims (Polleta 2000; Merry 1990). Indeterminacies, uncertainties, and contradictions constitute the pivotal points around which contest and interpretation can revolve, allowing for the development of discursive challenges designed to put indeterminacy to use in the construction of new meanings. Similarly, they reveal an awareness of the persuasiveness of claims identified in terms of prevailing principled norms, which work on states' identities to encourage norm acceptance and promotion (Thomas 2002; Finnemore and Sikkink 1998; Klotz 1995).

The terrain of international law has provided a critical framework for the framing of movement claims, but of course law can present both opportunities and constraints to social movements. Legal norms may invest a movement with ammunition, credibility, and legitimation, but they can also pose obstacles, and can be biased against certain types of claims. What we find in the body of international law evolving in the post-World War II era is the coexistence of statist and non-statist elements, presenting itself to indigenous activists as a site of exclusion and inclusion containing both hegemonic and counter-hegemonic elements (Falk et al. 2006, 711), and calling for the creative mobilization of counter-hegemonic elements in a 'war of position'. Statist elements revolve around the doctrine of state sovereignty and attendant notions of territorial integrity, which are central to international law, and which, as discussed in Chapter 4, constitute operative principles of the UN Charter. They are moderated in the Charter and subsequent international law by human rights precepts. Anaya (2004b, 53) paints the following picture:

> In sum, international law – the body of principles, norms and procedures that today function across national boundaries – remains state-centred, but it is increasingly pulled at by a discourse directly concerned with individuals and even groups. Notions of state sovereignty, although still very much alive in international law, are ever more yielding to an overarching normative trend defined by visions of world peace, stability, and human rights. This trend, promoted by modern international institutions and involving non-state actors in multilateral settings, enhances international law's competency over matters at one time considered within states' exclusive domestic domain.

Emphasizing the importance of legal forms in the language of indigenous discursive activism is to underline something distinctive in the strategic approach of the global indigenous movement. If on the face of it, however, a stress on the law as key to the framing enterprise suggests a comparison to the methods of interest groups, which work primarily with institutionally mandated authorities and which frequently engage in judicial and legislative lobbying to promote their concerns, it is important to note that the discursive work of the indigenous movement is much broader – more expressive – than interest group politics. Expressive dimensions infuse a much broader discursive undertaking that includes forms of identity politics and cultural politics (Muehlebach 2001), which are as integral to the movement's character and charisma as its affinity with the law.

Framing for Self-Determination

The Meaning of Self-Determination

As discussed in Chapter 4, the international law of self-determination features a good deal of uncertainty and indeterminacy. It is 'a conceptual morass in international law' (Kingsbury 2000, 20), 'a thorny topic … with remarkable contradictions' (Xanthaki 2007, 131), 'so hedged around by escape clauses that it is virtually meaningless as a basis for legal or political debate' (Ennals, cited in Stavenhagen 1996, 6). Stavenhagen (1996, 2) writes that, 'if I had a post-modernist inclination, I would be tempted to deconstruct the self-determination discourse, and end up by revealing it as nothing but a "text" whose only meaning is given to it by a succession of "readers"'. For the most part, the indeterminacy surrounding self-determination attaches itself to two questions: first, who can assert the right to self-determination, and second, what does the right entail? Clarifying the answers to these two questions has comprised the crux of the contest between indigenous peoples and states in UN negotiations aimed at elaborating indigenous peoples' rights, and has involved indigenous representatives in elaborate framing processes intended to remake the right to self-determination in a more universal and relational mould.

Evidently, questions of the scope and content of self-determination are substantially interlinked insofar as state objections to and constraints on the scope of application of the right have generally been related to assumptions regarding its content, which have taken secession and political independence as the paradigmatic exercise of the right. Equally, the gradual development of a consensus amongst states towards acceptance of the right of self-determination as applying to 'peoples' on a more universal basis has relied upon the development of a more tempered understanding of its modalities, whereby the relational, human rights, and democratic aspects of the right have been emphasized. In this latter respect, it is important to reiterate that the indigenous assertion of the right to self-determination at the UN has not involved simply 'stepping into' or occupying the right of self-determination understood as a static right with a fixed meaning, but rather taking part in its modification and evolution.

Extending the Scope of Application of Self-Determination: Contesting Discrimination

Questions surrounding the 'self' in self-determination find little textual clarity from relevant international instruments, which answer in terms that are 'as simple in formulation as chimerical in fact' (Daes 2000a, 76). As outlined in some detail in Chapter 4, international legal instruments liberally proclaim the universality of the right to self-determination, whilst also limiting its application. The Declaration on Colonial Countries of 1960 and the two International Human Rights Covenants of 1966, which form the cornerstone of the UN law of self-determination, provide that 'all peoples have the right to self-determination' (United Nations 1960a, Art. 2; United Nations 1966a, Art. 1; 1966b, Art. 1). Yet Resolution 1541 (XV), which accompanies Resolution 1514 (XV), identifies the holder of the right as the aggregate populations of territories under conditions of classical colonialism (United Nations 1960b, Principle IV) (United Nations 1960b, Principle IV). The Covenants are not explicit in their limitations, but the drafting history points to a restricted scope of 'peoples'.

Particularly in the earlier stages of the drafting process, Resolution 1541 (XV) was deployed by some states to oppose a right of self-determination for indigenous peoples on the basis that self-determination applied only to cases of 'domination or exploitation from outside' (e.g. Argentina, cited in Barsh 1996, 797) and 'had to be placed in the historical context of decolonization' (United Nations 1996b, para. 43). Apparent in this claim is an understanding of self-determination as a fixed rather than evolving norm, which in no way reflects the recognized view of the nature of general international legal principles as amenable to evolution (Cassese 1995, 128), and which indigenous delegates, legal experts, and some states challenged throughout the drafting process as 'freezing international law' (see. e.g. United Nations 1996a, para. 43). Relatedly, it fails to take account of two further applications emerging in later international law, including racial groups suffering oppression under a state of apartheid and whole populations of democratic states, as per Resolution 2396 (XXII) on apartheid (United Nations 1968b) and the Helsinki Declaration (Conference of Security and Cooperation in Europe 1975), respectively. More problematic still, such a claim fails to pay due regard to the basic principle of international law that human rights be applied universally, and is blind to the evident discrimination, not least political opportunism, involved in treating indigenous peoples, whose experiences have been for all intents and purposes comparable to that of colonial peoples in overseas colonies, as less equal to other peoples for the purposes of self-determination.

In both the WGIP and the WGDD, indigenous representatives consistently maintained that the right of self-determination must be applied universally and that to deny, limit, or place any qualification on the right in the context of indigenous peoples would be to create a double standard in international law. This latter objection featured time and again during negotiations on the UNDRIP, and can be thought of as constituting the basis of what we might describe as a 'discrimination frame'. The following interventions made by the representatives of ATSIC and the American Indian Law Alliance to the 3rd and 8th sessions of the WGDD in 1997 and 2002, respectively, are illustrative of its substantive content (statements on file with author):

> To proclaim self-determination as a right of 'all peoples', and at the same time to deny or seek to limit its application to indigenous peoples surely offends the prohibition of racial discrimination. The guarantee of non-discrimination is a norm of customary international law, on many accounts a peremptory norm from which no derogation is permitted.

> As virtually all participants in this working group acknowledge, the affirmation of the right to self-determination of indigenous peoples is a core element of the Draft Declaration and essential to its integrity. As provided in the International Human Rights Covenants, this right applies to 'all peoples'. Consequently, it would violate the peremptory norm prohibiting racial discrimination to create a different and lesser standard for the world's indigenous peoples concerning this crucial human right.

These interventions show the discrimination frame to be principled and morally persuasive, and to adhere to a logic of normative legitimation in the assertion of 'soft' (Keohane and Nye 1998) or 'communicative' (Dryzek 2000, 1999) power, whereby social movements articulating their claims in terms of principled international norms expand their influence over states concerned to gain or retain membership within the community of 'civilized' nations (Thomas 2002; Risse et al. 1999; Keck and Sikkink 1998). Its influence is very evident in the evolving positions of independent experts and states, and likely reflects the *jus cogens* status of the norm of non-discrimination, such norms being so fundamental that they cannot be departed from or set aside by treaty. Unlike rules of ordinary customary law, which normally allows states to apply reservations to treaties and thereby to modify their obligations, peremptory norms cannot be violated by any state, while treaties concluded in violation of *jus cogens* are considered null and void. Evidently, the accusation of alleged violation of *jus cogens* carries substantial weight, while transgressors face a weight of condemnation.

The impression of the frame can be seen to emerge in the thinking of both the independent experts and states. Erica-Irene Daes (1993c, paras. 24–25), for example, issuing an explanatory note on completion of the Draft Declaration in 1993, concluded that:

> With few exceptions, indigenous peoples were never a part of State-building. They did not have an opportunity to participate in designing the modern constitutions of the States in which they live, or to share, in any meaningful way, in national decision-making. In some countries they have been excluded by law or by force, but in many countries they have been separated by language, poverty, misery, and the prejudices of their non-indigenous neighbours. Whatever the reason, indigenous peoples in most countries have never been, and are not now, full partners in the political process and lack others' ability to use democratic means to defend their fundamental rights and freedoms. What, then, should be the response of the international community to the situation of indigenous peoples who lack effective partnership in governing the States in which they live? It would be inadmissible and discriminatory to argue that these peoples lack the right of self-determination because they are indigenous.

Certain states also took up the discourse of discrimination. At the eighth session of the WGDD in 2002, for example, a number of states, including Guatemala, Mexico, Norway, and Australia, registered their opposition to the US proposal to restrict Article 3 to a 'right to internal self-determination' by reference to the non-discrimination norm. Australia – proposing the even more unacceptable alternative of 'self-management' – described the US proposal as a 'constructive proposal', but regretted that (statement on file with author):

> The notion of an 'internal' right of self-determination is essentially a 'qualified right. It would seem to imply that indigenous peoples somehow have a lesser or inferior right of self-determination as compared to other peoples. However, this right is already guaranteed (in an unqualified form) to all peoples, by virtue of existing covenants.

The Battle of the 'S'

One of the most unrelenting features of negotiations of the past twenty years or so over the scope of application of the right of self-determination has been a contest over naming, centred around the question of whether indigenous peoples constitute 'peoples' with evident implications for self-determination. Involving a reluctance on the part of many states to recognize indigenous peoples as 'peoples' in favour of a language of 'populations' or 'people', the so-called 'battle of the "S"' has constituted a central site of discursive contest between state and indigenous representatives. The importance of the contest, to the uninitiated a seemingly superficial if not pedantic debate, is of course clear, for where 'populations' or 'people' carry no implications as to collective rights in international law, the term 'peoples' marries its holders to self-determination as a general human right. It is, therefore, an important linguistic symbol of indigenous peoples' identification as self-determining peoples.

A majority of states engaging in negotiations over the self-determination of indigenous peoples have at one time or another objected to the terminology of 'peoples' as applied to indigenous peoples. States' objections have generally turned on a narrow interpretation of 'peoples' for the purposes of self-determination, whereby 'peoples' refers to a limited universe of narrowly defined entities possessed of the 'actual or putative attributes of sovereignty or statehood' (Anaya 2000, 5; see also Anaya 1996, 77–80). The following statement of the United States to the fifth session of the WGDD in 1999 is indicative of this approach (United Nations 1999, para. 49):

> There is no international practice or instrument that accords indigenous groups everywhere the right to self-determination. The 'peoples' entitled to self-determination under international law are the entire peoples of a State or those that could constitute themselves as a sovereign independent state, and not particular groups within a State.

Evidently, this approach and others like it is not aimed at answering for scholarly purposes the question of 'who are peoples?' but on excluding indigenous peoples from the 'peoples' entitled to self-determination, and is arrived at completely independently of any consideration of objective definitional criteria. In this respect, it is of little intellectual merit, and is instead involved in rendering 'the promises of self-determination largely irrelevant to indigenous peoples' (Iorns 1992, 291). This is achieved by conflating the otherwise distinct entities of 'state' and 'people' for the purposes of establishing entitlement, thereby creating a legal fiction or 'semantic confusion … to avoid confronting … the various lamentable situations of indigenous peoples' (Falk 1988, 27).

Indigenous participants have been forceful in rejecting the claim that they do not constitute 'peoples'. Such efforts have turned on a range of arguments and justifications, including the issue of self-definition, whereby the subjective element of 'peoples' as recognized in a number of authoritative scholarly descriptions is insisted upon (e.g. Cristescu 1981; Espiell 1980). Indigenous perspectives have also challenged the rigid, limited understanding of human associational patterns inherent in the linkage of 'peoples' and 'states', as demonstrated in the following intervention by Dalee Sambo Dorough, formerly human rights specialist at the ILRC, to the fifteenth session of the WGIP in 1997 (statement on file with author):

> This limited conception of peoples largely ignores the multiple, overlapping spheres of community, authority, and interdependency that actually exist in human experience. This vision corresponds with the traditional Western perspective that limits humanity to two perceptual categories – the individual and the state – and which views states according to a model of mutually exclusive spheres of territory, community, and centralized authority.

International law lacks a formal definition of 'peoples' from which to definitively establish that indigenous peoples are 'peoples' with all the implications that attach to it in international law. Generally speaking, however, the indigenous position has found keen support in the opinions of international legal experts, amongst them former Chairperson-Rapporteur of the WGIP Erica-Irene Daes, who has taken the view that (2008, 13; see also Daes 2001, 2000, 1993b; see also Hannum 1996):

> Indigenous peoples are unquestionably 'peoples' in every social, cultural, and ethnological meaning of this term. They have their own long histories as distinct societies and nations; and a unique economic, religious, and spiritual relationship with the territories in which they have so long lived. It is neither logical nor scientific to treat them as their neighbours, who obviously have different languages, histories and cultures and who have often been their oppressors. The UN should not pretend, for the sake of convenient legal fiction, that these differences do not exist.

Indigenous claims have also found support in a number of well-accepted descriptions emerging from various UN studies and meetings. One such description is the so-called Kirby description produced by the UNESCO International Meeting of Experts on Further Study of the Concept of the Rights of Peoples, which attaches the following characteristics to an understanding of 'a people' (UNESCO 1989, para. 22):

1. a group of individual human beings who enjoy some or all of the following common features:
    a) a common historical tradition;
    b) racial or ethnic identity;
    c) cultural homogeneity;
    d) linguistic unity;
    e) religious or ideological affinity;
    f) territorial connection;
    g) common economic life.

2. the group must be of a certain number which need not be large (e.g. the people of micro States) but which must be more than a mere association of individuals within a State
3. the group as a whole must have the will to be identified as a people or the consciousness of being a people – allowing that groups or some members of such groups, though sharing the foregoing characteristics, may not have that will or consciousness; and possibly;
4. the group must have institutions or other means of expressing its common characteristics and will for identity.

A similar description is to be found in an earlier UN study by Aureliu Cristescu (1981), who describes a 'people' according to objective and subjective criteria. The objective requirements include characteristics of common language, race or ethnicity, culture, religion, and some relationship to territory, 'even if the peoples in question have been wrongfully expelled from it and artificially replaced by another population' (Cristescu 1981, para. 279). The subjective requirements include a consciousness as a distinct people and a collective will to exist as a distinct people. Such criteria clearly differentiate peoples from states, whilst also indicating that peoples may include subgroups existing within sovereign states, including indigenous peoples. Indigenous peoples in general enjoy characteristics such a common historical tradition, linguistic identity, cultural distinctiveness, and attachment to territory, even if the latter may have been interrupted in a physical sense. They also have the will to be identified as indigenous peoples and the desire to perpetuate their existence as distinct peoples. They may or may not possess active or extensive institutions expressing 'common characteristics and will for identity', but the political impetus for self-government is evidenced in claims to self-determination (Iorns 1992, 289).

The Content of Self-Determination: Tackling Secession Anxiety

As with the scope of application of self-determination, the question of what the right to self-determination entails has undergone maturation since its initial inclusion in the UN Charter in 1945. Yet much of the debate over the right of indigenous peoples to self-determination taking place in the last twenty years or so has been characterized by conservative if not static understandings of the content of the right, particularly on the part of certain very intransigent states, whereby the right to self-determination has been conceptualized as closely, indeed inextricably, linked with secession and political independence. Such a conception, carrying with it supposedly drastic implications for the territorial integrity and sovereignty of states, has arguably presented indigenous lawyers and activists with their biggest challenge, giving meaning to Christian Tomuschat's (1993, 11) reading that 'it is the tragedy of self-determination that it includes a right to independent statehood'.

State objections to and concerns about recognizing a right of indigenous peoples to self-determination based on a linkage between self-determination and secession have taken different forms. One, softer, variant has been to regard secession as included within the various modalities for the exercise of a right to self-determination. This view does not generally involve an outright objection to self-determination but a call for some form of limitation or qualification on its exercise, and is reflected in the summary of relevant debate at the third session of the WGDD in 1998 (United Nations 1998b, para. 44.e):

> Other States that also supported this principle [self-determination] expressed concern with respect to the implications that a wide recognition of that right in Article 3 might have, since it might be inclusive of the right to secession, therefore affecting the territorial integrity and political unity of States. They also expressed the need for these concerns to be reflected in the final version of Article 3.

Another, more extreme, variant has regarded self-determination as a fixed right with a single, predetermined meaning equivalent to secession, and relevant only to the period of decolonization. This view is reflected in the summary report of the first session of the WGDD in 1995, which states that (United Nations 1996a, para. 43):

> Many governments were of the view that article 3 went beyond existing international and national law and practice in that self-determination had to be placed in the historical context of decolonization.

To interpret self-determination as a synonym for secession and independent statehood is to adopt what Xanthaki (2007, 146) describes as a 'minimalist' approach to self-determination that is not supported by the evolutionary development of international law and that, in particular, overlooks the move since the mid-1970s or thereabouts towards emphasizing the internal, democratic aspects of self-determination. It is also to adopt a state-centred rather than a people-centred approach to self-determination, reducing the content of the norm to a process relating to states rather than a human right promoting the needs and aspirations of certain collective communities of cohesion and identity (Stavenhagen 1996, 4; see also Anaya 2000). As an approach to be overcome, it has involved indigenous activists in an exigent process of meaning transformation aimed at drawing states away from rigid and restrictive conceptualizations toward a more tempered understanding of self-determination whereby secession is de-emphasized and, concomitantly, a connection is established between the recognition of self-determination and the achievement of peace, security, and human rights.

A number of legal resources have been critical to discursive efforts to reconstruct the meaning of self-determination and to disassociate it from secession and associated concerns regarding territorial integrity. Particularly important are textual formulations linking self-determination with representative government, which can be regarded as playing an important role in advancing states towards a vision of indigenous peoples' self-determination exercised within states through an ongoing, dynamic relationship, and without the disorder and trauma of territorial separation. As outlined in Chapter 4, this understanding of self-determination in international law is evident as early as 1968 in Resolution 2396 (XXII) in relation to South Africa, in which self-determination was understood as involving 'majority rule based on universal suffrage', and can be regarded as becoming increasingly established in successive instruments, notably the 1970 Declaration on Friendly Relations, the Helsinki Declaration of 1975, and the 1993 Vienna Declaration. The Helsinki Declaration projects the right of self-determination as a continuous right of peoples – in this case European – to determine their 'internal status', that is, to determine the form of government under which they live (Conference of Security and Cooperation in Europe 1975). The Vienna Declaration endorses the right of 'all peoples' to self-determination and recalls the Declaration on Friendly Relations in taking up the so-called 'safeguard clause', though with a minor difference in that it expands on the distinctions established in the earlier Declaration – 'race, creed, or colour' – in calling for a government 'representing the whole people belonging to the territory without distinction of any kind' (United Nations 1993, Art. 2):

> All peoples have the right to self-determination. By virtue of that right they freely determine their political status, and freely pursue their economic, social and cultural development.
>
> In accordance with the Declaration on the Principles of International Law concerning Friendly Relations and Cooperation Among States in accordance with the Charter of the United Nations, this shall not be construed as authorizing or encouraging any action which would dismember or impair, totally or in part, the territorial integrity or political unity of sovereign and independent States conducting themselves in compliance with the principle of equal rights and self-determination of peoples and thus possessed of a Government representing the whole people belonging to the territory without distinction of any kind.

Of course, what is not necessarily entailed in the version of self-determination entailed above is a right of sub-state groups to self-determination; as discussed in Chapter 4, international law may point to the possibility of remedial secession under extreme circumstances of political exclusion and discrimination, but there is no *right* to secession as such, and indeed, the real novelty to the aforementioned instruments is in their extending the right to internal self-determination of entire populations living within sovereign states, *demos* rather than *ethnos*. As a basis to progress negotiations towards the acceptance of a right of indigenous peoples to self-determination, however, the norm of self-determination as representative or democratic government proved to be highly persuasive, leading states – and indeed to begin with the WGIP experts – towards an understanding of indigenous self-determination as involving a kind of 'belated State-building' (Daes 1993b, 375), and exercised with regard to the territorial integrity of democratic, representative states. This understanding is reflected in the following exert, which outlines the position arrived at by the longstanding WGIP Chair, Erica-Irene Daes (*ibid.*, 374–375):

> With regard to indigenous peoples, I believe that the right of self-determination should ordinarily be interpreted as the right of these peoples to negotiate freely their political status and representation in the States in which they live. This process might best be described as a kind of belated State-building, through which indigenous peoples are able to join with all the other peoples that make up the State on mutually agreed upon and just terms, after many years of isolation and exclusion. This process does not require the assimilation of individuals, as citizens like all others, but the recognition and incorporation of distinct peoples in the fabric of the State, on agreed terms.

The influence can also be discerned in the evolving positions of states, for example, the position of Guatemala as stated at the 8th session of the WGDD in 2002 (statement on file with author, own translation):

> In the era of decolonization, the right of self-determination gave rise to independence movements. Today, the right of self-determination enables peoples or national groups to determine, within States, their political status through processes of decentralization and autonomy, and to pursue their economic, social, and cultural development.

An evolving norm of self-determination as representative government can be thought of a constituting a core element of a broadly reassuring discourse aimed at tackling secession anxiety and encouraging the exploration of more nuanced meanings of self-determination. Another tenet of that discourse has involved highlighting a link between respect for the right to self-determination and the integrity of states' borders, which I have described elsewhere as constituting part of a 'peace and security frame' (Morgan 2004) aimed not only at neutralizing anxieties but at achieving a 'thoroughgoing conversion' (Snow et al. 1986, 247) – a radical shift – in the way in which states perceived self-determination. Involving an example of 'frame transformation' (*ibid.*, 240) supplanting old meanings with new and contrasting understandings that 'radically reconstitute what it is for participants that is going on' (*ibid.*, 245), this meaning work has drawn substantially on international law, in particular the 'safeguard clause' in the 1970 Declaration on Friendly Relations. As discussed in some detail in Chapter 4, this clause is broadly interpreted as allowing for the possibility of remedial secession in extreme cases of *carence de souveraineté*, in effect therefore establishing a relationship in international law between the recognition of the right to self-determination and the stability of states' borders. As reasoned by a speaker on behalf of the National Congress of American Indians and the Native

American Rights Fund in a joint statement to the 8th session of the WGDD in 2002 (statement on file with author):

> The right of secession is a dormant right that may only be triggered by extremes of political disenfranchisement, ruthless exploitation, or material dispossession. On the other hand the right may be neutralized by access to meaningful political participation. States 'conducting themselves in compliance with the principles of equal rights and self-determination of peoples' keep secession at bay. It makes no sense for the US to raise this obscure, well nigh, irrelevant issue of secession and use it to erect a barrier to indigenous peoples' rights to determine their own futures.

This linkage between the recognition of self-determination and the stability of states' borders is made around a clause of international law, but it also reflects the political reality of conflict prevention and resolution, which shows us that armed conflict and secessionist aspirations diminish with autonomy and self-government arrangements, while neglect of internal diversity breeds political violence (e.g. van Praag 1998; Gurr 1993). Beyond legal provision, and drawing on the empirical credibility of this claim, indigenous representatives and their supporters have pressed the wisdom of respecting self-determination. To quote Erica-Irene Daes (1996, 50) again:

> It is not realistic to fear indigenous peoples' exercise of the right to self-determination. It is far more realistic to fear that the denial of indigenous peoples' right to self-determination will leave the most marginalized and excluded of all the world's peoples without a legal, peaceful weapon to press for genuine democracy in the states in which they live.

This aspect of a 'peace and security frame' – raising as it does even remote circumstances justifying secession – might be regarded as involving indigenous representatives in a threatening posture otherwise at odds with indigenous identity as it is deployed in UN negotiations, with its emphasis on values of harmony, equilibrium, reciprocity, peace, and well-being. Cognizant of the possible disjuncture, indigenous representatives have approached the issue with care. This can be seen in the following statement by a representative of the Chittagong Hill Tracts NGO Forum to the 8th session of the WGDD in 2002 (statement on file with author):

> Personally I do not believe in violent methods and would never encourage it, but I am afraid that the qualification and reduction of the substance of the principle and the right to self-determination as it applies to indigenous peoples might reduce the confidence of indigenous peoples to seek redress through dialogue and peaceful methods. In such situations, people like myself may have little influence to talk about peace and dialogue.

Self-Determination and Environmental Stewardship

Another frame emerging in the meaning work of the indigenous movement in its pursuit of self-determination revolves around the connections between the upholding of indigenous rights and conservation of the natural environmental. Indigenous peoples are often regarded as exemplars of environmentally sustainable living, and their cultures, values, and ways of living thought to be environmentally sensitive. What we might term the 'environmental frame' turns on this, establishing a relationship between the cultural, economic, social, and physical integrity of indigenous peoples and ecological integrity and sustainability.

The discourse points to a number of aspects of indigenous cultures, values, and ways of life relevant to environmental stewardship, including a spiritual relationship with the natural world and a veneration for the 'whole of creation' as holding religious and cultural significance, resulting in a respectful relationship with and reverence for all living things and a view of the natural environment as containing meanings and teaching lessons. Another factor pointing to indigenous peoples' contribution to environmental sustainability is a sense of responsibility for future generations, expressed in indigenous peoples' role as 'caretakers' of the environment and in principles such as the 'seventh generation principle', a Haudenosuanee injunction to ensure that present actions are guided by consideration of the welfare and well-being of future generations. High levels of social cooperation and community cohesion, combined with forms of social and political organization inclined towards sustainability are also presented as pertinent, as is the possession of traditional environmental knowledge, understood as intimate knowledge of local ecology accumulated over generations of direct experience of sustainable environmental management. We find some of these features in the following interventions by representatives of the Apache Survival Coalition, Na Koa Ikaika O Ka Lahui Hawai'i, and the Cordillera Peoples Alliance to the 11th session of the WGIP, the 1st session of the PFII, and the 19th session of the WGIP in 1993, 2001 and 2002, respectively (statements on file with author):

> The sacred peaks of Mount Graham are part of our existence. Mount Graham is a foundation of the Apache culture, past, present, and future. The mountain has many meanings to the people because of its role in the cultural traditions. We learn from out sacred land. It gives information about life. Sacred peaks are like altars, libraries. There is sacred knowledge embedded in our landscape. We depend on our land as an essential part of our learning. We do not make the same separation between nature and people that is found in traditional Western thinking.

> Kanaka Maoli, who are the Indigenous People of Hawai'i, like other Indigenous Peoples of the world, understand that the state of our peoples inextricably depends on the state of the environment. Like all Pacific Islanders, our culture is both land and ocean based. Our genealogy informs us that we are the stewards of our homeland because Papahanaumoku, the Earth, is our mother, and Wakea

> is Sky Father. The kalo or taro that is our traditional staple sustains life, and is our older sibling. Therefore we have a sacred responsibility to take care of our environment as we would our family, because that is exactly what it is – an embodiment of our elders.
>
> It is not an accident that the last frontiers of the world's remaining resources are found in indigenous peoples' territories. This is because of the way we regard nature and all creation as our relations and not objects to be dominated and exploited excessively.

These and countless other similar interventions to relevant UN meetings display a pride and celebration of indigenous environmental values and practices, which are also presented as a valuable model for the rest of humanity and a potential saviour for the global environmental and climate crisis brought about by unsustainable development and growth. We find this in the following statement of Charmaine Whiteface to the first session of the PFII in 2002 (statement on file with author):

> Today, the global environment is being rapidly destroyed. It is imperative that the member states of the UN broaden perspectives now to see that the life ways of indigenous peoples are the only cure for the environmental sickness all over the world. Yet the very people who could teach the colonizers how to truly live with the Earth are being constantly pushed to change their identity and become like the colonizer.

The same message is contained in the Anchorage Declaration adopted at the Indigenous Peoples' Global Summit on Climate Change held in Anchorage, Alaska in April 2009:[1]

> Through our knowledge, spirituality, sciences, practices, experiences and relationships with our traditional lands, territories, waters, air, forests, oceans, sea ice, other natural resources and all life, Indigenous Peoples have a vital role in defending and healing Mother Earth. The future of Indigenous Peoples lies in the wisdom of our elders, the restoration of the sacred position of women, the youth of today and in the generations of tomorrow. … We offer to share with humanity our Traditional Knowledge, innovations, and practices relevant to climate change, provided our fundamental rights as intergenerational guardians of this knowledge are fully recognized and respected.

While celebrating the stewardship role of indigenous peoples and the value of traditional knowledge, the discourse also contains an implicit critique of states

1 This can be viewed on the Summit website at: http://www.indigenoussummit.com/servelet/content/declaration.

and Western values more generally. States emerge in terms much like the 'high modernist' state of James C. Scott's *Seeing Like a State* (1998), interested in controlling and commodifying nature and its resources, coercive, mistaken in its monstrous development goals, removed from consideration of local conditions, complexities, and realities, and unable to see the 'metis'. The critique is also made explicit, as we see in the following intervention by the IITC to the 1st Session of the PFII in 2002 (statement on file with author):

> Under the dominant statist vision of economy and value, a forest in balance with nature has no value just as it is. It only has value if it is exploited. It has value when it is converted into lumber for exportation, when it is destroyed. The earth, when providing traditional food for indigenous families, is considered badly utilized. It only has value in large farms producing for exportation.

Some aspects of the discourse on environmentalism might be seen as presenting 'framing hazards' (Snow et al. 1986). One line of thinking regards the framing of claims to self-determination in terms of environmental protection as inherently contradictory, requiring indigenous peoples to maintain high environmental standards that might be otherwise at odds with the option to change traditional values and to pursue resource ventures regardless of environmental consequences, compromising the right of self-determination (Tennant 1994; Brysk 1994b; Dallam 1991). Other concerns regarding the environmental frame point to the dangers of romanticizing and primitivizing indigenous peoples through a 'view of Indians as Nature' (Brysk 1994b, 37), impairing claims for self-determination and risking the surfacing of harmful stereotypes dangerously at odds with indigenous peoples' own representations emphasizing their political capacity (Tennant 1994). A very real concern given the way in which representational constructs of indigenous peoples have functioned in the historical and contemporary oppression of indigenous peoples, movement activists have offset the primitive stereotype with an emphasis on the role of indigenous peoples as environmental innovators, adapting to new environmental challenges and with a role in crafting a course for wider society to follow. This has been particularly evident in debates on climate change, which have seen indigenous representatives press their role as innovators leading the way in designing and implementing mitigation and adaptation measures based on their traditional knowledge and technologies, often in combination with modern science and technologies (McClean et al. 2009; Tauli-Corpuz et al. 2009; United Nations 2008a).

Indigenous activists have highlighted the mutually reinforcing relationship between indigenous self-determination and ecological preservation in number of contexts, including debates on indigenous rights, biodiversity, sustainable development, and climate change. Consequently, the contributions of indigenous peoples are affirmed in a number of international legal instruments and policy documents across a range of issues. It is particularly evident in international declarations, resolutions, and policies relating to environment and development.

Early recognition can be discerned in the so-called Bruntland Report prepared by the World Commission on Environment and Development, Our Common Future, which proclaimed that (United Nations 1987, Ch. 4, para. 74):

> These communities are the repositories of vast accumulations of traditional knowledge and experience that links humanity with its ancient origins. Their disappearance is a loss for larger society, which could learn a great deal from their traditional skills in sustainably managing very complex ecological systems.

As mentioned in Chapter 1, various instruments adopted at the 1992 Earth Summit affirm the role of indigenous peoples as stewards of global and national resources and biodiversity. Agenda 21, a 300 page plan for achieving sustainable development in the 21st century, acknowledges the 'interrelationship between the natural environment and its sustainable development and the cultural, social, economic, and physical well-being of indigenous peoples' (United Nations 1992a, Ch. 26, para. 1). The Rio Declaration on Environment and Development recognizes the 'vital role' of indigenous communities in sustainable development (United Nations 1992b, Principle 22), while the Convention on Biological Diversity, ratified by some 190 states, obliges state parties to (United Nations 1992d, Art. 8j):

> Respect, preserve, and maintain knowledge, innovations and practices of indigenous and local communities embodying traditional lifestyles relevant for the conservation and sustainable use of biological diversity and promote their wider application with the approval and involvement of the holders of such knowledge, innovations and practice and encourage the equitable sharing of benefits arising from the utilization of such knowledge, innovations, and practices.

Ten years later, the political declaration adopted at the WSSD reaffirms pronouncements made at Rio concerning the 'vital role' of indigenous peoples in sustainable development (2002a, para. 25), while the Plan of Implementation of the WSSD recognizes that 'traditional and direct dependence on renewable resources and ecosystems, including sustainable harvesting, continues to be essential to the cultural, economic and physical well-being of indigenous people and their communities' (2002e, II.e).

International human rights law also contains a number of provisions that mirror aspects of the discourse. For example, HRC General Comment No. 23 on minorities observes that 'culture manifests itself in many forms, including a particular way of life associated with the use of land resources, especially in the case of indigenous peoples' (HRC 1994, para. 7). Preambular paragraph 11 of the UNDRIP recognizes that 'respect for indigenous knowledge, cultures and traditional practices contributes to sustainable and equitable development' (United Nations 2007a). Article 25 recognizes the 'distinctive spiritual relationship' of indigenous peoples to their lands, territories, and resources, and recognizes the right of indigenous peoples to 'uphold their responsibilities to future generations in this regard' (*ibid.*). Policies and declarations of UN specialized agencies, in addition, affirm the value of traditional knowledge. UNDP's Policy of Engagement with Indigenous Peoples, for example, recognizes that (2001, para. 11):

> Indigenous cultures comprise a heritage of diverse knowledge and ideas that is a resource for the whole world. As UNDP pursues sustainable human development, attention has been placed on indigenous peoples largely owing to their sustainable development practices. This has led to an interest in indigenous peoples' ways of life, their cultures, sciences, land and resource management, governance, political and justice systems, knowledge and healing practices. Recognition of indigenous peoples' assets and traditional knowledge (such as terrestrial and marine ecosystems, naturally occurring medicines from plants and insects, cultivated plant varieties, and animal husbandry) can be helpful to national and international development.

Similarly, the UNESCO Universal Declaration on Cultural Diversity and accompanying Main Lines of an Action Plan for Implementation recognizes 'the contribution of traditional knowledge, particularly with regard to environmental protection and the management of natural resources, and fostering synergies between modern science and local knowledge' (UNESCO 2001, Action Plan, para. 14).

One issue area where the role of indigenous peoples is not integrated into the text of core instruments is climate change. Neither the United Nations Framework Convention on Climate Change (UNFCCC) (United Nations 1992f) nor the Kyoto Protocol (United Nations 1998c) recognize the contributions of indigenous peoples, something that movement activists have denounced in statements to the Conference of the Parties (COP) and in indigenous declarations issuing from summits of the International Indigenous Peoples Forum on Climate Change (IIPFCC).[2] Nor have efforts to secure recognition of indigenous peoples' rights or contributions in subsequent climate instruments proved particularly successful. The Copenhagen Accord adopted at the fifteenth Session of the COP in 2009 makes no reference to indigenous peoples or their rights. This is a particular concern and disappointment for indigenous representatives participating in and around the

2 These include: the Lyon Declaration of the First International Forum of Indigenous Peoples and Local Communities on Climate Change (2000); the Hague Declaration of the Second International Forum of Indigenous Peoples and Local Communities on Climate Change (2000); the Bonn Declaration of the Third International Forum of Indigenous Peoples and Local Communities on Climate Change (2001); the Marrakech Statement of the Indigenous Peoples Caucus to the Seventh Session of the COP (2001); the New Dehli Statement of the Indigenous Peoples Caucus to the Eighth Session of the COP (2002); the Milan Declaration of the Sixth International Forum of Indigenous Peoples and Local Communities on Climate Change (2003); the Statement of Indigenous Peoples Attending the Tenth Session of the COP, Buenos Aires (2004); and the Anchorage Declaration of the Indigenous Peoples Global Summit on Climate Change (2009).

UNFCCC and related processes, not least because, though contributing the least to global warming, indigenous peoples are amongst those most negatively impacted upon by climate change. Indigenous peoples also suffer the negative effects of mitigation measures promoted as solutions to climate change. Of particular concern is the UN Collaborative Initiative on Reducing Emissions from Deforestation and Forest Degradation on Developing Countries (REDD), under which it is feared that certain measure such as carbon trading might result in encroachment of indigenous peoples' territorial rights and threats to their livelihoods (Tauli-Corpuz et al. 2009).

Chapter 6

The Impact of the Global Indigenous Movement

The social movement literature offers a number of classifications of movement effects, most of which have focused on political outcomes, and more specifically policy impacts. Probably the most cited scholar on political outcomes is Gamson (1990 [1975]), who distinguished between acceptance and new advantages as key political outcomes, where the former refers to acceptance by authorities of protestors as legitimate challengers and the latter to the realization of a challenger's goals. In another early typology, Schumaker (1975) differentiates between two forms of acceptance by the political system, namely *access responsiveness*, indicating the extent to which authorities are willing to hear a group's claims, and *agenda responsiveness*, referring to the transformation of a claim into an issue and its placing on the political agenda. Substantive advantages or effects include *policy responsiveness* and *output responsiveness*, referring to the adoption and implementation of new policies, and finally *impact responsiveness*, or the 'degree to which the actions of the political system succeed in alleviating the grievances of protest groups' (Schumaker 1975, 495).

Scholars of transnational contention have also offered typologies of movement impacts. Keck and Sikkink (1998), for example, model the effectiveness of transnational advocacy networks in a series of five progressive stages. First, through effective framing, movements get their claims onto the agenda, after which they may encourage both procedural and discursive change. Procedural changes increase the opportunities for advocacy, allowing for networks to influence the discursive positions of target actors, which may be states or international institutions. The final test of influence is state behaviour. Discursive change and/or policy success does not guarantee that state or institutional practices will necessarily change, making state practice the ultimate, more rigorous, marker of network effectiveness (Keck and Sikkink 1998, 25, 201). In another progressive model, in their work on the socialization of international human rights norms into domestic practices and the important role of transnational human rights networks in that process, Risse, Ropp, and Sikkink (1999) adopt a 'spiral model' of human rights change that has states moving from: i) repression of social movements to; ii) denial of the validity of human rights norms to; iii) tactical concessions made to the human rights network to; iv) acceptance of prescriptive status for human rights norms; to v) behaviour consistent with human rights norms (Risse and Sikkink 1999, 20–35). 'Prescriptive status' describes states that ratify international treaties, acknowledge the validity of human rights norms, and have institutionalized norms in domestic law but which do not consistently comply with human rights standards. 'Rule-consistent behaviour' refers to a state of institutionalization, internalization and habitualization of human rights norms and standards (Risse and Sikkink 1999, 29–32).

We can assess the impacts of the global indigenous movement against these typologies of movement influence. It is clear that the movement has achieved a range of political and legal impacts. It has succeeded in securing acknowledgement and recognition to the extent that indigenous issues are firmly on the UN agenda, evidenced in all manner of initiatives, not least the holding of two successive UN Decades dedicated to the world's indigenous peoples, from 1995–2004 and 2005–2014 respectively, and the establishment of a number of mechanisms aimed at promoting and protecting the rights of indigenous peoples, including the position of UN Special Rapporteur. It has pressed for and achieved procedural innovations, gaining unprecedented levels of institutional access to and participation in norm creation, and, uniquely, a permanent institutional space consistent with the aspiration to acquire lasting voice and visibility in international society. Discursive changes, taking concrete form in the UNDRIP and other normative instruments, constitute perhaps the movement's most remarkable achievement, which has been to reshape and rework human rights to allow for the emergence of new specifications of rights supportive of indigenous peoples' distinctive communal and cultural patterns of association, and otherwise at odds with the individualistic tenets of the human rights discourse. New meanings associated with self-determination, in particular, break with longstanding dominant understandings linking self-determination to statehood, and reflect a transformed discourse of self-determination 'more tempered in its meaning but also more universal in its reach' (Lam 2000, 210).

All this is not to say, however, that the movement has secured benefits sufficient to the needs and challenges faced by indigenous peoples. International recognition to the extent achieved by the global indigenous movement is a remarkable accomplishment, but the movement has pursued that recognition not as an end in itself but as a means to empower indigenous communities against threats to their dignity and well-being, to contribute to cultural renewal and ethnic revival, and to secure advantages in national and local contexts. The ultimate goal of activism focused on the UN is the alleviation and remedy of grievances experienced in national and local settings. Yet it is precisely at the state and community level that it is less easy to demonstrate positive changes, leading some observers to question the impact of the movement (e.g. Corntassel 2007). This chapter centres predominantly on these concerns. It asks to what extent international responsiveness is reflected at the national or community level, what this means for an evaluation of movement impact, and considers prospects for securing further improvements where they really matter, that is, in the lives of indigenous peoples.

Co-optation or Stages of Impact?

The activities of the global indigenous movement over the past few decades have resulted in a very high level of international recognition and responsiveness, manifesting in such steps as the adoption of new international standards, the establishment of innovative spaces providing opportunities for representation, and an overall impetus to mainstream indigenous issues across the UN system. One question that we evidently need to ask of these international achievements, however, is what kind of changes they have effected at state and community level. The pursuit of international recognition and its attendant standards and institutional innovations has been driven by the need to see improvements in the conditions of indigenous peoples and the alleviation of grievances in national and local contexts, making this a critical question. Here, however, it is more difficult to speak convincingly of widespread improvements, as indigenous peoples worldwide continue to live in conditions of extreme disadvantage and to experience pervasive and prejudicial threats to their continued existence and ways of life from states, multinationals, rebels, and other harmful agents. Even a perfunctory look at the situation of indigenous peoples demonstrates that there is a long way to go before they are secure in the enjoyment of their human rights. Several decades ago, Special Rapporteur José Martínez Cobo concluded in the Study on the Problem of Discrimination Against Indigenous Populations that indigenous peoples in many countries were 'at the bottom of the socio-economic scale' (United Nations 1983, Add. 8). Today, indigenous peoples continue to be overrepresented amongst the disadvantaged, the poor, the unemployed, the unhealthy, and the illiterate, a situation that applies to indigenous peoples in both developed and developing countries. A recent report commissioned by the World Bank on socio-economic conditions amongst indigenous peoples in Asia and Africa found Millennium Development Goals (MDGs) indicators for indigenous groups to be significantly below population averages (Hall and Patrinos 2010). Combining with a similar study focusing on Latin America (Hall and Patrinos 2006), which also found poverty to be pervasive amongst indigenous peoples, the results cover over 85 per cent of the world's indigenous population (Hall and Patrinos 2010, 2). The situation as regards the achievement or otherwise of economic and social rights is closely related to the legacy of historical injustices, as well as to ongoing human rights abuses, notably discrimination, land and resource dispossession, displacement, marginalization in the political order, environmental contamination, and much more.

IWGIA's (2005) strategy document for the second International Decade on the World's Indigenous People concludes that, 'while indigenous peoples have been extremely efficient in carving out a niche for themselves within the UN system, the first Decade offers but few examples of indigenous peoples bringing the achievements from the UN home to their indigenous communities'. This conclusion was also noted in common in a number of evaluations of the impact of the first Decade, which, while able to catalogue an array of initiatives within the UN system relating to indigenous issues, were less able to demonstrate the permeation of UN activities down to the community level. A review carried out by the OHCHR, for example, surmised that, 'despite the important institutional developments that have taken place within the framework of the Decade, indigenous people in many countries continue to be among the poorest and the most marginalized' (United Nations 2004a, para. 8). Similarly, the Secretary-General's report on activities carried out during the first Decade, identifying implementation as a 'further challenge', noted that, 'this constitutes the real test of the Decade, for if there have been few or no measurable improvements in the living conditions of indigenous peoples in many communities, the work of the past 10 years may be deemed incomplete' (United Nations 2004e, para. 67). More emphatic still, a review conducted by the IITC concluded that 'it is difficult to quantify outcomes of the Decade that actually did improve the lives of Indigenous Peoples given the lack of data. But the many reports cited herein, and others found within the United Nations system, lead to the conclusion that Indigenous Peoples in general are no better off now than they were at the beginning of the Decade' (IITC 2004, 16). The mid-term review of the second International Decade has yet to be concluded, but submissions to the review process suggest an ongoing concern,[1] as do numerous other recent reports (see e.g. United Nations, Department of Economic and Social Affairs 2009).

One line of thinking regards the apparent lack of impact at community level as supporting an argument for cooptation, whereby 'in a system of power, the power holder intentionally extends some form of political participation to actors who pose a threat' (Lacy, in Corntassel 2007, 139). Corntassel (2007), for example, regards the indigenous movement centred around the UN as subject to the twin processes of 'blunting' and 'channelling', with the result that the UN promotes its own legitimacy while creating an 'illusion of inclusion for indigenous peoples' and a distraction from other forms of national or local mobilization that might otherwise directly challenge state or corporate practices. 'Blunting' refers to moderation of indigenous claims and agendas to fit the dominant norms of existing institutional structures (*ibid.*, 140). 'Channeling' describes a process by which the energies of transnational indigenous activists are channeled exclusively into UN activities rather than into grassroots or national mobilizations (*ibid.*). Corntassel concludes (*ibid.*, 140):

> Channeling effects occur when members of Indigenous groups, having accepted representation via global forums, confine their activities solely within these official structures and cease other forms of political mobilization outside of the UN system. For instance, rather than pursuing grassroots mobilization to stop encroachment of a logging company on Indigenous homelands…, an Indigenous community might channel most of their political efforts into publicizing human rights abuses within a global forum. … By pursuing such strategies, Indigenous efforts at political mobilization become co-opted by the very state-centric system that they seek to challenge.

1 See, for example, the submission for the North American region at: http://treatycouncil.org/PDFs/NA%20region%20mid%20term%20report%202nd%20Decade.pdf.

Certainly, the social movement literature indicates that processes of cooptation are to be taken into serious consideration in the trajectories of social movements (see e.g. Jimenez 1999, Kriesi et al. 1995, Meyer and Tarrow 1998, Roth 2004, Seippel 2001), particularly those that focus their protest in and around institutions. As discussed in Chapter 2, the paradigmatic view in the social movement literature is that social movements engaging in formal institutional politics undergo a process of 'institutionalization' that features social movements losing their spontaneity, moderating their claims, and giving up contentious forms of mobilization. A process that is thought to come about principally with the formalization and professionalization of SMO organizational structures, 'institutionalization' has commonly been presented as an inevitable consequence of institutional action, setting up a 'presumed inconsistency between movement politics and institutional politics' (Katzenstein 1998a, 195; see also Katzenstein 1998b). The problem with this paradigm, however, is that it allows for very little variation in terms of the dynamics of interaction between social movements and institutions, while, evidently, as Katzenstein (1998a, 197) has put it, 'a variety of things happen within institutional habitats'. This is amply demonstrated by empirical research, which evinces a range of outcomes, exchanges, and relationships between social movements and institutions, states, and political parties not reducible to the institutionalization paradigm (see e.g. Goldstone 2003a, Goldstone 2003b).

As for the global indigenous movement, the institutionalization or cooptation thesis does not sit well with the very complex and dialectical relationship that the movement has come to enjoy with the United Nations. In particular, there does not seem to be much substance in the idea that global indigenous political mobilization has seen a 'downgrading' of claims, a so-called 'blunting' of the indigenous political agenda. Throughout the drafting of the UNDRIP, indigenous representatives were firm and unyielding in their insistence on the inclusion of the right to self-determination, rejecting any approaches suggestive of limitations on what they argued was a universal right of all peoples, and, for some of the latter period of negotiations, adhering to a firm 'no change' strategy in relation to the entire draft text as drafted by the WGIP. To the extent that movement activists were able to resist the moderation of claims, this may reflect the success of a strategy based on invoking the normative context, whereby an otherwise challenging or anti-systemic claim or set of claims may be upheld by a process of framing drawing on the legitimation and authority inherent in international legal norms, as discussed at length in the previous chapter (see also Morgan 2007, 2009). Nor does the cooptation thesis concord with what is described in Chapter 3 in terms of the so-called 'SMO infrastructure' (Kriesi 1996, 153) of the global indigenous movement, which is characterized by high numbers of grassroots organizations typified by informal and decentralized structures existing alongside more formally constituted IPOs. A relevant observation insofar as institutionalization is thought to stem from a process of professionalization and formalization of SMOs, transforming vibrant, informal SMOs into hierarchical, bureaucratic organizations more concerned with their survival than their original goals, indigenous organizations accessing

UN spaces relevant to their core concerns are not under any obligation to make structural or procedural changes.

Another difficulty with casting the impact of the global indigenous movement in terms of cooptation is that higher forms of movement impact can be time-sensitive, calling for a more progressive or sequential understanding of impact that allows for a knock-on effect from one form of impact to another. In this way, just as acceptance and access are regarded as precursors to discursive changes and the adoption of new standards, meaningful impact at community level ought to be thought of as following strides in so-called 'output responsiveness' (Schumaker 1975), with implementation constituting the key issue. This understanding of impact is reflected in a number of NGO strategy statements and specialist assessments of impact. For example, summarizing the position following the adoption of the UNDRIP in 2007, former UN Special Rapporteur, Rodolfo Stavenhagen concluded that (Stavenhagen 2007, 16–17):

> As this stage nears to its end, we have now initiated the next stage which deals with the question, 'what do we do with all of this, where does it go?' This is the era of implementation. ... We should always remember that when working at this so-called high level of UN standard setting we are talking about the lives of people, of women, children, men, of communities and their lands, culture, spirituality, identity, and relationships. How can we make our standards, our declarations, our resolutions, our recommendations meaningful to the lives of people on an everyday basis? I think that is the great challenge before us.

Implementation and its Challenges

The question of human rights implementation is typically regarded first and foremost as a legal issue, an assumption that stems from a broader phenomenon of the 'legalization of human rights', understood as the permeation of human rights theory and practice with legal conceptions (Cali and Meckled-Garcia 2006). A somewhat problematic phenomenon (see e.g. Freeman 2006), there are nevertheless a number of reasons why a legal approach to implementation seems apposite. Law and legal process appear accessible, structured, and practicable. Law as a matter of authority offers the prospect of real resolution; moreover, beyond the formally coercive functions of law, the normativity of law promises to render it influential in efforts to implement human rights. Importantly, however, there is a need to recognize the limits of legalism in the implementation of human rights, both internationally and nationally, which depends upon the configuration of number of facets of social, political, economic, and cultural life for its realization. In what follows, I address the prospects for implementation through the law before progressing to a discussion of the implementation gap and measures for addressing it.

Implementing International Human Rights Law

When thinking about implementing international human rights law, how one assesses the extent to which we may regard it as effective depends in large part on whether we understand it as a matter of enforcement or norms (Donnelly 2006). Understood as international enforcement, that is, in terms of its formal supervisory and monitoring mechanisms, its powers of coercion are relatively weak. Understood as international legal norms, gaining influence through processes of social learning, persuasion, and acculturation, its transformative potential greatly increases to offer the promise of making a substantial contribution to the realization of human rights.

International enforcement mechanisms tend to be the first port of call for human rights advocates and scholars addressing the issue of the implementation of human rights. Yet it is widely accepted that UN exertions to devise procedures and mechanisms of enforcement have been less than successful, and have in no way matched up to efforts to elaborate international human rights standards (the 'what?' of human rights) (e.g. Bayefsky 2000). Implementation is tied to state consent, which means that limitations on state sovereignty in principle have not been reflected in stringent oversight procedures, as states have refused to submit to rigorous international scrutiny over matters traditionally deemed within their domestic jurisdiction. The main international enforcement mechanism is the reporting system attached to the UN treaty-based organs, involving the submission of periodic state reports to a treaty-based committee of experts for consideration. A system characterized by a number of serious limitations, a particular problem is that it is dependent on states reporting self-critically on measures taken to make national law and practices compatible with their obligations under a relevant treaty, whereas honest appraisal is frequently lacking (see e.g. Alston and Crawford 2000; Bayefsky 2000; Boerefijn 1999). In addition to the quality of reports received, the committees themselves lack adequate funding and resources, and importantly, the capacity to impose any kind of sanctions on states that are found wanting in respect of their obligations. Their response is limited to making formal comments, which reflect a non-adversarial culture and tend to be 'excessively deferential to states and quick to take refuge in technicalities' (Robertson 1999, 46). Other enforcement mechanisms include a system of individual petition and – under the ICCPR, ICERD, and ICAT – an inter-state complaints system allowing for the relevant committees to consider communications from state parties claiming that another state is failing in its obligations, as yet not invoked.

International law in the area of indigenous peoples' rights is subject to a degree of international enforcement or monitoring under the ILO conventions, which come under the description of so-called 'hard' law. Similar to the reporting system attaching to the UN treaty bodies, states ratifying ILO Convention No.169 are subject to a periodic reporting procedure one year after ratification and every five years thereafter. State reports are reviewed by the ILO Committee of Experts on the Application of Conventions and Recommendations (CEACR), which assesses the conformity of a country's law and practice with its obligations under the Convention. The Committee compiles its comments and conclusions, comprising recommendations for improved implementation, which it delivers to the relevant state party and publishes in its annual report. In addition to a reporting system, the ILO also allows for a system of complaints, whereby a so-called 'representation' alleging human rights abuses may be submitted to the ILO by a worker's or employer's organization. States that have ratified ILO Convention No. 107 are also subject to a reporting procedure, though reports submitted under Convention No. 107 are reviewed in the light of more contemporary norms as contained in Convention No. 169 and not in view of its paternalistic and integrationist elements, which are now roundly discredited.

Other international resolutions, statements, and declarations concerning indigenous peoples' rights, not taking the form of treaties, do not have any monitoring mechanisms attached to them. Indeed, much of what contributes to an overall normative build-up in respect of indigenous peoples' rights, as discussed in Chapter 1, might be thought of as constituting 'non-law', which may engender compliance from states, but 'not out of any sense of obligation vis-à-vis other states or international entities' and 'merely as a matter of national convenience' (Szasz 1997, 33). As for the UNDRIP, this constitutes a form of 'soft' law, defined as 'technically non-binding norms that states actually do follow or at least subscribe to' (*ibid.*, 29). The UNDRIP calls upon a number of actors to promote its implementation, particularly states (United Nations 2007a, Art.38) as well as UN bodies and specialized agencies (*ibid.*, Art. 42), and is framed in obligatory rather than hortatory language ('shall' rather than 'should'), but it does not have a legally binding effect per se and lacks any kind of oversight mechanism. Lacking formal 'enforcement', however, the UNDRIP is thought by some to enjoy – in part at least – the status of customary international law, lending it legal relevance beyond its status as a non-binding declaration. A process highlighting the normative effects of international law, customary international law develops principally from the widespread and consistent practice of states acting out of a sense of obligation that a certain form of behaviour is required as a matter of law (*opinio juris*), and purports to bind all states regardless of any formal implementation architecture. The 'practice of states' includes a wide remit of conduct reflected in a variety of acts, including making official statements at international conferences and in diplomatic exchanges, formal instructions to diplomatic agents, national court decisions, legislative measures, or other actions taken by governments to deal with matters of international concern (Buergenthal and Murphy 2002, 22–23).

UNDRIP as Customary International Law

There is a body of opinion, including amongst international legal experts, that the UNDRIP – not as a whole but in part – has legal bearing to the extent that it reflects and reaffirms customary international law. Determined as per Article 38(1) of the Statute of the International Court of Justice (ICJ) and the requirements as stated in the *North Sea Continental Shelf Case*, claims for the customary international law character of the UNDRIP require evidence of widespread practice of states in conjunction with *opinio juris*, referring to the belief that a certain conduct is required as a matter of legal obligation.[2] Key proponents of this view include Wiessner and Anaya, whose global comparative surveys of state practice and *opinio juris* conducted over a number of years since 1999 have pointed to obligations of customary international law in respect of a wide range of rights existing prior to the adoption of the UNDRIP in 2007 (e.g. Wiessner 2009, 2008, 1999; Anaya and Wiessner 2007; Anaya and Williams 2001; see also Lenzerini 2006; Wenzel 2008), and which the UNDRIP reaffirms (Wiessner 2009):

> The UNDRIP is a solemn, comprehensive, and authoritative response of the international community of States to the claims of indigenous peoples, with which maximum compliance is expected. Some of the rights therein may already form part of customary international law, others may become the *fons et origo* of later-emerging customary international law. Scholarly analyses of State practice and *opinio juris* have concluded that indigenous peoples are entitled to maintain and develop their distinct cultural identity, their spirituality, their language, and their traditional ways of life; that they hold the right to political, economic and social self-determination, including a wide range of autonomy; and that they have a right to the lands they have traditionally owned or otherwise occupied and used.

The opinion that the UNDRIP reaffirms pre-existing international customary law does not receive unanimous agreement. Many states, in particular, deny that any of its provisions have the status of customary international law – or indeed any kind of legal status – a position that was emphasized by several states voting on the Declaration in the General Assembly in 2007, both for and against. Thus, the UK, voting in favour of the Declaration, described it as an 'important policy tool' but 'not legally binding' (United Nations, 2007, 22), while Canada, voting against, stated that 'the Declaration is a non-binding document that does not reflect customary international law nor change Canadian laws', a position that Canada continues to hold following its endorsement of the UNDRIP in November 2010 (United Nations 2007, 13; Canada 2010). The United States, similarly, has strongly

2 Article 38(1) of the ICJ Statute defines customary international law as 'evidence of a general practice accepted as law'. The necessity of the presence of *opinio juris* in determining international customary norms is more explicitly stated in the case of the *North Sea Continental Shelf*, in which the Court concluded (ICJ Report 1969, 44, para. 77): 'Not only must the acts concerned amount to a settled practice, but they must also be such, ..., as to be evidence of a belief that this practice is rendered obligatory by the existence of a rule of law requiring it. The need for such a belief, i.e. the existence of a subjective element, is implicit in the very notion of *opinio iuris sive necessitates*. The States concerned must therefore feel that they are conforming to what amounts to a legal obligation. The frequency, or even habitual character of the acts, is not in itself enough'.

rejected the claim that the UNDRIP or any of its provisions can be regarded as international customary law. In its statement explicating the US vote opposing the Declaration, Robert Hagen of the U.S. Permanent Mission to the United Nations stated that (United States 2007):

> With respect to the nature of the declaration, it was the clear intention of all States that it be an aspirational declaration with political and moral, rather than legal, force. Its persuasiveness and usefulness to the international community therefore critically depends upon the extent to which it enjoys unqualified support among States. ... The United States rejects any possibility that this document is or can become customary international law. ... As this declaration does not describe current State practice or actions that States feel obliged to take as a matter of legal obligation, it cannot be cited as evidence of the evolution of customary international law. This declaration does not provide a proper basis for legal actions, complaints, or other claims in any international, domestic, or other proceedings.

States' grounds for the claim that the UNDRIP does not reflect customary international law are arguably based less on close legal analysis than political motive – to the extent that an argument for the customary international law status of specific provisions can be demonstrated, states may be considered legally bound – but then again, sound arguments can certainly be levelled against the view that particular of its provisions have crystallized into customary international law. Notably, we cannot ignore the fact that the UNDRIP took some 25 years to complete, and nor can we pretend that there are not widespread examples of state practice that violate the rights of indigenous peoples, which must be a serious consideration when making an argument based on the degree of acceptance by the international community of the norms in question. Equally, however, sources for relevant principles are very widespread in international and national law and practice, opening the door to debate as to whether a practice of sufficient density and uniformity has accumulated to make a case for the existence of general customary rules or whether in fact too much inconsistency between states in their practice exists to make such a claim, a difficult debate given the inherently informal nature of the customary process. As put by Lillich (1984, 44) in his classic discussion of the human rights of aliens in international law, 'the process is one of juridical osmosis, there being no identifiable moment at which a resolution suddenly bursts forth as a binding norm. As the process is necessarily a gradual one, disagreement will often occur over whether, at any given time, the magic point has been attained'.

It is beyond the scope of this book to offer a wide-ranging analysis of whether and which of the UNDRIP provisions may be regarded as an expression of customary international law. An authoritative assessment of this matter can be found in the recent report of the International Law Association Committee on the Rights of Indigenous Peoples, a committee of international experts tasked with providing authoritative clarification and guidance over the normative status of the UNDRIP provisions and indigenous rights in general, which has described state and international practice supportive of indigenous rights as progressively increasing over the last few decades 'like a flooding river under an unstoppable rain' (International Law Association 2010, 44):

> Overall, there is a massive amount of highly significant international practice recognizing the rights of indigenous peoples, which is accompanied and confirmed by the practice developed at domestic level by most countries in the territory of which a significant population of indigenous people live. This practice has developed both at the legislative (including constitutional) and jurisdictional level, affirming the right of indigenous peoples to the recognition and safeguarding of their cultural identity, their cultural rights, land rights, and their right to autonomy and participation in decisions affecting them. In addition, in recent years a number of governments have developed reparation policies aimed at redressing indigenous peoples for the lands they have been deprived of as well as for other wrongs suffered. … The practice in point constitutes a direct manifestation of the will of States or of international institutions that originate from the will of States, expressed through the adoption and ratification of the relevant international treaties that have established such institutions. In addition, the findings of these institutions have never been disputed by the States concerned on the merits. This confirms that the pertinent practice is accompanied by the 'evidence of a belief that [it] is rendered obligatory by the existence of a rule of law requiring it', making the requirement that the element of state practice is accompanied by the necessary *opinio juris* – in order to have customary international law – fully satisfied. It is therefore indisputable that indigenous peoples are of concern of customary international law (International Law Association 2010, 49).

The report cites a number of sources supportive of its conclusions, including domestic practice in the following countries and contexts: Argentina, Australia,[3] Bangladesh,

3 See e.g. *Mabo v. Queensland (No.2)*, which reversed the legal fiction that Australia was *terra nullius* before colonization, thereby paving the way for Aboriginal and Torres Strait Islander peoples to have their native title recognized under common law, and which led to the *Native Title Act 1993* (NTA 1993), the object of which was to provide for the recognition and protection of native title and to establish a mechanism for determining claims to native title. Also see *The Wik Peoples v. Queensland*, which held that pastoral leases did not extinguish native title (Wik Peoples v. Queensland [1996] HCA 40; (1996) 187 CLR 1). *Wik* triggered amendments to the *Native Title Act*, which were first formulated in the form of a 'Ten Point Plan' and then passed in July 1998 through the *Native Title Amendment Act* (Cth) (NTAA 1998). For a detailed analysis of the NTAA 1998, see Triggs 1999; Aboriginal and Torres Strait Islander Commission 1998; McDougall (no date); see also CERD 1999. The amendments drew particularly strong criticism from CERD, which issued a number of decisions criticizing the Act as discriminatory and as 'creating legal certainty for governments and third parties at the expense of indigenous title' (CERD 1999, 6).

Belize,[4] Bolivia,[5] Botswana, Brazil,[6] Cambodia, Canada,[7] Chile, Colombia,[8] Costa

---

4 See e.g. *Supreme Court of Belize, Cal v. Attorney General of Belize*, Claim No.171 of 2007, Judgement October 18, 2007. Note the conclusion of the Justice that, 'it is my considered view that both customary international law and general international law would require that Belize respect the rights of its indigenous peoples to their lands and resources' (para. 127).

5 See the new 'post neo-liberal constitution' of Bolivia, especially Articles 30 and 31, which recognize the right of indigenous peoples in their territories to control their own judicial institutions and social systems and to exercise distinct forms of communitarian democracy (Republic of Bolivia, Constitution of 2009).

6 See e.g. Article 231 of the amended Constitution of 1988, which provides that indigenous peoples are entitled to the permanent ownership of the lands traditionally occupied by them, including the exclusive fruition or enjoyment of existing soil resources, rivers and lakes (Constitution of the Federated Republic of Brazil 1988, Art. 231).

7 Important aboriginal rights are safeguarded at the level of the Canadian Constitution, which provides that 'the existing Aboriginal and treaty rights of Canada's Aboriginal peoples are hereby recognized and reaffirmed' (*Constitution Act 1982*, s.35.1). Evidence of a growing sensitivity to protecting indigenous land and title rights can be found in a number of legal decisions dating back to the 1990s. In *R v. Sparrow* (1990), for example, involving the rights of the Musqueam Nation to fish in British Columbian waters, the Court imposed a strict justificatory test for interference with existing aboriginal title, according to which only those objectives 'purporting to prevent the exercise of s. 35.1 rights that would cause harm to the general populace or to aboriginal peoples themselves' or otherwise found to be 'compelling and substantial' would be valid (*Sparrow* [1990] 1 S.C.R., 1113). The Court concluded that the conservation and management of fisheries constitutes sufficient enough objective, but rejected 'the public interest' as a basis for infringement, this being 'so vague as to provide no meaningful guidance and so broad as to be unworkable as a test for the justification of a limitation on constitutional rights' (*Sparrow*, 1113). See also *Delgamuukw vs. British Colombia* (1997), in which the Court considered aboriginal title to be 'inalienable' and to 'encompass the right to exclusive use and occupation of land' (*Delgamuukw* [1997] S.C.R., 1111). As for self-government arrangements, the federal government accepts the right of aboriginal peoples to govern themselves and has proceeded with a number of self-governing models with First Nation bands. Of particular note, the separation from the Northwest Territories of the territory of Nunavut in 1999 provided for an Inuit-run territory within the federal system, and represents a form of indigenous self-government involving a high level of sovereignty (Dahl et al. 2000). The government is elected by all citizens of the territory, including non-aboriginal citizens, but with Inuit making up some 85 per cent of the populace the Inuit have majority influence.

8 The 1991 reform of the Colombian constitution followed ratification of ILO Convention No.169 in the same year, and advanced the right of indigenous peoples to control the political and administrative affairs of their traditional *resguardos* (Political Constitution of Colombia 1991, Arts. 286, 287, 329). Legal recognition brings with it the right to be consulted regarding natural resource development on their territories (*ibid.*, Art. 330), which is regarded not solely as a practical intervention in an administrative process but as a fundamental right critical for the preservation of the social, cultural, and ethnic unity and survival of indigenous groups.

Rica, Ecuador,[9] European Union,[10] India, Japan, Laos, Malaysia, Mexico,[11] New Zealand, Nicaragua[12], Norway,[13] Paraguay,[14] Peru,[15] Philippines,[16] South Africa, Taiwan, United States of America,[17] and Venezuela. At the international level, relevant sources include the 'unequivocal' (*ibid.*, 43) judicial practice of the UN treaty bodies, which have affirmed the obligation of states in relation to a number of principles. The HRC, in particular, habitually scrutinizes state practice against Article 1, including Article 1(2) concerning the right to freely dispose of natural wealth and to be secure in the means of subsistence (see e.g. HRC 2005, 2006c). Further, in interpreting Article 27 of the ICCPR, the Committee has confirmed the

9 See e.g. Article 57 of the 2008 Ecuadorian Constitution, which recognizes the right of indigenous peoples to develop and strengthen their identities, to be free from discrimination and racism, to the collective ownership of traditional Indian lands, to participate in the use and conservation of the natural resources found in their territories, and to free, prior, and informed consent relating to any proposed development projects on the lands (Republic of Ecuador, Constitution of 2008).

10 See e.g. Council Resolution on Indigenous Peoples within the Framework of the Development Cooperation of the Community and the Member States of 30 November 1998 acknowledging 'the importance that indigenous peoples attach to the affirmation of their "self-development", that is to say, the shaping of their own social, economic and cultural development and their own cultural identities' (European Council 1998, para. 2), 'the key role played by indigenous peoples in the conservation and sustainable use of natural resources' (*ibid.*, para. 5), and 'the right to choose their own development paths, which includes the right to object to projects, in particular in their traditional areas' (*ibid.*). In November 2002 the Council adopted Conclusions on Indigenous Peoples, which recalled the commitment to the 1998 Resolution and invited states to continue its implementation.

11 See e.g. Articles 2 and 27 of the Constitution, recognizing the right to self-determination and autonomy and land rights, respectively (Political Constitution of Mexico, 2009).

12 See e.g. Articles 89–91 of the Constitution, which outline the land, resource, and cultural rights of the communities of the Atlantic coast (Political Constitution of the Republic of Nicaragua 1987, with reforms of 1995, 2000, and 2005).

13 See e.g. Article 110(a) stating that 'it is the responsibility of the authorities of the State to create conditions enabling the Sami people to preserve and develop its language, culture and way of life' (Constitution of Norway).

14 See e.g. Articles 63 and 64 of the Constitution recognizing the right of indigenous peoples to preserve their ethnic identity in their respective habitats and the right to collective ownership of their lands, which are indivisible imprescriptible, and non-transferable, and which cannot be sold (Political Constitution of 1992, Republic of Paraguay).

15 See e.g. Article 89 of the Constitution, which recognizes that native communities are 'autonomous in their organization, communal working, and the free use and disposal of their lands' (Political Constitution of Peru 1993).

16 See e.g. Indigenous Peoples Rights Act 1997.

17 In the United States, the federal government has a 'government-to-government' relationship with Indian nations and tribes that involves recognition of tribal self-government over a range of internal affairs, including administration of justice, tribal membership, culture and language, and land and resource management.

link between cultural identity and the respect of land and resource rights (see e.g. HRC 1994, paras. 3.2 and 7); the right to restitution of ancestral lands has also been stressed (see e.g. HRC 2006d). Other relevant jurisprudence emerges from the CERD, which has time and again pressed the requirement that states recognize and protect indigenous peoples' rights to their traditional lands (see. e.g. CERD 1997, 2007a, 2007b), as well as the obligation of states to respect the right of indigenous peoples to 'practice and revitalize their cultural traditions and customs and to preserve and practice their languages' (CERD 1997, para. 4.e). The CESCR, similarly, has pressed the interconnections between the cultural life of indigenous peoples and the protection of their lands and resources, as well as, in a number of contexts, the strong communal dimension of indigenous peoples' cultural life (see. e.g. CESCR 2008a, 2009). The jurisprudence of the CRC also emerges as relevant, particularly where it emphasizes the 'cultural significance of the traditional land and the quality of the natural environment while ensuring the children's right to life, survival, and development to the maximum extent possible' (CRC 2009, para. 35).

Other sources cited by the ILA include judicial practice at the regional level, notably the jurisprudence of the Inter-American Court of Human Rights (IACHR) and the African Commission on Human and Peoples Rights (ACHPR). The IACHR has in its recent jurisprudence proclaimed a number of important principles relating to land rights and cultural rights, including the right of indigenous peoples to the protection of their customary land and resource tenure, the right to resources used by indigenous peoples and upon which their physical and cultural survival depends, and the right to enjoy property in accordance with their communal tradition (see e.g. Inter-American Court of Human Rights 2001, 2007). In its most celebrated judgement of *Awas Tingni v. Nicaragua* of 31 August 2001, the Court observed that (Inter-American Court of Human Rights 2001, paras. 148–149):

> Through an evolutionary interpretation of international instruments for the protection of human rights, taking into account applicable norms of interpretation and pursuant to Article 29(b) of the Convention – which precludes a restrictive interpretation of rights – it is the opinion of this Court that Article 21 of the Convention protects the right to property in a sense which includes, among others, the rights of members of the indigenous communities within the framework of communal property, which is also recognized by the Constitution of Nicaragua.
>
> Given the characteristics of the instant case, some specifications are required on the concept of property in indigenous communities. Among indigenous peoples there is a communitarian tradition regarding a communal form of collective property of the land, in the sense that ownership of the land is not centred on an individual but rather on the group and its community. Indigenous groups, by the fact of their very existence, have the right to live freely in their own territory; the close ties of indigenous people with the land must be recognized and understood as the fundamental basis of their cultures, their spiritual life, their integrity, and

> their economic survival. For indigenous communities, relations to the land are not merely a matter of possession and production but a material and spiritual element which they must fully enjoy, even to preserve their cultural legacy and transmit it to future generations.

Other relevant practice cited as testifying to the 'special concern of the international community for the rights of indigenous peoples' (International Law Association 2010, 49) include a plethora of soft law instruments, and the various policy and operational initiatives developed by intergovernmental organizations and international agencies. The World Bank, for example, recently revised its operational directive regarding indigenous peoples to pay closer regard to the inextricable link between the identities and cultures of indigenous peoples and the complete and undisturbed enjoyment of their lands and natural resources.[18] Article 2 of the current Operational Policy OP 4.10 states that (World Bank 2005a):

> The Bank recognizes that the identities and cultures of Indigenous Peoples are inextricably linked to the lands on which they live and the natural resources on which they depend. These distinct circumstances expose Indigenous Peoples to different types of risks and levels of impacts from development projects, including loss of identity, culture, and customary livelihoods, as well as exposure to disease. … As social groups with identities that are often distinct from dominant groups in their national societies, Indigenous Peoples are frequently among the most marginalized and vulnerable segments of the population. As a result, their economic, social, and legal status often limits their capacity to defend their interests in and rights to lands, territories, and other productive resources, and/or restricts their ability to participate in and benefit from development. At the same time, the Bank recognizes that Indigenous Peoples play a vital role in sustainable development and that their rights are increasingly being addressed under both domestic and international law.

During the process of revision, the Bank undertook a legal review of 'emerging principles of international law on indigenous peoples, and the extent to which the proposed Bank Policy is consistent with such principles' (World Bank 2005b, para. 1). The review concluded that (*ibid.*, para. 28):

> The international instruments and practices surveyed above, including the General Assembly Resolutions, indicate the emergence of international principles and practices, particularly with regard to (i) consultation with, and participation of indigenous peoples on decisions affecting them, and (ii) recognition and

18 Operational Policy (OP) and Bank Procedure (BP) 4.10 together replace Operational Directive (OD) 4.20, Indigenous Peoples, dated September 1991, which in turn replaced its Operational Manual Statement (OMS) 2.34, Tribal People in Bank-Financed Projects, of 1982.

> protection of the rights of indigenous peoples, including land rights and rights to natural and cultural resources. In addition, other sources for these emerging principles can be found in national legislation and court decisions on the rights of indigenous peoples.

The argument that customary international norms concerning indigenous peoples are a 'reality in the context of the contemporary international legal order' (International Law Association 2010, 51) is arguably a convincing one. As for the future role of the UNDRIP in engendering new customary rules, all the signs point to its role as a catalysing force, not least the clear trend toward seeing the UNDRIP as an authoritative guide in legal and policy decision-making at international, regional and national levels. Within the UN system, the UNDRIP has become a guide for a number of bodies and agencies, including the UN treaty bodies, which are using the Declaration in order to interpret states' obligations under the relevant treaties. For example, in February 2009, the CRC issued General Comment 11 (2009): Indigenous Children and their Rights under the Convention, which urged 'State parties to adopt a rights-based approach to indigenous children based on the Convention and other relevant international standards, such as ILO Convention No. 169 and the United Nations Declaration on the Rights of Indigenous Peoples' (CRC 2009, para. 82). Similarly, in its concluding observations on Nicaragua, the CESCR called on the state party to 'continue with its efforts to promote and implement the principles of the United Nations Declaration on the Rights of Indigenous Peoples' (CESCR 2008a, para. 35). More emphatic still, in its response to the fifth and sixth periodic reports of the United States of America in 2008, CERD recommended that the state party view the UNDRIP as a normative framework to interpret its obligations, *regardless of* the United States vote opposing the Declaration (CERD 2008, para. 29):

> While noting the position of the State party with regard to the United Nations Declaration on the Rights of Indigenous Peoples (A/RES/61/295), the Committee finally recommends that the declaration be used as a guide to interpret the State party's obligations under the Convention relating to indigenous peoples.

Other UN bodies to use the UNDRIP as a guiding framework include the PFII, which affirmed at its seventh session in 2008 that the Declaration 'will be its legal framework' (United Nations 2008a, para. 132). Both the Special Rapporteur and the EMRIP have indicated that the UNDRIP will form the main framework for substantive work; the latter mechanism has made the implementation of the UNDRIP a permanent item on its agenda (United Nations 2009b, paras. 61–83). Wide support for the UNDRIP and its guiding role can also be discerned across the diverse UN specialized agencies, and is reflected in particular in the IASG statement on the Declaration adopted in September 2007:

> The Declaration sends out a clear message to the entire international community, reaffirming the human rights of the world's indigenous peoples. This landmark action of the United Nations bears political, legal, symbolic and moral significance, as well as constituting a crucial opportunity for the UN System and other inter-governmental organizations to critically reflect upon their engagement with indigenous peoples' issues and, according to Article 42 of the Declaration, to promote respect for and full application of its provisions and follow-up its effectiveness. The IASG pledges to advance the spirit and letter of the Declaration within our agencies' mandates and to ensure that the Declaration becomes a living document throughout our work.[19]

At the regional level, the Inter-American Court on Human Rights referred to the Declaration in its decision of 28 November 2007 in *Saramaka People v. Suriname*, in which it cites Article 32 in determining that the Saramaka people have 'the right to give or withhold their free, informed and prior consent, with regards to development or investment projects that may affect their territory' (Inter-American Court, 2007). In the Organization of American States (OAS), a majority of participants in the negotiations towards the drafting of an American Declaration on the Rights of Indigenous Peoples have supported the use of the UNDRIP 'as the baseline for negotiations' and 'a minimum standard for the OAS Declaration' (Organization of American States, 2008). In 2007, the African Commission on Human and Peoples' Rights (ACHPR) issued a communiqué in which it states that the UNDRIP is 'in line with the position and work of the African Commission on indigenous peoples' rights' and that 'the Declaration will become a very valuable tool and a point of reference for the African Commission's efforts to ensure the promotion and protection of indigenous peoples' rights on the African continent' (African Commission on Human and Peoples' Rights, 2007).

National responses to the UNDRIP also underline its widespread use as a guide for legal action. Examples include the October 2007 ruling by the Supreme Court of Belize in the case of *Aurelio Cal v. Attorney General of Belize*, in which the Court drew upon the UNDRIP and other international legal sources in arriving at its decision to uphold the collective right of the Maya people to their land, resources, and environment. Citing in particular Article 26 of the UNDRIP, the Chief Justice described the Declaration as 'reflecting… the growing consensus and the general principles of international law on indigenous peoples and their lands and resources…and importing significant obligations for the State of Belize in so far as the indigenous Maya rights to their land and resources are concerned' (at paras.131 and 133).[20] Another arresting example can be found in the adoption in

19 The complete IASG 'Statement on the Declaration on the Rights of Indigenous Peoples' can be found at: www.un.org/esa/socdev/unpfii/en/iasg.html.

20 Other international sources cited by the Chief Justice include ILO Convention No.169, CERD General Recommendation XXIII (1997), and the decision of the Inter-

November 2007 in Bolivia of the *National Law No. 3760 on Indigenous Peoples*, making the UNDRIP binding as national law. Also, in June 2008, the Japanese Diet voted unanimously to recognize the Ainu as indigenous people and called upon the government to refer to the UNDRIP in advancing Ainu policies. Further examples predate the adoption of the UNDRIP; for example, in its draft form, the Declaration formed the basis for the drafting of the 1997 *Indigenous Peoples' Rights Act* in the Philippines.

Closing the Implementation Gap

Whilst emphasizing the role of law in the implementation of indigenous peoples' rights, there is evidently a danger in entrusting all to the function of law, which on its own is rarely able to secure respect for human rights. Beyond the law, a host of social, economic, political, and cultural factors determine the reality of action on human rights, rendering legal recognition and judicial action potential preconditions rather than sufficient for their realization, and accounting for an oft discerned 'implementation gap' between the legal recognition of human rights at both international and national levels and the realities of human rights on the ground. In the area of indigenous peoples' rights, the implementation gap is both marked and persistent, as such measures have not been sufficient to overcome the serious and deeply entrenched concerns of indigenous peoples and to ensure the realization of rights in practice. As observed by the former UN Special Rapporteur Rodolfo Stavenhagen (United Nations 2007d, para. 5), 'a persistent, and even widening, *implementation gap* remains between the good intentions frequently expressed in constitutional reforms and various forms of legislation and the effective enjoyment of human rights at the practical, everyday level' (see also United Nations 2006c).

An implementation gap is discernible in relation to a range of indigenous rights, but it is arguably in the area of land and natural resource rights that the gap is most apparent, reflecting the conflict between indigenous peoples' territorial and resource rights – so closely related to their cultural integrity – and state and corporate interests in resource extraction and infrastructure development, interests that prioritize short-term growth and profit over the survival and viability of indigenous peoples. A particular problem in this dynamic is that it often involves private corporations in a range of violations of indigenous peoples' rights, whereas private entities are not – as yet anyway – direct bearers of human rights obligations. Notwithstanding an emerging international consensus that transnational corporations should bear some responsibilities for human rights, evidenced in initiatives such as the UN

American Court of Human Rights in the case of *Awas Tingni Community vs. Nicaragua* (2001). *Aurelio Cal et al. v. Attorney General of Belize*, Supreme Court of Belize (Claim 121/2007) (18 October 2007).

Global Compact[21] and the UN Sub-Commission Norms on the Responsibilities of Transnational Corporations and Other Business Enterprises with Regard to Human Rights (United Nations 2003b), transnational corporations and other business enterprises assume no real accountability for human rights abuses. To the extent that guidelines do exist, these fall within the framework of voluntarism and self-regulation and do not therefore promise to prove effective, particularly with the worst offenders, as economic benefits are judged to outweigh the human costs. In the case of extractive and infrastructure projects affecting indigenous peoples, the human costs are 'very often devastating' (United Nations 2003a, 2), with loss of subsistence, degradation of the traditional environment, social disorganization and breakdown of communal life, and demise of indigenous peoples' cultural and religious ways of life counting amongst the potential negative impacts. This strongly points to the need for the direct imposition of human rights obligations on TNCs. As indicated by one author (Miranda 2007, 170), 'if self-regulation was the best means to ensure human rights, then one might have expected the number of abuses attributable to businesses to have diminished'.

The state duty to take appropriate measures to prevent and respond to human rights violations committed by third parties finds a number of holds in international law, both under the law of state responsibility and in international human rights law.[22] The international human rights treaties, in particular, firmly establish a state duty to protect against human rights abuses by non-state actors within their territory or jurisdiction, which is understood as part of a state's overall responsibility to ensure the enjoyment of human rights.[23] Yet there is a serious

21 The UN Global Compact is a UN initiative aimed at encouraging businesses to adopt environmentally and socially responsible policies in line with the so-called Ten Principles in the areas of human rights, labour, anti-corruption, sustainable development, and the environment. Visit the Global Compact website: http://www.unglobalcompact.org.

22 See *Report of the Special Representative of the Secretary General on the Issue of Human Rights and Transnational Corporations and Other Business Enterprises*, John Ruggie, which provides a comprehensive summary of the most relevant provisions and interpretations on the state duty to eliminate and remedy abuse by third parties (United Nations 2009e). See also Ruggie's report focusing specifically on state responsibilities to regulate and adjudicate corporate activities under the international human rights treaties (United Nations 2007e).

23 Relevant treaty provisions abound across the nine treaties and may or may not make specific reference to business or corporations. Guidance from the treaty bodies in the form of general comments and/or concluding observations is also extensive, and covers the state duty to protect against abuse by a wide range of non-state actors, including corporate enterprises. A recent, unambiguous example can be found in HRC General Comment No. 31, which states that 'the positive obligations on States Parties to ensure Covenant rights will only be fully discharged if individuals are protected by the State, not just against violations of Covenant rights by its agents, but also against acts committed by private persons or entities' (HRC 2004b, para. 8). There is also guidance specific to a state duty to protect indigenous peoples from certain industries and corporate ventures. CERD General

concern that, because of their economic power, transnational corporations have in effect outgrown the ability of states to regulate them efficiently. It is for a variety of reasons difficult for states to control the activities of corporations within their territories, not least the fact that corporations can easily relocate their operations if threatened with tough regulations. Very often, moreover, it is the case that development projects are state-corporate hybrids arising from an alignment of state and corporate interests, and are therefore positively encouraged by states. In such cases, extractive or development operations are commonly invoked by the state as serving the public or general interest, whether as a means of boosting the overall economy, creating income and employment opportunities, generating energy resources, improving transport networks, or some other supposed national benefit, and regardless of the interests of specific constituencies such as indigenous peoples. As expressed by Rodolfo Stavenhagen, 'the concerns of indigenous peoples, who are seldom consulted on the matter, take a back seat to an overriding "national interest", or to market-driven business objectives aimed at developing new economic activities, and maximizing productivity and profits' (United Nations 2003a, para. 8). Legal incoherence and ambiguity, where there is a lack of consistency between legislation on indigenous rights and sectoral legislation on, say, mining or logging, compound the situation and allow for the disregard of indigenous rights. Racism and discriminatory attitudes, moreover, make it possible for elites to proceed with harmful actions (Daes 2001b, para. 4):

> To attract foreign investment and trade, many developing countries have opened to extractive industries, such as mining and logging, hitherto isolated parts of their territories which are often the last refuges of indigenous peoples and their cultural diversity. By such means, indigenous peoples are collectively sacrificed in order to increase the income of other citizens. Racism against indigenous peoples makes it relatively easy for national political and business leaders to contemplate such measures and to mobilize wider public support for them. If indigenous communities resist dispossession, racism makes it easier for politicians to justify the use of violence to crush the protestors.

Racism also makes it easier to dispense with the need for prior consultation with indigenous groups likely to be affected by proposed development. The state duty to consult and cooperate in good faith with indigenous peoples through their own representative institutions in order to obtain their free, prior and informed consent prior to the approval of development projects affecting their lands, territories, and resources is contained in Article 32 of the UNDRIP, but is overlooked where indigenous peoples are regarded as second-class citizens, a perception

Recommendation No. 23 on indigenous peoples, for example, observes that indigenous peoples have lost lands and resources as a result of the activities of commercial companies and calls upon states to 'take steps to return those lands and territories' (CERD 1997).

that continues to linger in many countries as a result of deep-rooted attitudes and structural racism.

Other factors contribute to difficulties of implementation: the low levels of participation and representation of indigenous peoples in the legislature; a lack of political will to prioritize indigenous concerns, to allocate funds to address them, or to give effect to constitutional reforms through new laws; problems in the public administration such as bureaucratic inertia, corruption, a lack of efficiency, or an administrative culture unaccustomed to multiculturalism; a lack of coordinated or systematic policy across the various ministries and organs of the state relevant to indigenous issues in the areas of education, administration of justice, health, environmental policy, and economic development; distrust or ignorance of international norms on the part of domestic institutions; a lack of adequate mechanisms for consultation with indigenous peoples prior to the development or implementation of new laws; and more (see e.g. United Nations 2006c, at paras. 14–50; United Nations 2006d, at paras. 39–46).

Closing the Gap

Closing the gap calls for the concerted involvement of a wide range of actors. States, of course, as both the principal violators and the central protectors in respect of human rights, must play a fundamental role, a responsibility that is, according to Anaya, made more pivotal by the essentially reparative nature of indigenous rights, which require that states take concrete, affirmative measures to 'attack the systemic problems that indigenous peoples face in the enjoyment of their human rights in ways that are consistent with their specific cultural characteristics and their own expressed wishes' (United Nations 2008b, para. 44). Indigenous rights are inclusive of both negative rights, such as those to enjoyment of lands and territories or to culture, and positive rights, for example regarding the improvement of indigenous peoples' social and economic conditions. The need for an active role for the state is especially clear for positive rights, but a decisive role may be no less critical in respect of negative rights that call for zones of state exclusion and non-interference. This is true, for example, in relation to indigenous peoples' rights to autonomy and self-governance in matters relating to their internal and local affairs, which, at a minimum, call for state support in the form of financial and technical assistance. Articles 4 and 39 of the UNDRIP together call upon states to offer this support, and without prejudice to assistance received through international cooperation (United Nations 2007a, Art. 4 and Art. 39). The same holds true for indigenous rights over their lands, territories and resources, which call for active state recognition and protection enacted through an assortment of legal, policy, administrative, and other measures necessary to create effective mechanisms for official delimitation, demarcation and titling of indigenous lands, in accordance with indigenous peoples customs, traditions, and land tenure systems. Legislative action as envisaged by Article 38 of the UNDRIP is simply the first step towards operationalization of the spectrum of indigenous rights and must be followed up by the 'concerted, goal-oriented action of a myriad of governmental actors within the scope of their respective fields of competence' (United Nations 2008b, para. 55).

Across the UN system, diverse organs and mechanisms have a role to play in implementation. Of those bodies and mechanisms specifically concerning indigenous peoples, all have distinctive, complementary functions in the operationalization of indigenous rights. The EMRIP, under its mandate to provide thematic expertise on the rights of indigenous peoples to the Council, is well placed to contribute practical guidance as to the implementation of specific articles; to date the EMRIP has produced a detailed *Study on Lessons Learned and Challenges to Achieve the Right of Indigenous Peoples to Education* (United Nations 2009c), which provides an indication of the EMRIP's potential role in this respect. Future thematic work might also involve a focus on the production of codes of good practice, such codes being 'a bridge between a norm and its implementation in practice' (United Nations 2006c, para. 6). As for the Special Rapporteur, his/her mandate since the establishment of the EMRIP – and indeed the adoption of the UNDRIP – is more clearly directed at monitoring and the investigation of country-specific cases of human rights violations, as well as identifying and promoting best practices, a role with a clear opportunity to encourage implementation (United Nations 2007b). For its part, the PFII promises to perform a number of functions relevant to the implementation of indigenous rights. Meeting in January 2009 to consider its role, members of the forum and international experts highlighted three clear responsibilities and areas of work: (i) awareness-raising and education, with a focus on capacity building amongst indigenous peoples, informing non-indigenous publics about indigenous peoples, and training of relevant actors from UN staff to private sector actors and national parliamentarians; (ii) promotion of the integration of indigenous rights into programmes and activities of the UN system; and (iii) consideration of written reports and submissions from states, UN agencies, and indigenous peoples on the implementation of the Declaration at national and local levels (United Nations 2009d). This latter role represents an extended mandate for the PFII based on Article 42 of the Declaration, which stipulates that, 'the United Nations, its bodies, including the Permanent Forum on Indigenous Issues, and specialized agencies, including at the country level, and States shall promote respect for and full application of the provisions of this Declaration and follow up the effectiveness of this Declaration' (United Nations 2007a). Notwithstanding its promise as a mechanism for operationalizing indigenous rights, the PFII will need the input of more resources than it currently receives, which must come from states first and foremost, as well as from outside donors and the NGO community.

Other UN bodies with an ongoing role in implementation include the UN treaty bodies, which will continue to monitor states' compliance with their human rights commitments, a process that, though lacking teeth, nevertheless throws light on violations of human rights while contributing to the development of a body of jurisprudence on indigenous peoples' rights. The Universal Periodic Review

(UPR), further, stands to offer a potential tool in the advancement of indigenous rights. Established in 2006 with the creation of the Human Rights Council (United Nations 2006b), the UPR process aims to appraise the human rights records of all UN member states every four years. Reviews are conducted by the UPR Working Group, consisting of the representatives of the 47 members of the Council, and are based upon information provided by states, reports of independent human rights experts, including information provided by the human rights treaty bodies, and NGOs. According to the current Special Rapporteur, S. James Anaya, the likelihood is that, over time, the UNDRIP will become entrenched in the UPR process, meaning that states given the task of reviewing country reports will utilize the Declaration as the basis for evaluation and recommendation (United Nations 2008b, para. 63).

It is also expected that the UN specialized agencies play a key role in the operationalization of indigenous rights, principally through the mobilization of financial cooperation and technical assistance. An important step is the reform of their policies to enhance the effectiveness of their engagements with indigenous peoples within their remit, a step that has been made by a number of agencies. Relevant policy developments include the UNDP's Practice Note on Engagement (United Nations Development Program 2001) and the World Bank's 2005 Operational Policy and Bank Procedure on Indigenous Peoples 4.10 (World Bank 2005a). More recently, the International Fund for Agricultural Development (IFAD) adopted the IFAD Policy on Engagement with Indigenous Peoples (International Fund for Agricultural Development 2009). Another positive development in this respect is the adoption in February 2008 of the United Nations Development Group Guidelines for Indigenous Peoples Issues, which aim to assist the UN system to mainstream and integrate indigenous peoples' issues into operational activities and programmes at the country level. The Guidelines apply to the 32 funds, agencies and programmes united through the United Nations Development Group (UNDG). They set out the normative framework for implementing a human rights-based approach to development for and with indigenous peoples and provide lines of action against which to plan, implement and evaluate programmes involving indigenous peoples (United Nation Development Group 2008).

Lastly, critical responsibilities for implementing international indigenous rights standards must fall on the rights-holders themselves, who will need to be proactive in exercising responsibilities for the fulfillment of self-determination at the community level. The operationalization of indigenous rights requires indigenous peoples to pursue local, community-based initiatives that enact – 'breathe life into' (Sambo Dorough 2009) – the right to self-determination at the local level, and in a way that does not necessarily involve the direct participation of the state. As Anaya has pointed out, such community-based assertions of self-determination are particularly important in relation to those rights that accord indigenous peoples a large degree of autonomy in managing their local and internal affairs, and which therefore call for the exercise of inherent governance, whether in relation to the establishment of institutions and mechanisms of self-government, the development of indigenous justice systems, the preservation of cultural heritage, or environmental stewardship (United Nations 2008b, paras. 75–77; see also Sambo Dorough 2009).

In addition to the exercise of inherent authority, it is incumbent on indigenous peoples, together with their allies in civil society, to continue to be energetic in the defence of their human rights through various forms of social, legal, and political mobilization. The vocal and visible mobilization of indigenous organizations and communities will be critical to bringing rights home to indigenous localities, subjecting governments to pressures of exposure and condemnation. The success of mobilizations will depend upon organization, as well as an awareness in indigenous communities of all the tools at their disposal, allowing for leverage over the political process and for forms of accountability politics that expose governments to embarrassment and hypocrisy, and, in the case of TNCs and businesses, that call into question their 'social license to operate' (United Nations, 2009e). The task at hand will be a challenging one, but what seems clear is that indigenous peoples seeking to influence the outcome of contests in domestic contexts are empowered today in ways that were unimaginable thirty years ago, and that a politics of implementation is an emboldened politics that confronts target actors with a weight of international opinion and action, and that, more particularly, equips local and national movements with legitimation, credibility, and authority. What is hardly in doubt is that indigenous peoples will rise to this ongoing challenge with the same tenacity, energy, and ability that they have applied to the pursuit of their goals in the international arena.

References

Aboriginal and Torres Strait Islander Commission (1998), 'Detailed Analysis of the Native Title Amendment Act 1998' [website]. At: <http://pandora.nla.gov.au/pan/41033/20060106-0000/ATSIC/issues/land/native_title/detailed_analysis_of_the_native_.html> accessed 3 June 2009.

African Commission on Human and Peoples' Rights (2007a), *Resolution on the Composition and Renewal of the Mandate of the Working Group on Indigenous Populations/Communities in Africa*, ACHPR/Res.123 (XXXXII) 07, 28 November 2007.

African Commission on Human and Peoples' Rights (2007b), *Communiqué on the UN Declaration on the Rights of Indigenous Peoples, Annex,* ACHPR/Res.121 (XXXXII) 07, 28 November 2007.

African Union (2007), *Decision on the United Nations Declaration on the Rights of Indigenous Peoples*, Doc. Assembly/AU/Dec. 141 (VIII).

Ahren, M. (2007), 'The UN Declaration on the Rights of Indigenous Peoples: How was it adopted and why is it significant?' in *Galdu Cala, Journal of Indigenous Peoples Rights* 4, 84–128.

Alfonso Martínez, M. (1999), *Study on Treaties, Agreements, and Other Constructive Arrangements between States and Indigenous Peoples, Final Report by Miguel Alfonso Martínez, Special Rapporteur*, U.N. Doc. E/CN.4/Sub.2/1999/20, 22 June 1999.

Alfred, T. (1999), *Peace, Power, and Righteousness: An Indigenous Manifesto* (Don Mills, Ontario: Oxford University Press).

Alston, P., and Crawford, J. (eds) (2000), *The Future of UN Human Rights Treaty Monitoring* (Cambridge: Cambridge University Press).

Amenta, E. and Young, M.P. (1999), 'Democratic States and Social Movements: Theoretical Arguments and Hypotheses', *Social Problems* 46, 153–68.

American Anthropological Association (1999), *Declaration on Anthropology and Human Rights, Committee for Human Rights, American Anthropological Association, Adopted by the AAA Membership June 1999.*

Anaya, J. (1996), *Indigenous Peoples in International Law* (Cambridge: Cambridge University Press).

Anaya, J. (2004a), 'International Human Rights and Indigenous Peoples: The Move Towards the Multicultural State', *Arizona Journal of International and Comparative Law* 21:1, 13–61.

Anaya, J. (2004b) *Indigenous Peoples in International Law*, 2nd Edition. (Cambridge: Cambridge University Press).

Anaya, J. (2008), 'Summary', in Henriksen (ed.) *Saami Self-Determination: Scope and Implementation, Galdu Cala Journal of Indigenous Peoples Rights*, 2, 7–10.

Anaya, J. (2009), 'The Right of Indigenous Peoples to Self-Determination in the Post-Declaration Era', in Charter and Stavenhagen (eds) *Making the Declaration Work: The United Nations Declaration on the Rights of Indigenous Peoples* (Copenhagen: IWGIA).

Anaya, J. and Weissner, S. (2007), 'The UN Declaration on the Rights of Indigenous Peoples: Towards Re-Empowerment', *Jurist* October 2007, 1–7 [website]. At: <http://jurist.law.pitt.edu/forumy/2007/10/un-declaration-on-rights-of-indigenous.php> accessed 18 May 2009.

Anaya, J. and Williams, R.A. Jr. (2001), 'The Protection of Indigenous Peoples' Rights over Lands and Natural Resources Under the Inter-American Human Rights System', *Harvard Human Rights Journal* 14, 33–87.

Ashworth, G. (1999), 'The Silencing of Women', in Dunne and Wheeler (eds), *Human Rights in Global Politics* (Cambridge: Cambridge University Press).

Assembly of First Nations (2010), 'Description of the AFN' [website]. At: <http://www.afn.ca/article.asp?id=58> accessed 15 February 2010.

Australia (2009), 'The Hon Jenny Macklin MP, Statement on the United Nations Declaration on the Rights of Indigenous Peoples, 03 April 2009', *The Hon Jenny Macklin MP, Minister for Families, Housing, Community Services and Indigenous Affairs* [website]. At: <http://www.jennymacklin.fahcsia.gov.au/statements/Pages/un_declaration_03apr09.aspx> accessed 25 May 2009.

Baehr, P. (1999), *Human Rights: Universality in Practice* (Basingstoke: Macmillan).

Barsh, R. (1996), 'Indigenous Peoples and the UN Commission on Human Rights: A Case of the Immoveable Object and the Irresistible Force', *Human Rights Quarterly* 18:4, 782–813.

Baxi, U. (2002), *The Future of Human Rights* (New Delhi: Oxford University Press).

Bayefsky, A. (ed.) (2000), *The UN Human Rights Treaty System in the 21st Century* (The Hague: Kluwer).

Behera, D.K. (1998), '"So-Called Development" and its Impact on the Human Rights of Indigenous People in India', in Price-Cohen (ed.) *The Human Rights of Indigenous Peoples* (Ardsley: Transnational Publishers).

Berman, H. (1988), 'The International Labour Organisation and Indigenous Peoples: Revision of ILO Convention No. 107 at the 75th Session of the International Labour Conference, 1988', *The Review of the International Commission of Jurists* 41, 48–57.

Bernstein, M. (2003), 'The Strategic Uses of Identity by the Lesbian and Gay Movement', in Jasper (ed.) *The Social Movements Reader: Cases and Concepts* (Oxford: Blackwell).

Black, D. (1999), 'The Long and Winding Road: International Norms and Domestic Political Change in South Africa', in Risse, Ropp, and Sikkink (eds)

The Power of Human Rights: International Norms and Domestic Change (Cambridge: Cambridge University Press).

Bob, C. (2007), 'Dalit Rights are Human Rights: Caste Discrimination, International Activism, and the Construction of a New Human Rights Issue', *Human Rights Quarterly* 29:1, 167–93.

Bodley, J.H. (1990), *Victims of Progress* (Mountain View, Cal.: Mayfield Publishing Company).

Boerefijn, I. (1999), *The Reporting Procedure Under the Covenant on Civil and Political Rights* (Antwerp: Intersentia).

Boutcher, S. (2005), 'Making Lemonade: Turning Adverse Decisions into Opportunities for Mobilization', *Amici* 13:1, 8–13.

Brockett, C.D. (1991), 'The Structure of Political Opportunities and Peasant Mobilization in Central America', *Comparative Politics* 23, 253–74.

Brown, C. (1999), 'Universal Human Rights: A Critique', in Dunne and Wheeler (eds) *Human Rights in Global Politics* (Cambridge: Cambridge University Press).

Brown, W. (2004), '"The Most We Can Hope For...": Human Rights and the Politics of Fatalism', *South Atlantic Quarterly* 103, 451–63.

Brownlie, I. (1990), *Principles of Public International Law*, 4th Edition. (Oxford: Clarendon Press).

Brownlie, I. (1998), *Principles of Public International Law*, 5th Edition. (Oxford: Clarendon Press).

Brysk, A. (1994a), *The Politics of Human Rights in Argentina: Protest, Change, and Democratization* (Stanford, Cal.: Stanford University Press).

Brysk, A. (1994b), 'Acting Globally: Indian Rights and International Politics in Latin America', in Van Cott (ed.) *Indigenous Peoples and Democracy in Latin America* (London: Macmillan).

Brysk, A. (2000), *From Tribal Village to Global Village: Indian Rights and International Relations in Latin America* (Stanford: Stanford University Press).

Brysk, A. (ed.) (2002), *Globalization and Human Rights* (Berkeley: University of California Press).

Buchanan, A. (2004), *Justice, Legitimacy and Self-Determination: Moral Foundations for International Law* (Oxford: Oxford University Press).

Buergenthal, T. and Murphy, S. (2002), *Public International Law in a Nutshell* (St. Paul: West Group).

Burger, J. (1987), *Report from the Frontier: The State of the World's Indigenous Peoples* (London: Zed Books).

Burger, J. (1990), *The Gaia Atlas of First Peoples: A Future for the Indigenous World* (Toronto: Doubleday).

Burnstein, P. (1991), 'Legal Mobilization as a Social Movement Tactic: The Struggle for Equal Employment Opportunity', *American Journal of Sociology* 96:5, 1201–25.

Burnstein, P., Einwohner R.L., and Hollander J.A. (1995), 'The Success of Political Movements: A Bargaining Perspective', in Jenkins and Klandermans (eds) *The Politics of Social Protest: Comparative Perspectives on States and Social Movements* (Minneapolis: University of Minnesota Press).

Buxton, N. (2009), 'Bolivia's New Constitution', *Transnational Institute: A Worldwide Fellowship of Committed Scholar-Activists* [website]. At: <http://www.tni.org/detail_page.phtml?act_id=19180> accessed 9 June 2009.

Cali, B., and Meckled-Garcia, S. (2006), 'Human Rights *Legalized* – Defining, Interpreting and Implementing an Ideal', in Meckled-Garcia and Cali (eds) *The Legalization of Human Rights: Multidisciplinary Perspectives on Human Rights and Human Rights Law* (Abingdon, Oxon.: Routledge).

Cambell, T. (2006), *Rights: A Critical Introduction* (Abingdon, Oxon.: Routledge).

Canada (2010), 'Canada's Statement of Support on the United Nations Declaration on the Rights of Indigenous Peoples', *Foreign Affairs and International Trade Canada* [website]. At: < http://www.international.gc.ca/indig-autoch/un_declaration_nov2010/onu.aspx?lang=eng> accessed 24 January 2010.

Carey, S.C. and Poe, S.C. (eds) (2004), *Understanding Human Rights Violations: New Systematic Studies* (Aldershot: Ashgate).

Cassese, A. (1995), *Self-Determination of Peoples: A Legal Reappraisal* (Cambridge: Cambridge University Press).

Children's Rights Committee (2009), *General Comment No.11 (2009): Indigenous Children and their Rights Under the Convention*, U.N. Doc. CRC/C/GC/11, 12 February 2009.

Clark, A.M. (2001), *Diplomacy of Conscience: Amnesty International Changing Human Rights Norms* (Princeton: Princeton University Press).

Clarkson, L. et al. (1992), *Our Responsibility to the Seventh Generation: Indigenous Peoples and Sustainable Development* (Winnipeg: International Institute for Sustainable Development).

Cohen, J.L. (1985), 'Strategy or Identity: New Theoretical Paradigms and Contemporary Social Movements', *Social Research* 52, 663–716.

Cohen, R. and Rai, S. (eds) (2000), *Global Social Movements* (London: Athlone Press).

Coicaud, J.-M. (2003), 'Conclusion: Human Rights in Discourse and Practice: The Quandry of International Justice', in Coicaud et al. (eds) *The United Nations System in the 21st Century: The Globalization of Human Rights* (Tokyo: United Nations University Press).

Committee on Economic, Social, and Cultural Rights (1999), *General Comment No.12 (1999): The Right to Adequate Food, U.N. Doc. E/C.12/1999/5*, 12 May 1999.

Committee on Economic, Social, and Cultural Rights (2000), *General Comment No. 14 (2000): The Right to the Highest Attainable Standard of Health,* U.N. Doc. E/C.12/2000/4, 11 August 2000.

Committee on Economic, Social, and Cultural Rights (2002), *General Comment No. 15 (2003): The Right To Water,* U.N. Doc. E/C.12/2002/11, 20 January 2002.

Committee on Economic, Social, and Cultural Rights (2008a), *Concluding Observations of the Committee on Economic, Social and Cultural Rights, Nicaragua*, U.N. Doc. E/C.12/NIC/CO/4, 28 November 2008.

Committee on Economic, Social, and Cultural Rights(2008b), *Concluding Observations of the Committee on Economic, Social and Cultural Rights, Philippines*, U.N. Doc. E/C.12/PHL/CO/4.

Committee on Economic, Social, and Cultural Rights (2009), *General Comment No. 21: The Right of Everyone to Take Part in Cultural Life*, U.N. Doc. E/G.12/C/21, 21 December 2009.

Colchester, M. (1997), *Guyana: Fragile Frontier – Loggers, Miners, and Forest Peoples* (Montevideo: World Rainforest Movement and Latin American Bureau with Ian Randle Publishers).

Colchester, M. (2001), *Forest Industries: Indigenous Peoples and Human Rights* (Moreton-in-Marsh: Forest Peoples Programme).

Committee on the Elimination of Dicrimination Against Women (1999), *General Recommendation 24: Women and Health (Chapter 1)*, U.N. Doc. A/54/38/ Rev.1 (SUPP), 5 February 1999.

Committee on the Elimination of Discrimination (1997), *General Recommendation No: 23: Indigenous Peoples (Annex V)*, U.N. Doc. A/52/18 (SUPP), 18 August 1997.

Committee on the Elimination of Discrimination (1999), *Report of the Committee on the Elimination of Racial Discrimination (Fifty-fourth Session, 1–19 March 1999) (Fifty-fifth Session, 2–27 August 1999), General Assembly, Official Records, Fifty-fourth Session, Supplement No.18,* U.N. Doc. A/54/18.

Committee on the Elimination of Discrimination (2005), *Committee on the Elimination of Racial Discrimination, Concluding Observations, Nigeria*, U.N. Doc. CERD/C/NGA/CO/18, 1 November 2005.

Committee on the Elimination of Discrimination (2007), *Committee on the Elimination of Racial Discrimination, Concluding Observations, Nigeria*, U.N. Doc. CERD/C/NGA/CO/18, 27 March 2007.

Committee on the Elimination of Discrimination (2006), *Committee for the Elimination of Racial Discrimination Early Warning and Urgent Action Procedure, Decision 1 (68) United States of America.*

Committee on the Elimination of Discrimination (2007a), *Concluding Observations of the Committee on the Elimination of Racial Discrimination, Canada,* U.N. Doc. CERD/C/CAN/CO/18, 25 May 2007.

Committee on the Elimination of Discrimination (2007b), *Concluding Observations of the Committee on the Elimination of Racial Discrimination, Nigeria*, U.N. Doc. CERD/C/NGA/CO/18, 27 March 2007.

Committee on the Elimination of Discrimination (2007c), *Concluding Observations of the Committee on the Elimination of Racial Discrimination, India*, U.N. Doc. CERD/C/IND/CO/19, 5 May 2007.

Committee on the Elimination of Discrimination (2008), *Concluding Observations of the Committee on the Elimination of Racial Discrimination, United States of America*, U.N. Doc. CERD/C/USA/CO/6, 8 May 2008.

Conference on Security and Cooperation in Europe (1975), *Final Act of the Conference on Security and Cooperation in Europe*, August 1, 1975, 14 ILM 1292.

Corntassel, J. (2007), 'Partnership in Action? Indigenous Political Mobilization and Co-optation During the First UN Indigenous Decade (1995–2004)', *Human Rights Quarterly* 29:1, 137–66.

Crees, D. and Snow, D. (2000), 'The Outcomes of Homeless Mobilization: The Influence of Organization, Disruption, Political Mediation and Framing', *American Journal of Sociology* 105, 1063–104.

Cristescu, A. (1981), *The Right to Self-Determination: Historical and Current Developments on the Basis of United Nations Instruments*, UN Doc. E/CN.4/Sub.2/404/Rev.1.

Cunningham, Myra (2009), 'Health', in *State of the World's Indigenous Peoples* (New York: United Nations Department of Economic and Social Affairs). United Nations Publication Sales No. 09.VI.13.

Daes, E.-I. (1993a), *Study on the Protection of the Cultural and Intellectual Property of Indigenous Peoples by Erica-Irene Daes, Special Rapporteur of the UN Sub-Commission on the Prevention of Discrimination and Protection of Minorities and Chairperson of the Working Group on Indigenous Populations*, U.N. Doc. E/CN.4/Sub.2/1993/28.

Daes, E.-I. (1993b), 'Some Considerations on the Right of Indigenous Peoples to Self-Determination', *Transnational Law and Contemporary Problems* 3:1, 367–77.

Daes, E.I. (1993c), *Explanatory Note Concerning the Draft Declaration on the Rights of Indigenous Peoples*, U.N. Doc. E/CN.4/Sub.2/1993/26/Add.1, 1993.

Daes, E.-I. (1995), *Report on the Protection of the Heritage of Indigenous Peoples*, U.N. Doc. E/CN.4/Sub.2/1995/26.

Daes, E.-I. (1996a), *Working Paper by the Chairperson-Rapporteur, Mrs Erica-Irene A. Daes on the Concept of "Indigenous Peoples"*, U.N. Doc. E/CN.4/Sub.2/AC.4/1996/2.

Daes, E.-I. (1996b), 'The Right of Indigenous Peoples to "Self-Determination" in the Contemporary World Order', in Clark et al. (eds) *Self-Determination: International Perspectives* (London: Macmillan Press).

Daes, E.-I. (2000a), 'Reflections on the Making of the UN Draft Declaration on the Rights of Indigenous Peoples: The Spirit and Letter of the Right to Self-Determination', in Aikio and Scheinin (eds) *Operationalizing the Right of Indigenous Peoples to Self-Determination* (Turku, Abo: Institute for Human Rights, Abo Akademi University).

Daes, E.-I. (2000b), 'Protection of the World's Indigenous Peoples and Human Rights', in Symonides (ed.) *Human Rights: Concepts and Standards* (Paris: UNESCO Publishing, in association with Ashgate).

Daes, E.-I. (2001a), *Indigenous Peoples and their Relationship to Land, Final Working Paper Prepared by the Special Rapporteur, Mrs. Erica-Irene A. Daes*, U.N. Doc. E/CN.4/Sub.2/2001/21.

Daes, E.-I. (2001b), *Working Paper on Combating Racism Against Indigenous Peoples, submitted by Mrs. Erica-Irene A. Daes, Member of the Working Group on Indigenous Populations of the Sub-Commission on the Promotion and Protection of Human Rights*, U.N. Doc. A/CONF.189/PC.3/4, 20 July 2001.

Daes, E.-I. (2002), 'Article 3 of the Draft Declaration on the Rights of Indigenous Peoples: Obstacles and Consensus'. Paper presented at International Seminar on the Right to Self-Determination of Indigenous Peoples, Rights and Democracy, New York, May 18, 2002.

Daes, E.-I. (2004a), *Indigenous Peoples' Permanent Sovereignty Over Natural Resources, Final Report of the Special Rapporteur*, Erica-Irene A. Daes, U.N. Doc. E/CN.4/Sub.2/2004/30, 13 July 2004.

Daes, E.-I. (2004b), *'The Participation of Indigenous Peoples in the United Nations System's Political Institutions*', Lecture by Professor Erica-Irene A Daes at the Castan Centre for Human Rights, Monash University, 27 June 2004 [website]. At: <http://www.hreoc.gov.au/about/media/speeches/social_justice/un_political_institutions.html> accessed 5 March 2010.

Daes, E.-I. (2008), 'An Overview of the History of Indigenous Peoples: Self-Determination and the United Nations', *Cambridge Review of International Affairs* 21(1): 7–26.

Dahl, J. et al. (eds) (2000), *Nunavut: Inuit Regain Control of their Land and their Lives* (Copenhagen: IWGIA).

Dalton, R. and Kuechler, M. (eds) (1990), *Challenging the Political Order: New Social and Political Movements in Western Democracies* (Cambridge: Polity Press).

Dallam, E. (1991), 'The Growing Voice of Indigenous Peoples: Their Use of Storytelling and Rights Discourse to Transform Multilateral Development Bank Policies', *Arizona Journal and International and Comparative Law* 8, 117–48.

Darrow, M. (2003), *Between Light and Shadow: The World Bank, the International Monetary Fund and International Human Rights Law* (Oxford: Hart Publishing).

della Porta, D. and Diani, M. (1999), *Social Movements: An Introduction* (Oxford: Blackwell).

della Porta, D. et al. (eds) (1999), *Social Movements in a Globalizing World* (London: Macmillan).

della Porta, D. and Tarrow, S. (2005), 'Transnational Processes and Social Activism', in della Porta and Tarrow (eds) *Transnational Protest and Global Activism* (Lanham: Rowman and Littlefield).

Dembour, M.B. (2006), *Who Believes in Human Rights? Reflections on the European Convention* (Cambridge: Cambridge University Press).

Dodson, M. (1998a), 'Linking International Standards with Contemporary Concerns of Aboriginal and Torres Strait Islander Peoples', in Pritchard (ed.) *Indigenous Peoples, the United Nations, and Human Rights* (London: Zed Books).

Dodson, M. (1998b), 'Comment: Mick Dodson, Aboriginal and Torres Strait Islander Commissioner', in Pritchard (ed.) *Indigenous Peoples, the United Nations, and Human Rights* (London: Zed Books).

Donnelly, E.A. (2002), 'Proclaiming Jubilee: The Debt and Structural Adjustment Network', in Khagram et al. (eds) *Restructuring World Politics: Transnational Social Movements, Networks and Norms* (Minneapolis: University of Minnesota Press).

Donnelly, J. (1989), *Universal Human Rights in Theory and Practice* (Ithaca: Cornell University Press).

Donnelly, J. (1999), 'The Social Construction of International Human Rights', in Dunne and Wheeler (eds) *Human Rights in Global Politics* (Cambridge: Cambridge University Press).

Donnelly, J. (2003), *Universal Human Rights in Theory and Practice*, 2nd Edition (Ithaca: Cornell University Press).

Donnelly, J. (2006), 'The Virtues of Legalization', in Meckled-Garcia and Cali (eds) *The Legalization of Human Rights: Multidisciplinary Perspectives on Human Rights and Human Rights Law* (Abingdon, Oxon.: Routledge).

Downing, T. et al. (2002), *Indigenous Peoples and Mining Encounters: Strategies and Tactics, Report Commissioned by Minerals, Mining, and Sustainable Development Project* (London: International Institute for Environment and Development and World Business Council for Sustainable Development).

Dryzek, J. (1999), 'Transnational Democracy', *The Journal of Political Philosophy* 7:1, 30–51.

Dryzek, J. (2000), *Deliberative Democracy and Beyond: Liberals, Critics, Contestations* (Oxford: Oxford University Press).

Dunbar-Oritz, R. (2006), 'The First Decade of Indigenous Peoples at the United Nations', *Peace and Change* 31:1, 58–74.

Duyvendak, J. W and Guigni, M. (1995), 'Social Movement Types and Policy Domains', in Kriesi et al. (eds) *New Social Movements in Western Europe: A Comparative Analysis* (Minneapolis: University of Minnesota Press).

Earl, J. (2000), 'Methods, Movements, and Outcomes: Methodological Difficulties in the Study of Extra-Movement Outcomes', *Research in Social Movements, Conflicts, and Change* 22, 3–25.

Earl, J. (2000), 'The Cultural Consequences of Social Movements', in Snow et al. (eds) *The Blackwell Companion to Social Movements* (Oxford: Blackwell).

Eide, A. (2007), 'Rights of Indigenous Peoples: Achievements in International Law during the Last Quarter of a Century', *Galdu Cala Journal of Indigenous Peoples' Rights*, 4, 40–82.

Eide, A. (2009), 'The Indigenous Peoples, the Working Group on Indigenous Populations, and the Adoption of the UN Declaration on the Rights of

Indigenous Peoples', in Charters and Stavenhagen (eds) *Making the Declaration Work: The United Nations Declaration on the Rights of Indigenous Peoples* (Copenhagen: IWGIA).

Engle, K. (2001), 'From Scepticism to Embrace: Human Rights and the American Anthropological Association from 1947–1999', *Human Rights Quarterly* 23:3, 536–59.

Espiell, H.G. (1980), *The Right to Self-Determination: Implementation of United Nations Resolutions*, UN Doc. E/CN.4/Sub.2/405/Rev.1.

Evans, T. (2003), 'Universal Human Rights: "As Much Round and Round As Ever Onward"', *International Journal of Human Rights* 7:4, 155–68.

European Council (1998), 'Council Resolution on Indigenous Peoples within the Framework of the Development Cooperation of the Community and the Member States', *European Commission External Relations* [website]. At: <http://ec.europa.eu/external_relations/human_rights/ip/docs/council_resolution1998_en.pdf> accessed 11 June 2009.

Falk, R. (1988), 'The Rights of Peoples (In Particular Indigenous Peoples)', in Crawford (ed.) *The Rights of Peoples* (Oxford: Clarendon Press).

Falk, R. (2000), *Human Rights Horizons: The Pursuit of Justice in a Globalizing World* (London: Routledge).

Falk, R. et al. (2006), 'Reshaping Justice: International Law and the Third World: An Introduction', *Third World Quarterly*, 27:5, 711–12.

Falk, R. (2010), 'The Kosovo Advisory Opinion: Conflict Resolution and Precedent', *American Journal of International Law*, 105:1, 50–60.

Feldman, A. (2002), 'Making Space at the Nations' Table: Mapping the Transformative Geographies of the International Indigenous Movement', *Social Movement Studies* 1, 31–46.

Finnemore, M. (1993), 'International Organizations as Teachers of Norms: The United Nations Educational, Scientific, and Cultural Organization and Science Policy', *International Organization* 47:4, 565–98.

Finnemore, M. (1996), *National Interests in International Society* (Ithaca: Cornell University Press).

Finnemore, M. and Sikkink, K. (1998), 'International Norm Dynamics and Political Change', *International Organization*, 52, 887–917.

Forest Peoples Programme (2003), *Extracting Promises: Indigenous Peoples, Extractive Industries, and the World Bank* (Manila: Tebtebba and the Forest Peoples Programme).

Forest Peoples Programme (2007), *Indigenous Peoples' Rights and Transnational and Other Business Enterprises: A Review of International Law and Jurisprudence, Submission to the African Commission on Human and Peoples' Rights at its 41st Session* (Moreton-in-Marsh: Forest Peoples Programme).

Forsythe, D. (2006), *Human Rights in International Relations*, 2nd Edition. (Cambridge: Cambridge University Press).

Freeman, M. (2006), 'Putting Law in its Place: An Interdisciplinary Evaluation of National Amnesty Laws', in Meckled-Garcia and Cali (eds) *The Legalization of Human Rights: Multidisciplinary Perspectives on Human Rights and Human Rights Law* (Abingdon, Oxon.: Routledge).

Gamson, W. (1989), 'Media Discourse and Public Opinion on Nuclear Power', *American Journal of Sociology* 95, 1–38.

Gaer, F. (1995), 'Reality Check: Human Rights Nongovernmental Organizations Confront the United Nations', *Third World Quarterly* 16, 389–404.

Gamson, W. (1990 [1975]), *The Strategy of Social Protest*, 2nd Edition. (Belmont, CA: Wadsworth).

Gamson, W. and Meyer, D. (1996), 'Framing Political Opportunity', in McAdam et al. (eds) *Comparative Perspectives on Social Movements: Political Opportunities, Mobilizing Structures, and Cultural Framing* (Cambridge: Cambridge University Press).

Gamson, W. (1998), 'Social Movements and Cultural Change', in Giugni et al. (eds) *From Contention to Democracy* (Lanham, MD: Rowman and Littlefield).

Gamson, W. (2006), 'Movement Impact on Cultural Change', in Pfohl et al. (eds) *Culture, Power, and History: Studies in Critical Sociology* (Leiden: Brill).

García-Alix, L. (ed.) (1999), *The Permanent Forum for Indigenous Peoples: The Struggle for a New Partnership* (Copenhagen: IWGIA).

Gearty, C. (2006), *Can Human Rights Survive?* (Cambridge: Cambridge University Press).

Geer, M. (1998), 'Foreigners in their Own Land: Cultural Land and Transnational Corporations – Emergent Rights and Wrongs', *Virginia Journal of International Law* 38, 331.

Gelb, J. (1989), *Feminism and Politics: A Comparative Perspective* (Berkeley: University of California Press).

Glendon, M.A. (1991), *Rights Talk: The Impoverishment of the Political Discourse* (New York: Free Press).

Goldstone, J. (2003a), 'Bridging Institutionalized and Noninstitutionalized Politics', in Goldstone (ed.) *States, Parties, and Social Movements* (Cambridge: Cambridge University Press).

Goldstone, J. (ed.) (2003b), *States, Parties, and Social Movements* (Cambridge: Cambridge University Press).

Grand Council of the Crees (2001), *Pushed to the Edge of Extinction: Racism Against Indigenous Peoples in Canada* (Ottawa: Grand Council of the Crees).

Granzer, S. (1999), 'Changing Discourse: Transnational Advocacy Networks in Tunisia and Morocco', in in Risse, Ropp, and Sikkink (eds) *The Power of Human Rights: International Norms and Domestic Change* (Cambridge: Cambridge University Press).

Gray, A. (1997), *Indigenous Rights and Development: Self-Determination in an Amazonian Community* (Oxford: Berghahn Books).

Guidry, J. et al (eds) (2000), *Globalizations and Social Movements: Culture, Power, and the Transnational Public Sphere* (Anne Arbour: University of Michigan Press).

Gurr, T. (1993), *Minorities at Risk: A Global View of Ethnopolitics* (Washington D.C.: United States Institute of Peace Press).

Guzman Bouvard, M. (1996), *Women Reshaping Human Rights: How Extraordinary Activists are Shaping the World* (Wilmington, DE: SR Books).

Haas, P. (1992), 'Introduction: Epistemic Communities and International Policy Coordination', *International Organization* 46:1, 1–35.

Habermas, J. (1996), *Between Facts and Norms: Contributions to a Discourse Theory of Law and Democracy* (Cambridge, Mass.: MIT Press).

Haebich, A. (1998), *For Their Own Good: Aborigines and Government in South West of Western Australia, 1900–1940* (Nedlands: University of Western Australia Press).

Hall, G. and Patrinos, H. (2006), *Indigenous Peoples, Poverty and Human Development in Latin America* (London: Palgrave).

Hall, G. and Patrinos, H. (2010), 'Indigenous Peoples, Poverty, and Development', *World Bank: Indigenous Peoples* [website]. At: <http://www.siteresources.worldbank.org> accessed 29 June 2010.

Hannum, H. (1990), *Autonomy, Sovereignty, and Self-Determination: The Accommodation of Conflicting Rights* (Philadelphia: University of Pennsylvania Press).

Hannum, H. (1996), 'Self-Determination in the Postcolonial Era', in Clark and Williamson (eds) *Self-Determination: International Perspectives* (London: St. Martin's Press).

Hannum, H (2011), 'The Advisory Opinion on Kosovo: An Opportunity Lost, or a Poisoned Chalice Refused?, *Leiden Journal of International Law* 24:1, 155–61.

Harding, S. (1984), 'Reconstructing Order through Action: Jim Crow and the Southern Civil Rights Movement', in Bright and Harding (eds) *Statemaking and Social Movements* (Ann Arbour: University of Michigan Press).

Havemann, P. (2000), 'Enmeshed in the Web? Indigenous Peoples' Rights in the Network Society', in Cohen and Rai (eds) *Global Social Movements* (London: Athlone Press).

Hawkins, D. (2002), 'Human Rights Norms and Networks in Authoritarian Chile', in Khagram et al. (eds) *Restructuring World Politics: Transnational Social Movements, Networks and Norms* (Minneapolis: University of Minnesota Press).

Henriksen, J. (ed.) (2008), 'Introduction: Sami Self-Determination: Scope and Implementation', *Galdu Cala Journal of Indigenous Peoples Rights*, 2, 7–10.

Higgins, R. (1994), *Problems and Processes: International Law and How We Use It* (Oxford: Clarendon Press).

Hoffer, E. (1951), *The True Believer* (New York: Harper and Row).

Hoover, D.R., and Den Dulk, K.R. (2004), 'Christian Conservatives Go to Court: Religion and Legal Mobilization in the United States and Canada', *International Political Science Review* 25:1, 9–34.

Howitt, R. et al. (eds) (1996), *Resources, Nations, and Indigenous Peoples: Case Studies from Australasia, Melanesia, and South-East Asia* (Oxford: Oxford University Press).

Howitt, R. et al. (1996), 'Resources, Nations, and Indigenous Peoples', in Howitt et al. (eds) *Resources, Nations, and Indigenous Peoples: Case Studies from Australia, Melanesia, and South-East Asia* (Oxford: Oxford University Press).

Human Rights Committee (1981), *Sandra Lovelace v. Canada, Communication No. R.6/24 (29 December 1977)*, U.N. Doc. Supp. No.40 (A/36/40), at 166.

Human Rights Committee (1994), *General Comment No. 23: The Rights of Minorities (Art. 27)*, U.N. Doc. CCPR/C/21/Rev.1/Add.5.

Human Rights Committee (1999a), *Concluding Observations of the Human Rights Committee, Norway*, U.N. Doc. CCPR/C/79/Add.112, 1 November 1999.

Human Rights Committee (1999b), *Concluding Observations of the Human Rights Committee, Canada*, U.N. Doc. CCPR/C/79/Add.105, 7 April 1999.

Human Rights Committee (1999c*), General Recommendation 24: Women and Health (Chapter 1)*, U.N. Doc. A/54/38/Rev.1 (SUPP), 5 February 1999.

Human Rights Committee (2003), *Concluding Observations of the Human Rights Committee, Philippines*, U.N. Doc. CCPR/CO/79/PHL, 1 December 2003.

Human Rights Committee (2004b), *General Comment No.31 [80] Nature of the General Legal Obligation Imposed on States Parties to the Covenant: 26/05/2004*, U.N. Doc. CCPR/C/21/Rev.1/Add. 13, 26 May 2004.

Human Rights Committee (2005), *Concluding Observations of the Human Rights Committee, Brazil*, U.N. Doc. CCPR/C/BRA/CO/2, 1 December 2005

Human Rights Committee (2006a), *Concluding Observations of the Human Rights Committee, Norway*, U.N. Doc. CCPR/C/NOR/CO/5, 25 April 2006.

Human Rights Committee (2006b), *Concluding Observations of the Human Rights Committee, Canada*, U.N. Doc. CCPR/C/CAN/CO/5, 20 April 2006.

Human Rights Committee (2006c), *Concluding Observations of the Human Rights Committee, United States of America*, U.N. Doc. CCPR/C/USA/CO/3/Rev.1, 18 December 2006.

Human Rights Committee (2006d) *Concluding Observations of the Human Rights Committee, Paraguay*, U.N. Doc. CCPR/C/PRY/CO/2, 24 April 2006.

Human Rights and Equal Opportunities Commission (1997), *Bringing Them Home: Report of the National Inquiry into the Separation of Aboriginal and Torres Strait Islander Children from Their Families* (Canberra: AGPS).

Hurwitz, D. (2005), 'Politics of the People, Human Rights, and What's Hidden from View', *George Washington International Law Review*.

International Court of Justice (1975), *Western Sahara, Advisory Opinion of 1975*.

International Fund for Agricultural Development (2009), 'Engagement with Indigenous Peoples: Policy' *International Fund for Agricultural Development: Indigenous Peoples* [website]. At: <http://www.ifad.org/indigenous/documents/ip_policy_e.pdf> accessed May 26 2010.

International Labour Organization (1957), *Convention No. 107 Concerning the Protection and Integration of Indigenous and Other Tribal and Semi-Tribal Populations in Independent Countries.*

International Labour Organization (1989), *Convention No. 169 Concerning Indigenous and Tribal Peoples in Independent Countries.*

International Labour Organization (2003), *ILO Convention No.169 Concerning Indigenous and Tribal Peoples in Independent Countries: A Manual* (Geneva: International Labour Office).

International Labour Organization (2008a) *Convention No. 107 List of Ratifications* (Geneva: ILOLEX, Database of International Labour Standards).

International Labour Organization (2008b) *Convention No. 169 List of Ratifications* (Geneva: ILOLEX, Database of International Labour Standards).

International Labour Organization (2009), *Indigenous and Tribal Peoples' Rights in Practice: A Guide to ILO Convention No. 169* (Geneva: ILO).

Ignatieff, M. (2001), *Human Rights as Politics and Idolatry* (Princeton: Princeton University Press).

Indian Law Resource Centre (2009), 'Centre Milestones' [website]. At: <http://www.indianlaw.org/en/about> accessed 15 March 2009.

Inter-American Court of Human Rights (2001), *The Mayagna (Sumo) Awas Tingni Community v. Nicaragua*, Judgment of August 31, 2001, Inter-Am. Ct. H.R., (Ser. C) No.79 (2001).

Inter-American Court of Human Rights (2007), *I/A HR Court, Saramaka People v. Suriname*, Series C (No. 172) (2007).

Inter-American Development Bank (2006a), *Operational Policy on Indigenous Peoples.*

Inter-American Development Bank (2006b), *Strategy for Indigenous Development.*

International Forum on Globalization (2009), 'Globalization: Effects on Indigenous Peoples' [website]. At: < http://www.ifg.org > accessed 20 March 2010.

International Indian Treaty Council (2003), 'Another Perspective on the Process Towards Adoption of the Declaration for the Rights of Indigenous Peoples', [website]. At: <http://www.treatycouncil.org/PDF/Support_for_the_Declaration_paper.pdf> accessed 1 March 2011.

International Indian Treaty Council (2004), 'Assessment of the Implementation of the Programme of Activities of the International Decade' [website]. At: <http://www.treatycouncil.org/IITC%20Review%20of%20the%20Decade.2.pdf> accessed 25 March 2009.

International Law Association (2010), *The Hague Conference: Rights of Indigenous Peoples, Interim Report* [website]. At: <http://www.ila-hq.org/en/committees/index.cfm/cid/1024> accessed 20 January 2011.

Iorns, C. (1992), 'Indigenous Peoples and Self-Determination: Challenging State Sovereignty', *Case Western Reserve Journal of International Law* 24, 199–348.

Ishay, M. (2008), *The History of Human Rights: From Ancient Times to the Globalization Era,* 2nd Edition. (Berkeley: University of California Press).

International Work Group for Indigenous Affairs (2005), 'IWGIA: Strategy for the 2nd Decade on Indigenous Peoples' [website]. At: <http://iwgia.org.synkron.com/graphics/Synkron-Library/Documents/Noticeboard/News/SecondDecadeStrategy.htm> accessed 27 February 2010.

International Work Group for Indigenous Affairs (2009), 'Human Rights Activities: International Advocacy Work' [website]. At: <http://www.iwgia.org/sw17660.asp> accessed 15 Feb 2010.

International Work Group for Indigenous Affairs (2009a), 'IWGIA's Project Activities' [website]. At: <http://www.iwgia.org/sw17654.asp> accessed 15 Feb 2010.

Jepperson, R., Wendt, A, and Katzenstein, P. (1996), 'Norms, Identity and Culture in National Security', in Katzenstein (ed.) *The Culture of National Security: Norms and Identity in World Politics* (New York: Colombia Press).

Jimenez, M. (1999), 'Consolidation through Institutionalisation? Dilemmas of the Spanish Environmental Movement in the 1990s', *Environmental Politics* 8, 149–69.

Jones, P. (1994), *Rights* (London: MacMillan).

Jorge, A. (1998), 'Indigenous Peoples in Papua New Guinea', in Price-Cohen (ed.) *The Human Rights of Indigenous Peoples* (Ardsley: Transnational Publishers).

Katzenstein, M.F. (1995), 'Discursive Politics and Feminist Activism in the Catholic Church', in Ferree and Martin (eds) *Feminist Organizations: Harvest of the New Women's Movement* (Philadelphia: Temple University Press).

Katzenstein, M.F. (1998a), 'Stepsisters: Feminist Movement Activism in Different Institutional Spaces', in Meyer and Tarrow (eds) *The Social Movement Society: Contentious Politics for a New Century* (Lanham, MD: Rowman and Littlefield).

Katzenstein, M.F. (1998b), *Faithful and Fearless: Moving Feminist Protest Inside the Church and the Military* (Princeton: Princeton University Press).

Katzenstein, P. (1996), 'Introduction: Alternative Perspectives on National Security', in Katzenstein (ed.) *The Culture of National Security: Norms and Identity in World Politics* (New York: Colombia Press).

Keal, P. (2003), *European Conquest and the Rights of Indigenous Peoples: The Moral Backwardness of International Society* (Cambridge: Cambridge University Press).

Keck, M. and Sikkink, K. (1998), *Activists Beyond Borders: Advocacy Networks in International Politics* (Ithaca: Cornell University Press).

Kennedy, D. (2002), 'The International Human Rights Movement: Part of the Problem?', *Harvard Human Rights Journal* 14, 101–26.

Kennedy, D. (2004), *The Dark Sides of Virtue: Reassessing International Humanitarianism* (Princeton: Princeton University Press).

Kenrick, J. and Lewis, J. (2004), 'Indigenous Peoples' Rights and the Politics of the Term "Indigenous"', *Anthropology Today* 20:2, 4–9.

Keohane, R. and Nye, J. (1998), 'Power and Interdependence in the Information Age', *Foreign Affairs* 77:5, 81–94.

Khagram, S. (2002), 'Restructuring the Global Politics of Development: The Case of India's Narmada Valley Dams', in Khagram et al. (eds) *Restructuring World Politics: Transnational Social Movements, Networks and Norms* (Minneapolis: University of Minnesota Press).

Khagram, S. et al. (2002), 'From Santiago to Seattle: Transnational Advocacy Groups Restructuring World Politics', in Khagram et al. (eds) *Restructuring World Politics: Transnational Social Movements, Networks and Norms* (Minneapolis: University of Minnesota Press).

Kingsbury, B. (1998), 'The Applicability of the International Legal Concept of "Indigenous Peoples" in Asia', in Bauer and Bell (eds) *The East Asian Challenge for Human Rights* (Cambridge: Cambridge University Press).

Kingsbury, B. (2000), 'Restructuring Self-Determination: A Relational Approach', in Aikio and Scheinin (eds) *Operationalizing the Right of Indigenous Peoples to Self-Determination* (Turku, Abo: Institute for Human Rights, Abo Akademi University).

Kirgis Jnr., F.L. (1994), 'The Degrees of Self-Determination in the United Nations Era', *American Journal of International Law* 88:2, 304–10.

Kitschelt, H.P. (1986), 'Political Opportunity Structures and Political Protest: Anti-Nuclear Protest in Four Democracies', *British Journal of Political Science* 16, 57–85.

Klímová-Alexander, I. (2005), *The Romani Voice in World Politics: The United Nations and Non-State Actors* (Aldershot: Ashgate).

Klotz, A. (1995), *Norms in International Relations: The Struggle Against Apartheid* (Ithaca: Cornell University Press).

Knop, K. (2002), *Diversity and Self-Determination in International Law* (Cambridge: Cambridge University Press).

Korey, W. (1998), *NGOs and the Universal Declaration of Human Rights* (Princeton: Princeton University Press).

Kornhauser, W. (1959), *The Politics of Mass Society* (New York: Free Press).

Krasner, S. (1999), *Sovereignty: Organized Hypocrisy* (Princeton, N.J.: Princeton University Press).

Kriesi, H. et al. (1992), 'New Social Movements and Political Opportunities in Western Europe', *European Journal of Political Research* 22, 219–44.

Kriesi, H. et al. (1995), *The Politics of New Social Movements in Western Europe: A Comparative Analysis* (Minneapolis and St. Paul: University of Minnesota Press).

Kriesi, H. (1996), 'The Organizational Structure of New Social Movements in a Political Context', in McAdam et al. (eds) *Comparative Perspectives on Social Movements: Political Opportunities, Mobilizing Structures, and Cultural Framing* (Cambridge: Cambridge University Press).

Kukathas, C. (2003), *The Liberal Archipelago: A Theory of Diversity and Freedom* (Oxford: Oxford University Press).

Kuper, A. (2003), 'The Return of the Native', *Current Anthropology* 44:3, 389–402.

Kymlicka, W. (1991), *Liberalism, Community, and Culture* (Oxford: Oxford University Press).

Kymlicka, W. (1996), *Multicultural Citizenship: A Liberal Theory of Minority Rights* (Oxford: Oxford University Press).

Lam, M.C. (2000), *At the Edge of the State: Indigenous Peoples and Self-Determination* (Ardsley: Transnational Publishers).

Lam, M.-C. (2002), 'The Self-Determination of Indigenous Peoples: Past Debate and Future Promise'. Paper presented at the International Seminar on the Right to Self-Determination of Indigenous Peoples, Rights and Democracy, New York, May 18, 2002.

Lam, M.-C. (2004), 'Remembering the County of their Birth: Indigenous Peoples and Territoriality', *Journal of International Affairs*, 57(2), 129–50.

Landman, T. (2005), *Studying Human Rights* (Abingdon: Routledge).

Lenzerini, F. (2006), 'Sovereignty Revisited: International Law and the Parallel Sovereignty of Indigenous Peoples', *Texas International Law Journal* 42, 155–89.

Lillich, R. (1984), *The Human Rights of Aliens in Contemporary International Law* (Manchester: Manchester University Press).

Lloyd, J. et al. (2006), 'Infrastructure Development in the South American Amazon', in Mander and Tauli-Corpuz (eds) *Paradigm Wars: Indigenous Peoples' Resistance to Globalization* (Berkeley and Los Angeles: University of California Press).

Lo, C. (1992), 'Communities of Challengers in Social Movement Theory', in Morris and Mueller (eds), *Frontiers in Social Movement Theory* (New Haven, CT.: Yale University Press).

MacKay, F. (2005), *Indigenous Peoples and United Nations Human Rights Treaty Bodies: A Compilation of Treaty Body Jurisprudence (Volume I) 1993–2004* (Moreton-in-Marsh: Forest Peoples Programme).

MacKay, F. (2006), *Indigenous Peoples and United Nations Human Rights Treaty Bodies: A Compilation of UN Treaty Body Jurisprudence (Volume II) 2005–2006* (Moreton-in-Marsh: Forest Peoples Programme).

MacKay, F. (2009), *Indigenous Peoples and United Nations Human Rights Treaty Bodies: A Compilation of UN Treaty Body Jurisprudence (Volume III) 2007–2008* (Moreton-in-Marsh: Forest Peoples Programme).

Macklem, P. (2001), 'Indigenous Rights and Multinational Corporations at International Law', *Hastings International and Comparative Law Review* 24:3, 475–84.

Maiguashca, B. (1994), 'The Transnational Indigenous Movement in a Changing World Order', in Sakamoto (ed.) *Global Transformation: Challenges to the State System* (Tokyo: UN University Press).

Mandat International (2010), 'Welcome and Accommodation at Valvaran' [website]. At: <http://www.mandint.org/en/welcome> accessed 15 February 2010.

Mander, J. (2006), 'Introduction: Globalization and the Assault on Indigenous Resources', in Mander and Tauli-Corpuz (eds) *Paradigm Wars: Indigenous Peoples' Resistance to Globalization* (Berkeley and Los Angeles: University of California Press).

Mander, J. and Tauli-Corpuz, V. (eds) (2006), *Paradigm Wars: Indigenous Peoples' Resistance to Globalization* (Berkeley and Los Angeles: University of California Press).

Maybury-Lewis, D. (1984), 'Demystifying the Second Conquest', in Schmink and Wood (eds) *Frontier Expansion in Amazonia* (Gainesville: University of Florida Press).

McAdam, D. (1982), *Political Process and the Development of Black Insurgency, 1930–1970* (Chicago: Chicago University Press).

McAdam, D. (1983), 'Tactical Innovation and the Pace of Insurgency', *American Sociological Review* 48, 735–54.

McAdam, D. (1996a), 'Conceptual Origins, Current Problems, and Future Directions', in McAdam et al. (eds) *Comparative Perspectives on Social Movements: Political Opportunities, Mobilizing Structures, and Cultural Framing* (Cambridge: Cambridge University Press).

McAdam, D. (1996b), 'The Framing Function of Movement Tactics: Strategic Dramaturgy in the American Civil Rights Movement', in McAdam et al. (eds) *Comparative Perspectives on Social Movements: Political Opportunities, Mobilizing Structures, and Cultural Framing* (Cambridge: Cambridge University Press).

McAdam, D. et al. (eds) (2001), *Dynamics of Contention* (Cambridge: Cambridge University Press).

McAdam, D. and Su, Y. (2002), 'The War at Home: Antiwar Protests and Congressional Voting, 1965–1973', *American Sociological Review* 67, 696–721.

McAdam, D. et al. (2005), '"There Will Be Fighting in the Streets": The Distorting Lens of Social Movement Theory', *Mobilization* 10:1, 1–18.

McCamant, J.F. (1981), 'Social Science and Human Rights', *International Organization* 35:3, 531–52.

McCann, M. (1994), *Rights at Work: Pay Equity Reform and the Politics of Legal Mobilization* (Chicago: Chicago University Press).

McCarthy, J., and Zald, M. (1973), *The Trend of Social Movements in America: Professionalization and Resource Mobilization* (Morristown, N.J.: General Learning Press).

McCarthy, J., and Zald, M. (1977), 'Resource Mobilization in Social Movements: A Partial Theory', *American Journal of Sociology* 82, 1212–41.

McClean, G. et al. (2009), *Report of the Indigenous Peoples' Global Summit on Climate Change, 20–24 April 2009, Anchorage, Alaska* (Darwin: UNU).

McDougall, G. (no date), 'Meeting of the Committee on the Elimination of Racial Discrimination, Report by Ms Gail McDougall, Country Rapporteur' [website]. At: <http://www.faira.org.au/cerd/racial_discrimination.html> accessed 3 June 2009.

McIntyre, A. (1984), *After Virtue* (London: Duckworth).

McNeil, K. (2004), 'The Vulnerability of Indigenous Land Rights in Australia and Canada', *Osgoode Hall Law Journal*, 42:2, 271–301.

Melucci, A. (1989), *Nomads of the Present: Social Movements and Individual Needs in Contemporary Society* (Philadelphia: Temple University Press).

Merry, S.E. (1990), *Getting Justice and Getting Even: Legal Consciousness Among Working-Class Americans* (Chicago: University of Chicago Press).

Merry, S.E. (2006), *Human Rights and Gender Violence: Translating International Law into Local Justice* (Chicago: Chicago University Press).

Meyer, D. and Tarrow, S. (1998a), 'A Movement Society: Contentious Politics for a New Society', in Meyer and Tarrow (eds) *The Social Movement Society: Contentious Politics for a New Century* (Lanham, MD: Rowman and Littlefield).

Meyer, D. and Tarrow, S. (eds) (1998b), *The Social Movement Society: Contentious Politics for a New Century* (Lanham, MD: Rowman and Littlefield).

Michels, R. (1960), *Political Parties* (New York: Collier).

Milner, N (1986), 'The Dilemmas of Legal Mobilization: Ideologies and Strategies of Mental Patient Liberation Groups', *Law and Policy* 8:1, 105–29.

Minde, H (2007), 'The Destination and the Journey: Indigenous Peoples and the United Nations from the 1960s through 1985', *Galdu Cala Journal of Indigenous Peoples' Rights*, 4, 9–38.

Mingst, K.A. and Karns, M.P (2000), *The United Nations in the Post-Cold War Era* (Boulder, Col.: Westview Press).

Miranda, L.A. (2007), 'The Hybrid State-Corporate Enterprise and Violations of Indigenous Land Rights: Theorizing Corporate Responsibility and Accountability Under International Law', *Lewis and Clark Law Review* 135, 135–83.

Morgan, R. (2004), 'Advancing Indigenous Rights at the United Nations: Strategic Framing and its Impact on the Normative Development of International Law', *Social and Legal Studies* 13:4, 481–500.

Morgan, R. (2007), 'On Political Institutions and Social Movement Dynamics: The Case of the United Nations and the Global Indigenous Movement', *International Political Science Review* 28:3, 273–92.

Morgan, R. (2009), 'Forging Indigenous Rights at the United Nations: A Social Constructionist Account', in Morgan and Turner (eds) *Interpreting Human Rights: Social Science Perspectives* (Abingdon, Oxon: Routledge).

Morinsk, J. (1999), *The Universal Declaration of Human Rights: Origins, Developing, and Intent* (Philadelphia: University of Pennsylvania Press).

Morris, A. (1984), *The Origins of the Civil Rights Movement* (New York: Free Press).

Morris, A., and Staggenborg, S. (2007), 'Leadership in Social Movements', in Snow et al (eds) *Blackwell Companion to Social Movements* (Oxford: Blackwell).

Moses, T. (2000), 'The Right to Self-Determination and its Significance to the Survival of Indigenous Peoples', in Aikio and Scheinin (eds) *Operationalizing the Right of Indigenous Peoples to Self-Determination* (Turku, Abo: Institute for Human Rights, Abo Akademi University).

Muehlebach, A. (2001), '"Making Place" at the United Nations: Indigenous Cultural Politics at the U.N. Working Group on Indigenous Populations', *Cultural Anthropology*, 16:3, 415–48.

Muehlebach, A. (2003), 'What Self in Self-Determination? Notes From the Frontiers of Transnational Indigenous Activism', *Identities: Global Studies in Culture and Power* 10, 241–68.

Mutua, M. (2002), *Human Rights: A Political and Cultural Critique* (Philadelphia: University of Pennsylvania Press).

Nash, K. (2000), *Contemporary Political Sociology: Globalization, Politics, and Power* (Oxford: Blackwell).

National Congress of American Indians (2010), 'NCAI: Policy Issues' [website]. At: <http://www.ncai.org/Policy-Issues.6.0.html> accessed 15 February 2010.

New Zealand (2010), 'Hon Pita Sharpe, Minister for Maori Affairs, New Zealand Permanent Mission to the United Nations, Statement to the Ninth Session of the United Nations Permanent Forum on Indigenous Issues, 19 April 2010', *United Nations Permanent Forum on Indigenous Issues* [website, link]. At: <www.docip.org> accessed 15 January 2011.

Niezen, R. (2000), 'Recognizing Indigenism: Canadian Unity and the International Movement of Indigenous Peoples', *Comparative Studies in Society and History* 42:1, 119–48.

Neizen, R. (2003), *The Origins of Indigenism: Human Rights and the Politics of Identity* (Berkeley: University of California Press).

O'Brien, R. et al. (2000), *Contesting Global Governance: Multilateral Economic Institutions and Global Social Movements* (Cambridge: Cambridge University Press).

Olson, M. (1965), *The Logic of Collective Action* (Cambridge, Mass.: Harvard University Press).

Organization of American States (2008), *Working Group to Prepare the Draft American Declaration on the Rights of Indigenous Peoples, Report of the Chair on the Meeting for Reflection on the Meeting of Negotiations in the Quest for Points of Consensus, OEA/Ser.K/XVI, GT/DADIN/doc.321/08, 14 January 2008.*

Orton, F. and Beach, H. (1998), 'A New Era for the Saami People of Sweden', in Price-Cohen (ed.) *The Human Rights of Indigenous Peoples* (Ardsley: Transnational Publishers).

Otto, D. (1996), 'Non-Governmental Organizations in the United Nations System: The Emerging Role of International Civil Society', *Human Rights Quarterly* 18, 107–41.

Parisi, L. and Corntassel, J. (2005), 'A Tale of Two UN Decades: Transnational Networks and Mobilization During the Women's and Indigenous Peoples' Decades', paper presented at the annual meeting of the International Studies Association, Honolulu, Hawai'i, March 2005.

Passy, F. (1999), 'Supranational Political Opportunities as a Channel of Globalization of Political Conflicts: The Case of the Rights of Indigenous Peoples', in della Porta (ed.) *Social Movements in a Globalizing World* (London: Macmillan).

Pedriana, N. (2004), 'Help Wanted NOW: Legal Resources, the Women's Movement, and the Battle Over Sex-Segregated Job Advertisements', *Social Problems* 51, 182–201.

Peterson, V.S. and Parisi, L. (1998), 'Are Women Human? It's Not an Academic Question', in Evans (ed.) *Human Rights Fifty Years On: A Reappraisal* (Manchester: Manchester University Press).

Piven, F.F. and Cloward, R. (1977), *Poor People's Movements: Why They Succeed, How They Fail* (New York: Pantheon).

Plummer, K. (2006), 'Rights Work', in Morris (ed.) *Rights: Sociological Perspectives* (London: Routledge).

Polleta, F. (2000), 'The Structural Context of Novel Rights Claims: Southern Civil Rights Organizing, 1961–1966', *Law and Society Review* 34, 367–407.

Raic, D. (2002), *Statehood and the Law of Self-Determination* (The Hague: Martinus Nijhoff Publishers).

Rajagopal, B. (2003), *International Law from Below: Development, Social Movements, and Third World Resistance* (Cambridge: Cambridge University Press).

Rajagopal, B. (2006), 'Counter-Hegemonic International Law: Rethinking Human Rights and Development as a Third World Strategy', *Third World Quarterly* 27:5, 767–83.

Republic of Serbia (2009), 'International Court of Justice, Accordance with International Law of the Unilateral Declaration of Independence by the Provisional Institutions of Self-Government of Kosovo (Request for an Advisory Opinion), Written Statement of the Republic of Serbia, 15 April 2009', *International Court of Justice* [website]. Available at: <http://www.icj-cij.org/docket/files/141/15642.pdf> accessed 1 March 2011.

Risse, T. (1999), 'International Norms and Domestic Change: Arguing and Communicative Behaviour in the Human Rights Area', *Politics and Society* 27:4, 529–59.

Risse, T. et al. (eds) (1999), *The Power of Human Rights: International Norms and Domestic Change* (Cambridge: Cambridge University Press).

Risse, T., and Ropp, S.C. (1999), 'International Human Rights Norms and Domestic Change: Conclusions', in Risse et al. (eds) *The Power of Human*

Rights: International Norms and Domestic Change (Cambridge: Cambridge University Press).

Risse, T., and Sikkink, K. (1999), 'The Socialization of International Human Rights Norms into Domestic Practices: Introduction', in Risse et al. (eds) *The Power of Human Rights: International Norms and Domestic Change* (Cambridge: Cambridge University Press).

Roach Anleu, S. (1999), 'Sociologists Confront Human Rights: The Problem of Universalism', *Journal of Sociology* 35:2, 198–212.

Robertson, G. (1999), *Crimes Against Humanity: The Struggle for Global Justice* (London: Allen Lane).

Robinson, F. (2003), 'Human Rights and the Global Politics of Resistance: Feminist Perspectives', *Review of International Studies* 29, 161–80.

Rodríguez-Garavito, C.A. and Arenas, L.C. (2005), 'Indigenous Rights, Transnational Activism, and Legal Mobilization: The Struggle of the U'wa People in Colombia', in de Sousa Santos and Rodríguez-Garavito (eds) *Law and Globalization from Below: Towards a Cosmopolitan Legality* (Cambridge: Cambridge University Press).

Rubin, E.L. (2001), 'Passing Through the Door: Social Movement Literature and Legal Scholarship', University of Pennsylvania Law Review 150:1.

Rodriguez-Pinero, L. (2006), *Indigenous Peoples, Postcolonialism, and International Law: the ILO Regime (1919–1989)* (Oxford: Oxford University Press).

Roth, B. (2004), 'Thinking About Challenges to Feminist Activism in Extra-Feminist Settings', *Social Movement Studies* 3:2, 147–66.

Rucht, D. (1990), 'Campaigns, Skirmishes, and Battles: Anti-Nuclear Movements in the USA, France, and West Germany', *Industrial Crisis Quarterly* 4, 193–222.

Rucht, D. (1996), 'The Impact of National Contexts on Social Movement Structures: A Cross-Movement and Cross-National Comparison', in McAdam et al. (eds) *Comparative Perspectives on Social Movements: Political Opportunities, Mobilizing Structures, and Cultural Framing* (Cambridge: Cambridge University Press).

Rucht, D. (1998), 'The Structure and Culture of Collective Protest', in Meyer and Tarrow (eds) *The Social Movement Society: Contentious Politics for a New Society* (Lanham, MD.: Rowman and Littlefield).

Rucht, D. (1999), 'The Transnationalization of Social Movements: Trends, Causes, Problems', in della Porta, D. et al. (eds) *Social Movements in a Globalizing World* (London: Macmillan).

Salamon, L. et al. (1999), *Global Civil Society: Dimensions of the Non-Profit Sector* (Baltimore: John Hopkins University Press, Institute for Policy Studies).

Sambo Dorough, D. (2002), 'Indigenous Peoples and the Right to Self-Determination: The Need for Equality: An Indigenous Perspective'. Paper presented at the International Seminar on the Right to Self-Determination of Indigenous Peoples, Rights and Democracy, New York, May 18, 2002.

Sambo Dorough, D. (2009), 'The Significance of the Declaration on the Rights of Indigenous Peoples and its Future Implementation', in Charters and Stavenhagen (eds) *Making the Declaration Work: The United Nations Declaration on the Rights of Indigenous Peoples* (Copenhagen: IWGIA).

Samson, C. (2003), *A Way of Life that Does Not Exist: Canada and the Extinguishment of the Innu* (London: Verso Press).

Sanders, D. (1980), 'The Formation of the World Council of Indigenous Peoples' [website]. At: <http://cwis.org/fwdp/International/wcipinfo.txt> accessed 12 January 2010.

Sanders, D. (1998), 'The Legacy of Deskaheh: Indigenous Peoples as International Actors', in Price-Cohen (ed.) *The Human Rights of Indigenous Peoples* (Ardsley: Transnational Publishers).

Sanders, D. (1999), 'Indigenous Peoples: Issues of Definition', *International Journal of Cultural Property*, 8:1, 4–13

Santos, B. de S. (2002), *Toward a New Legal Common Sense: Law, Globalization, and Emancipation* (London: Butterworths LexisNexis).

Saugestad, S. (2004), 'Comment on Kuper's "Return of the Native"', *Current Anthropology* 45:2, 263–4.

Scheingold, S. (1974), *The Politics of Rights: Lawyers, Public Policy, and Political Change* (New Haven, Ct.: Yale University Press).

Scheingold, S. (2004), *The Politics of Rights: Lawyers, Public Policy, and Political Change* (Ann Arbour: University of Michigan Press).

Schumaker, P.D. (1975), 'Policy Responsiveness to Protest-Group Demands', *The Journal of Politics* 37, 488–521.

Scott, C. (1996), 'Indigenous Self-Determination and Decolonization of the International Imagination: A Plea', *Human Rights Quarterly* 18, 814–20.

Scott, J.C. (1998), *Seeing Like a State: How Certain Schemes to Improve the Human Condition Have Failed* (New Haven: Yale University Press).

Seippel, O. (2001), 'From Mobilization to Institutionalization? The Case of Norwegian Environmentalism', *Acta Sociologica* 44, 123–37.

Sharma, S.P. (1997), *Territorial Acquisition, Disputes, and International Law* (The Hague: Martinus Nijhoff Publishers).

Shaw, M. (2000), 'Report by Malcolm N. Shaw: "Re: Order in Council P.C 1996–1997 of 30 September 1996', in Bayefsky *Self-Determination in International Law: Quebec and Lessons Learned* (Dordrecht: Kluwer Law International).

Shelton, D. (2000), (ed.), *Commitment and Compliance: The Role of Non-Binding Norms in the International Legal System* (Oxford: Oxford University Press).

Sikkink, K. (2002), 'Restructuring World Politics: The Limits and Asymmetries of Soft Power', in Khagram et al. (eds) *Restructuring World Politics: Transnational Social Movements, Networks and Norms* (Minneapolis: University of Minnesota Press).

Smith, J., Pagnucco, R., and Lopez, G.A. (1998), 'Globalizing Human Rights: The Work of Transnational Human Rights NGOs in the 1990s', *Human Rights Quarterly* 20:2, 379–412.

Smith, J. (2004), 'Transnational Processes and Movements', in Snow et al. (eds) *The Blackwell Companion to Social Movements* (Oxford: Blackwell Publishers).

Smith, R.K.M. (2007), *Textbook on International Human Rights*, 3rd Edition. (Oxford: Oxford University Press).

Smitz, H.P. (1999), 'Transnational Activism and Political Change in Kenya and Uganda', in Risse, Ropp, and Sikkink (eds) *The Power of Human Rights: International Norms and Domestic Change* (Cambridge: Cambridge University Press).

Snow, D. et al. (1986), 'Frame Alignment Processes, Micromobilization, and Movement Participation', *American Sociological Review* 51, 464–81.

Snow, D., and Benford, R. (1988), 'Ideology, Frame Resonance, and Participant Mobilization', *International Social Movements Research* 1, 197–217.

Snow, D., and Benford, R. (1992), 'Master Frames and Cycles of Protest', in Morris and Mueller (eds) *Frontiers in Social Movement Theory* (New Haven, CT.: Yale University Press).

Soule, S.A., et al. (1999), 'Protest Events: Cause or Consequence of State Action? The U.S. Women's Movement and Federal Congressional Activities, 1956–1979', *Mobilization* 4:2, 239–56.

Sousa Santos and Rodríguez-Garavito (eds) *Law and Globalization from Below: Towards a Cosmopolitan Legality* (Cambridge: Cambridge University Press).

Stamatopoulou, E (1994), 'Indigenous Peoples and the United Nations: Human Rights as a Developing Dynamic', *Human Rights Quarterly* 16: 58–81.

Stammers, N. (1993), 'Human Rights and Power', *Political Studies* 41:1, 70–82.

Stammers, N. (1999), 'Social Movements and the Social Construction of Human Rights', *Human Rights Quarterly* 21, 980–1008.

Stavenhagen, R. (1996), 'Self-Determination: Right or Demon?', in Clark and Williamson (eds) *Self-Determination: International Perspectives* (London: St. Martin's Press).

Stavenhagen, R. (2007), 'The Role of the Special Rapporteur in Realizing Human Rights for Indigenous Peoples', in IWGIA (ed.) *The UN Special Rapporteur, Indigenous Peoples' Rights: Experiences and Challenges* (Copenhagen: IWGIA).

Stavenhagen, R. (2009), 'Making the Declaration Work', in Charters and Stavenhagen (eds) *Making the Declaration Work: The United Nations Declaration on the Rights of Indigenous Peoples* (Copenhagen: IWGIA).

Steiner, H. et al. (2008), *International Human Rights in Context: Law, Politics, Morals* (Oxford: Oxford University Press).

Stewart-Harawira, M. (2005), *The New Imperial Order: Indigenous Responses to Globalization* (London and New York: Zed Books).

Stiles, A. (2001), *The Network Inside Out* (Michigan: University of Michigan Press).

Szasz, P. (1997), 'General Law-Making Processes', in Joyner (ed.) *The United Nations and International Law* (Cambridge: Cambridge University Press).

Tarrow, S. (1994), *Power in Movement: Social Movements, Collective Action, and Mass Politics in the Modern State* (Cambridge: Cambridge University Press).

Tarrow, S. (1998), *Power in Movement: Social Movements and Contentious Politics* (Cambridge: Cambridge University Press).

Tarrow, S. (2001), 'Transnational Politics: Contention and Institutions in International Politics', *Annual Review of Political Science*, 4, 1–20.

Tatz, C. (1999), 'Genocide in Australia', *Australian Institute of Aboriginal and Torres Strait Islander Studies Research Discussion Papers*, 8, 1–58.

Tatz, C. (2005), *Aboriginal Suicide is Different: A Portrait of Life and Self-Destruction* (Canberra: Aboriginal Studies Press).

Tauli-Corpuz, V. (2006), 'Our Right to Remain Separate and Distinct', in Mander and Tauli-Corpuz (eds) *Paradigm Wars: Indigenous Peoples' Resistance to Globalization* (Berkeley and Los Angeles: University of California Press).

Tauli-Corpuz, V. et al. (2009), *Guide on Climate Change and Indigenous Peoples*, 2nd Edition. (Baguio City: Tebtebba Foundation).

Taylor, V. And Van Dyke, N. (2007), '"Get up, Stand up": Tactical Repertoires of Social Movements', in Snow et al. (eds) *Blackwell Companion to Social Movements* (Oxford: Blackwell).

Tebtebba (2009), 'Concept Paper: International Conference on Indigenous Peoples and Extractive Industries', *Tebtebba Indigenous Peoples' International Centre for Research and Education* [website]. At: <http://www.tebtebba.org> accessed 20 May 2010.

Tebtebba (2010), 'Tebtebba: Our Programmes', *Tebtebba Indigenous Peoples' International Centre for Research and Education* [website]. At: <www.tebtebba.org> accessed 10 May 2010.

Tennant, C. (1994), 'Indigenous Peoples, International Institutions, and the International Legal Literature from 1945–1993', *Human Rights Quarterly* 16:1, 1–57.

Tilly, C. (1978), *From Mobilization to Revolution* (Reading, MA.: Addison-Wesley).

Thomas, D. (1999), 'The Helsinki Accords and Political Change in Eastern Europe', in Risse et al. (eds) (1999), *The Power of Human Rights: International Norms and Domestic Change* (Cambridge: Cambridge University Press).

Thomas, D. (2002), 'Human Rights in U.S. Foreign Policy', in Khagram et al. (eds) *Restructuring World Politics: Transnational Social Movements, Networks and Norms* (Minneapolis: University of Minnesota Press).

Thornberry, P. (2000), 'Self-Determination and Indigenous Peoples: Objections and Responses', in Aikio and Scheinin (eds) *Operationalizing the Right of Indigenous Peoples to Self-Determination* (Turku, Abo: Institute for Human Rights, Abo Akademi University).

Thornberry, P. (2002), *Indigenous Peoples and Human Rights* (Manchester: Manchester University Press).

Trask, M. (2005), 'Untitled', in *Advancing the Human Rights of Indigenous Peoples: A Critical Challenge for the International Community, Voices from a*

Forum at the 61st Session of the UN Commission on Human Rights, 13 April 2005 (Montreal: Rights and Democracy).

Triggs, G. (1999), 'Australia's Indigenous Peoples and International Law: Validity of the *Native Title Amendment Act* 1998 (Cth)', *Melbourne University Law Review* 372–415.

Turner, B.S. (1993), 'Outline of a Theory of Human Rights', *Sociology* 27:3, 489–512.

Turner, B.S. (1997), 'A Neo-Hobbesian Theory of Human Rights: A Reply to Malcolm Waters', *Sociology* 31:3, 565–71.

Turner, B.S. (2006), *Vulnerability and Human Rights* (Pennsylvania: Pennsylvania State University Press).

Turner, B.S., and Rojek, C. (2001), *Society and Culture: Principles of Scarcity and Solidarity* (London: Sage).

United Kingdom (2009), 'Request for an Advisory Opinion of the International Court of Justice on the Question "Is the Unilateral Declaration of Independence by the Provisional Institutions of Self-Government of Kosovo in Accordance with International Law?", Written Statement of the United Kingdom, 17 April 2009', *International Court of Justice* [website]. Available at: <http://www.icj-cij.org/docket/files/141/15638.pdf> accessed 1 March 2011.

United Nations (1945), *United Nations Charter*.

United Nations (1948), *Convention on the Prevention and Punishment of the Crime of Genocide*, G.A. Res. 260(III) A, 9 December 1948.

United Nations (1960a), *Declaration on the Granting of Independence to Colonial Countries and Peoples*, G.A. Res. 1514 (XV), 14 December 1960.

United Nations (1960b), *Principles Which Should Guide Members in Determining Whether or not an Obligation Exists to Transmit the Information Called for in Article 73e of the Charter of the United Nations*, G.A. Res. 1514 (XV).

United Nations (1966a), *International Covenant on Civil and Political Rights*, G.A. Res. 2200A (XXI), U.N. Doc. A/6316.

United Nations (1966b), *International Covenant on Economic, Social, and Cultural Rights*, G.A. Res. 2200A (XXI), U.N. Doc. A/6316.

United Nations (1967), *ECOSOC Resolution 1235 (XLII)*.

United Nations (1968a), *ECOSOC Resolution 1296 (XLIV)*, U.N. Doc. E/4548, 23 May 1968.

United Nations (1968b), *General Assembly Resolution 2396 (XXIII)*.

United Nations (1970), *Declaration on the Principles of International Law Concerning Friendly Relations and Co-operation Among States in Accordance with the Charter of the United Nations*, G.A. Res. 2625 (Xxv).

United Nations (1972), *Preliminary Martinez-Cobo Report*, U.N. Doc. E/CN.4/Sub.2/L.566, 29 June 1972.

United Nations (1974), *General Assembly Resolution 3292 (XXIX) Question of Spanish Sahara*, 13 December 1974.

United Nations (1981), *International NGO Conference on Indigenous Peoples and the Land*, U.N. Doc. E/CN.4/Sub.2/476/Add.5, 1981.

United Nations (1983), *Study of the Problem of Discrimination Against Indigenous Populations: Conclusions, Proposals, and Recommendations*, U.N. Doc. E/CN.4/Sub.2/1983/21/Add.8.

United Nations (1985a), *Report of the Working Group on Indigenous Populations at its Fourth Session*, U.N. Doc. E/CN.4/Sub.2/1985/22.

United Nations (1985b), *General Assembly Resolution 40/131 Establishing the United Nations Voluntary Fund for Indigenous Populations*, U.N. Doc. A/40/131, 13 December 1985).

United Nations (1986a), *Study on the Problem of Discrimination Against Indigenous Populations*, U.N. Doc. E/CN.4/Sub.2/1986/7/ and Add.1–4.

United Nations (1986b), *Declaration on the Right to Development, General Assembly Resolution 41/128*, 4 December 1986.

United Nations (1987), *Report of the World Commission on Environment and Development: Our Common Future*, U.N. Doc. A/42/427, Annex.

United Nations (1988), *Universal Declaration on Indigenous Rights: A Set of Preambular Paragraphs and Principles*, U.N. Doc. E/CN.4/Sub.2/1988/25.

United Nations (1991), *Study on the Rights of Persons Belonging to Ethnic, Religious and Linguistic Minorities*, United Nations publication, Sales No. E.91.XIV.2, Geneva, 1991.

United Nations (1992a), *Agenda 21, United Nations Conference on Environment and Development*, U.N. Doc. A/CONF.151/26/REF.1, Vols 1, II, and III., Annex II.

United Nations (1992b), *Rio Declaration on Environment and Development, United Nations Conference on Environment and Development,* U.N.Doc. A/CONF.151/26 (Vol.1), Annex 1, 12 August 1992.

United Nations (1992c), *Non-Legally Binding Authoritative Statement of Principles for a Global Consensus on the Management, Conservation, and Sustainable Development of All Types of Forest, United Nations Conference on Environment and Development* U.N. Doc. A/CONF.151/26 (Vol. III), Annex III, 14 August 1992.

United Nations (1992d), *Convention on Biological Diversity (with Annexes).*

United Nations (1992e), *Declaration on the Rights of Persons Belonging to National or Ethnic, Religious and Linguistic Minorities*, U.N. Doc. A/RES/47/135 (1992).

United Nations (1992f), *United Nations Framework Convention on Climate Change.*

United Nations (1993), *Vienna Declaration and Programme of Action, World Conference on Human Rights*, A/CONF./157/23, 12 July 1993.

United Nations (1994a), *Report of the Working Group on Indigenous Populations at its Twelfth Session*, U.N. Doc. E/CN.4/Sub.2/1994/30.

United Nations (1994b), *Programme of Action of the International Conference on Population and Development*, U.N. Doc. A/CONF.171/13, 18 October 1994.

United Nations (1994c), *International Decade of the World's Indigenous People*, U.N. Doc. A/RES/48/163, 18 February 1994.

United Nations (1994d), *Transnational Investments and Operations on the Lands of Indigenous Peoples, Report of the Centre on Transnational Corporations, submitted pursuant to Sub-Commission Resolution 1990/26*, UN. Doc. E/CN.4/Sub.2/1994/40.

United Nations (1995a), *Establishing a Working Group of the Commission on Human Rights to Elaborate a Draft Declaration in Accordance with Paragraph 5 of GA Res. 49/214 of 23 December 1994*, U.N. Doc. E/CN.4/Res/1995/32.

United Nations (1995b), *Beijing Declaration and Platform of Action*, U.N. Doc. A/CONF.177/20/Rev.1

United Nations (1996a), *Report of the Working Group Established in Accordance with Commission on Human Rights Resolution 1995/32 of 3 March 1995*, U.N. Doc. E/CN.4/1996/84.

United Nations (1996b), *Programme of Activities for the International Decade of the World's Indigenous People*, U.N. Doc. A/RES/50/157, 29 February 1996.

United Nations (1996c), *ECOSOC Resolution 1996/31: Consultative Relationship Between the United Nations and Non-Governmental Organizations, 25 July 1996.*

United Nations (1996d), *Review of the Existing Mechanisms, Procedures and Programmes within the United Nations Concerning Indigenous People, Report of the Secretary-General*, U.N. Doc. A/51/493, 14 October 1996.

United Nations (1997a), *Report of the UN Working Group on Indigenous Populations on its Fifteenth Session*, U.N. Doc. E/CN.4/Sub.2/1997/14.

United Nations (1997b), *Report of the Working Group established in accordance with Commission on Human Rights resolution 1995/32 of 3 March 1995*, U.N. Doc. E/CN.4/1997/102.

United Nations (1998a), *Report of the Workshop of Indigenous Journalists, Madrid, 26–28 January 1998*, U.N. Doc. E/CN.4/Sub.2/AC.4/1998/6, 18 May 1998.

United Nations (1998b), *Report of the Working Group Established in Accordance with Commission on Human Rights Resolution 1995/32*, U.N. Doc. E/CN.4/1998/106, 15 December 1997.

United Nations (1998c), *Kyoto Protocol to the United Nations Framework Convention on Climate Change.*

United Nations (1999a), *Report on the Workshop on Higher Education and Indigenous Peoples, Costa Rica, 28 June-2 July 1999*, U.N. Doc. E/CN.4/Sub.2/AC.4/1995/5, 22 July 1999.

United Nations (1999b), *Report of the Working Group Established in Accordance with Commission on Human Rights Resolution 1995/32*, U.N. Doc. E/CN.4/1999/82, 20 January 1999.

United Nations (2000a), *Report of the Working Group Established in Accordance with Commission on Human Rights Resolution 1995/32*, U.N. Doc. E/CN.4/2000/84, 6 December 1999.

United Nations (2000b), *Report on the Seminar on Multiculturalism in Africa: Peaceful and Constructive Group Accommodation in Situations Involving Minorities and Indigenous Peoples*, U.N. Doc. E/CN.4/Sub.2/AC.5/2000/3.

United Nations (2000c), *Establishment of a Permanent Forum on Indigenous Issues, Economic and Social Council Resolution 2000/22*, 28 July 2000.

United Nations (2000d), *Establishment of a Permanent Forum on Indigenous Issues, Commission on Human Rights Resolution 2000/87*, U.N. Doc. E/CN.4/RES/2000/87, 28 April 2000.

United Nations (2001a), *World Conference Against Racism, Racial Discrimination, Xenophobia, and Related Intolerance Declaration and Programme of Action*, U.N. Doc. A/CONF.189/12.

United Nations (2001b), *Report of the Second Workshop on Multiculturalism in Africa: Peaceful and Constructive Group Accommodation in Situations Involving Minorities and Indigenous Peoples*, U.N. Doc. E/CN.4/Sub.2/AC.5/2001/3.

United Nations (2001c), *Human Rights and Indigenous Issues, Commission on Human Rights Resolution 2001/57*, 24 April 2001.

United Nations (2002a), *Johannesburg Declaration on Sustainable Development, World Summit on Sustainable Development 26 August-4 September 2002*, Chapter 1, Resolution 1, U.N. Doc. A/CONF.199/20.

United Nations (2002b), *Report of the Third Workshop on Multiculturalism in Africa: Peaceful and Constructive Group Accommodation in Situations Involving Minorities and Indigenous Peoples*, U.N. Doc. E/CN.4/Sub.2/AC.4/2002/4.

United Nations (2002c), *Report of the Workshop on Indigenous Peoples, Private Sector Natural Resource, Energy and Mining Companies and Human Rights*, U.N. Doc. E/CN.4/Sub.2/AC.4/2002/3.

United Nations (2002d), *Draft Report of the Working Group Established in Accordance with Commission on Human Rights Resolution 1995/32*, U.N. Doc. E/CN.4/2002/WG.15/CRP.1.

United Nations (2002e), *Plan of Implementation of the World Summit on Sustainable Development*, Chapter 1, Resolution 2, U.N. Doc. A/CONF.199/20.

United Nations (2003a), *Report of the Special Rapporteur on the Situation of Human Rights and Fundamental Freedoms of Indigenous People, Rodolfo Stavenhagen, The Impact of Large-Scale or Major Development Projects on the Human Rights and Fundamental Freedoms of Indigenous Communities*, U.N. Doc. E/CN.4/2003/90, 21 January 2003.

United Nations (2003b), *Norms on the Responsibilities of Transnational Corporations and Other Business Enterprises with Regard to Human Rights*, U.N. Doc. E/CN.4/Sub.2/2003/12/Rev.2, 26 August 2003.

United Nations (2004a), *Implementation of the Programme of Activities for the International Decade of the World's Indigenous People, Report of the United Nations High Commissioner for Human Rights on the Implementation of the*

Programme of Activities for the International Decade of the World's Indigenous People, 1995–2004, U.N. Doc. A/59/277, 17 August 2004.

United Nations (2004b), *Report on the Expert Seminar on Indigenous Peoples and the Administration of Justice, Madrid, 12–14 November 2003*, U.N. Doc. E/CN.4/Sub.2/AC.4/2004/6.

United Nations (2004c), *Report on the Seminar on Treaties, Agreements, and Other Constructive Relations Between States and Indigenous Peoples, Geneva, 15–17 December 2003*, U.N. Doc. E/CN.4/Sub.2/AC.4/2004/7.

United Nations (2004d), *Report of the Special Rapporteur on the Situation of Human Rights and Fundamental Freedoms of Indigenous People, Rodolfo Stavenhagen, Administration of Justice, Indigenous Peoples and Human Rights*, U.N. Doc. E/CN.4/2004/80, 26 January 2004.

United Nations (2004e), *Report of the Secretary General on the Preliminary Review by the Coordinator of the International Decade of the World's Indigenous People on the Activities of the United Nations System in Relation to the Decade*, U.N. Doc. E/2004/82, 25 June 2004.

United Nations (2005a), *Second International Decade of the World's Indigenous People*, U.N. Doc. A/RES/59/174, 24 February 2005.

United Nations (2005b), *Final Report of the United Nations High Commissioner for Human Rights Reviewing the Activities within the United Nations System Under the Programme for the International Decade of the World's Indigenous People*, U.N. Doc. E/CN.4/2005/87, 4 January 2005.

United Nations (2005c), *Report of the Special Rapporteur on the Situation of Human Rights and Fundamental Freedoms of Indigenous People, Rodolfo Stavenhagen, Indigenous Peoples and Education Systems: Human Rights Challenges*, U.N. Doc. E/CN.4/2005/88, 6 January 2005.

United Nations (2006a), *Report of the Working Group Established in Accordance with Commission on Human Rights Resolution 1995/32*, U.N. Doc. E/CN.4/2006/79, 22 March 2006.

United Nations (2006b), *Human Rights Council Resolution 2006/2, Working Group of the Commission on Human Rights to Elaborate a Draft Declaration in Accordance with Paragraph 5 of the General Assembly Resolution 49/214 of 23 December 1994.*

United Nations (2006c), *Resolution Adopted by the General Assembly, Human Rights Council*, U.N. Doc. A/RES/60/251, 3 April 2006.

United Nations (2006d), *Report of the Special Rapporteur on the Human Rights and Fundamental Freedoms of Indigenous People*, U.N. Doc. E/CN.4/2006/78, 16 February 2006.

United Nations (2006e), *Report of the Special Rapporteur on the Human Rights and Fundamental Freedoms of Indigenous People: Addendum*, U.N. Doc. E/CN.4/2006/78, Add. 5, 16 February 2006.

United Nations (2007a), *United Nations Declaration on the Rights of Indigenous Peoples*, U.N. Doc. A/RES/61/295, Annex 1.

United Nations (2007b), *Human Rights and Indigenous Peoples: Mandate of the Special Rapporteur on the Situation of Human Rights and Fundamental Freedoms of Indigenous People*, U.N. Doc. A/HRC/RES/6/12, 28 September 2007.

United Nations (2007c), *Human Rights Council, Expert Mechanism on the Rights of Indigenous Peoples*, U.N. Doc. A/HRC/RES/6/36, 14 December 2007.

United Nations (2007d), *Report of the Special Rapporteur on the Situation of Human Rights and Fundamental Freedoms of Indigenous People*, U.N. Doc. A/HRC/4/32, 27 February 2007.

United Nations (2007e), *Report of the Special Representative of the Secretary General on the Issue of Human Rights and Transnational Corporations and Business Enterprises, State Responsibilities to Regulate and Adjudicate Corporate Activities under the Core Human Rights Treaties: An Overview of Treaty Commentaries*, U.N. Doc. A/HRC/4/35/Add 1.

United Nations (2007f), *United Nations General Assembly, 61st Session, 107th Plenary Meeting, Official Records*, U.N.Doc. A/61/PV.107.

United Nations (2008a), *Permanent Forum on Indigenous Issues, Report on the Seventh Session, 21 April-2 May 2008*, U.N. Doc. E/2008/43, E/C.19/2008/13.

United Nations (2008b), *Report of the Special Rapporteur on the Situation of Human Rights and Fundamental Freedoms of Indigenous People, S. James Anaya*, U.N. Doc. A/HRC/9/9, 11 August 2008.

United Nations (2009a), *Report of the Special Rapporteur on the Situation of Human Rights and Fundamental Freedoms of Indigenous People, S. James Anaya*, U.N. Doc. A/HRC/12/34, 15 July 2009.

United Nations (2009b), *Report of the Expert Mechanism on the Rights of Indigenous Peoples on its First Session*, U.N. Doc. A/HCR/10/56, 8 January 2009.

United Nations (2009c), *Study on Lessons Learned and Challenges to the Implementation of the Rights of Indigenous Peoples to Education*, U.N. Doc. A/HRC/EMRIP/2009/2, 26 June 2009.

United Nations (2009d), *Report of the International Expert Group Meeting on the Role of the Permanent Forum on Indigenous Issues in the Implementation of Article 42 of the United Nations Declaration on the Rights of Indigenous Peoples*, U.N. Doc. E/C.19/2009/2, 4 February 2009.

United Nations (2009e), *Report of the Special Representative of the Secretary-General on the Issue of Human Rights and Transnational Corporations and Other Business Enterprises, John Ruggie, State Obligations to Provide Access to Remedy for Human Rights Abuses by Third Parties, Including Business: An Overview of International and Regional Provisions, Commentary and Decisions*, U.N. Doc A/HRC/11/13/Add.1, 15 May 2009.

United Nations, Department of Economic and Social Affairs (2009), *The State of the World's Indigenous Peoples*, STA/ESA/328, United Nations Publication, Sales No.09.VI.13, ISBN 92-1-130283-7.

United Nations, Department of Public Information (2007), 'General Assembly Adopts UN Declaration on the Rights of Indigenous Peoples; 'Major Step Forward' Towards Human Rights for All, Says President' *United Nations Department of Public Information.* At: <http://www.un.org/News/Press/docs/2007/ga10612.doc.htm> accessed 10 June 2010.

United Nations Development Group (2008), 'United Nations Development Group Guidelines on Indigenous Peoples' Issues', *United Nations Development Group* [website]. At: <http://ohchr.org/Documents/Publications/undg_training_16EN.pdf> accessed 15 April 2010.

United Nations Development Program (2001), 'UNDP and Indigenous Peoples: A Practice Note on Engagement' *United Nations Development Program* [website]. At: <http://www.undp.org/partners/civil_society/indigenous/shtml> accessed 20 June 2009.

United Nations Educational, Scientific, and Cultural Organization (1981), *Declaration of San José,* UNESCO Doc. FS 82/WF.32 (1982).

United Nations Educational, Scientific, and Cultural Organization (1989), *International Meeting Of Experts on Further Study of the Concept of the Rights of Peoples, UNESCO Paris 27–30 November 1989: Final Report and Recommendations*, UNESCO Doc. SHS-89/CONF.602/7, 22 February 1990.

United Nations Educational, Scientific, and Cultural Organization (2001), *UNESCO Universal Declaration on Cultural Diversity*, 2 November 2001.

United Nations Educational, Scientific, and Cultural Organization (2003), *Convention on the Safeguarding of the Intangible Cultural Heritage*, October 2003.

United States (2007), 'Observations of the United States with Respect to the Declaration on the Rights of Indigenous Peoples: Explanation of Vote by Robert Hagen, U.S. Advisor, on the Declaration on the Rights of Indigenous Peoples, to the UN General Assembly, September 13 2007, USUN Press Release #204(07)' *US Mission to the United Nations in New York* [website]. At: <http://www.usunnewyork.usmission.gov/press_releases/20070913_204.html> accessed 10 June 2009.

United States (2010), 'Statement by Ambassador Susan E. Rice, U.S. Permanent Representative to the United Nations, on the Announcement of U.S. Support for the United Nations Declaration on the Rights of Indigenous Peoples, December 16 2010', *United States Mission to the United Nations* [website]. At: <www.usun.state.gov/briefing/statements/2010/153009> accessed 1 March 2011.

Varese, Stefano (1997), 'Memories of Solidarity: Anthropology and the Indigenous Movement in Latin America', *Cultural Survival Quarterly* 23:3 (Fall 1997).

Waldron, J. (1987), *Nonsense Upon Stilts: Bentham, Burke, and Marx on the Rights of Man* (London: Methuen).

Wallerstein, I. (1996), *Open the Social Sciences: Report of the Gulbenkian Commission on the Restructuring of the Social Sciences* (Stanford: Stanford University Press).

Waltz, S. (2001), 'Universalizing Human Rights: The Role of Small States in the Construction of the Universal Declaration of Human Rights', *Human Rights Quarterly* 23, 44–72.

Waltz, S. (2004), 'Universal Human Rights: The Contribution of Muslim States', *Human Rights Quarterly* 26, 799–844.

Waters, M. (1996), 'Human Rights and the Universalization of Interests: Towards a Social Constructionist Approach', *Sociology* 30:3, 593–600.

Weller, M. (2008a), *Contested Statehood: Kosovo's Struggle for Independence* (Oxford: Oxford University Press).

Weller, M. (2008b), 'Negotiating the Final Status of Kosovo', *Chaillot Paper No.114, Institute for Security Studies* [website]. Available at: <http://www.iss.europa.eu/uploads/media/cp114> accessed 25 February 2011.

Weller, M. (2011), 'Modesty can be a Virtue: Judicial Economy in the ICJ Kosovo Opinion?, *Leiden Journal of International Law* 24:1, 127–47.

Wenzel, N. (2008), *Das Spannungsverhaltnis zwischen Gruppensschutz und Individualschutz im Volkerrecht* (New York: Springer).

Werum, R., and Winders, B. (2001), 'Who's "In" and Who's "Out": State Fragmentation and the Struggle over Gay Rights, 1974–1999', *Social Problems* 48:3, 386–410.

Wiesel, E. (1999), 'A Tribute to Human Rights', in Danieli et al. (eds) *The Universal Declaration of Human Rights: Fifty Years and Beyond* (Amityville, N.Y.: Baywood).

Wiessner, S. (1999), 'Rights and Status of Indigenous Peoples: A Global Comparative and International Legal Analysis', *Harvard Human Rights Journal* 12, 57–128.

Wiessner, S. (2008), 'Indigenous Sovereignty: A Reassessment in the Light of the UN Declaration on the Rights of Indigenous Peoples', *Vanderbilt Journal of Transnational Law* 41, 1141–76.

Wiessner, S. (2009), 'United Nations Declaration on the Rights of Indigenous Peoples', *United Nations Audiovisual Library of International Law* [website]. At: <www.un.org.law/avl> accessed 25 May 2010.

Wilde, R. (2011), 'Self-Determination, Secession, and Dispute Resolution after the Kosovo Advisory Opinion', *Leiden Journal of International Law* 24:1, 149–54.

Williams, R.A. Jnr. (1990), *The American Indian in Western Legal Thought* (Oxford: Oxford University Press)

Wilmer, F. (1993), *The Indigenous Voice in World Politics: Since Time Immemorial* (Newbury Park, CA: Sage Publications).

Wilmer, F. (1996), 'Indigenous Peoples, Marginal Sites and the Changing Context of World Politics' in Beer and Hariman (eds) *Post-Realism: The Rhetorical Turn in International Relations* (East Lansing, MI.: Michigan State University Press).

Wilson, J. (1998), *The Earth Shall Weep: A History of Native America* (London: Picador).

Wilson, R.A. (ed.) (2005), *Human Rights in the 'War on Terror'* (Cambridge: Cambridge University Press).

Wilson, R.A. (2001), *The Politics of Truth and Reconciliation in South Africa: Legitimizing the Post-Apartheid State* (Cambridge: Cambridge University Press).

Woodiwiss, A. (1998), *Globalization, Human Rights, and Labour Law in Pacific Asia* (Cambridge: Cambridge University Press).

Woodiwiss, A. (2003), *Making Human Rights Work Globally* (London: Glasshouse Press).

World Bank (1991), *Operational Directive 4.20 on Indigenous Peoples.*

World Bank (2005a), *Operational Policy and Bank Procedure on Indigenous Peoples 4.10.*

World Bank (2005b), 'Legal Note on Indigenous Peoples', *The World Bank* [website]. At: <http://siteresources.worldbank.org/INTINDPEOPLE/Publications/20571167/Legal%20Note.pdf> accessed 10 June 2009.

World Council of Indigenous Peoples (1981a), 'Transnational Corporations and their Effect on the Resources and Lands of Indigenous Peoples', *Fourth World Documentation Project* [website]. At: <http://ftp.halcyon.com/pub/FWDP/International/transnat.txt> accessed 21 January 2010.

World Council of Indigenous Peoples (1981b), 'Indigenous Homelands and Transnational Corporations', *Centre for World Indigenous Studies* [website]. At: <http://www.cwis.org/fwdp/International/trnscorp.html> accessed 11 May 2010.

World Health Organization (1999), *The Geneva Declaration on the Health and Survival of Indigenous Peoples.*

World Rainforest Movement (2002), *The Pulp Invasion: The International Pulp and Paper Invasion in the Mekong Region* (Montevideo: World Rainforest Movement).

World Rainforest Movement (2005), Indigenous Peoples: Their Forests, Struggles and Rights (Montevideo: World Rainforest Movement).

Xanthaki, A. (2007), *Indigenous Rights and United Nations Standards: Self Determination, Culture and Land* (Cambridge: Cambridge University Press).

Xanthaki, A. (2010), 'Multiculturalism and International Law: Discussing Universal Standards', *Human Rights Quarterly* 32:1, 21–48.

Young, I.M. (2007), *Global Challenges: War, Self-Determination and Responsibility for Justice* (Cambridge: Polity).

Zemans, F. (1983), 'Legal Mobilization: the Neglected Role of the Law in the Political System', *American Political Science Review* 77:3, 690–703.

Index